PRAISE FOR HENNING MANKELL

QUICKSAND

"[*Quicksand*] defines life not by its ending but by the creative and humanitarian content that filled—and fulfilled—Mankell's life. . . . The essays . . . sharpen with resounding poignancy."
—*Financial Times*

"An extremely moving swan song. . . . The reader realizes that Mankell has never really been driven by anger but by the tiny, fragile hope that his words and deeds will help in the fight for a fairer world." —*The Independent* (London)

"Uplifting and, as a memoir, as unusual a creation as [Mankell's] Nordic detective, Kurt Wallander." —*British GQ*

"Throughout *Quicksand*, there are scenes [of] joy and triumph in the midst of suffering and loss. This grave book . . . takes us to these places in the thoughtful company of a great soul."
—*New Statesman*

"[An] absorbing addition to the work of Sweden's most internationally famous writer since August Strindberg. . . . *Quicksand*, a hybrid of essay and memoir, reflects knowledgeably on art, religion, childhood, and the 'final insensibility' that is our dying. Rarely has a writer contemplated the mystery of the end of life with such a wide-ranging curiosity."
—*London Evening Standard*

HENNING MANKELL

QUICKSAND

Henning Mankell's novels have been translated into forty-five languages and have sold more than forty million copies worldwide. He was the first winner of the Ripper Award and also received the Glass Key and the Crime Writers' Association's Gold Dagger, among other awards. His Kurt Wallander mysteries have been adapted into a PBS television series starring Kenneth Branagh. During his life, Mankell divided his time between Sweden and Mozambique, where he was the artistic director of the Teatro Avenida in Maputo. He died in 2015.

www.henningmankell.com

Laurie Thompson taught modern languages at universities in Sweden and Wales. He was a founding member of SELTA (the Swedish-English Literary Translators' Association) and edited the journal *Swedish Book Review* from its launch until 2002. As a freelance translator of Swedish literature, he translated more than fifty books, the last of which was Henning Mankell's *Quicksand*. He died in 2015.

QUICKSAND

QUICKSAND

What It Means to Be a Human Being

HENNING MANKELL

TRANSLATED FROM THE SWEDISH
BY LAURIE THOMPSON
WITH MARLAINE DELARGY

VINTAGE BOOKS
A Division of Penguin Random House LLC
New York

A VINTAGE BOOKS ORIGINAL, JANUARY 2017

English translation copyright © 2016 by Laurie Thompson

All rights reserved. Published in the United States by Vintage Books,
a division of Penguin Random House LLC, New York. Originally published
in Sweden as *Kvicksand* by Leopard förlag, Stockholm, in 2014.
Copyright © 2014 by Henning Mankell. This translation originally published
in hardcover in Great Britain by Harvill Secker, an imprint of Vintage Publishing,
a division of Penguin Random House Ltd., London, in 2016.

Vintage and colophon are registered trademarks of Penguin Random House LLC.

The Cataloging-in-Publication Data is on file at the Library of Congress.

Vintage Books Trade Paperback ISBN: 978-0-525-43215-9
eBook ISBN: 978-0-525-43216-6

www.vintagebooks.com

Printed in the United States of America

To Eva Bergman

This book is also dedicated to the memory of the baker Terentius Neo and his wife, whose name we don't know. Their faces can be seen in a fresco painting at their house in Pompeii.

Two people in the prime of life. Their expressions are solemn, but they also appear to have a spiritual dimension. She is very beautiful, but looks unsure of herself. He gives the impression of modesty.

They seem to be two people who take their lives extremely seriously.

When the volcano erupted in AD 79, they can't have had much time to grasp what was happening. They died there, in the middle of their lives, buried underneath the ash and the glowing lava.

Don't be ashamed because you are a human being, be proud!
Inside you is an endless series of strong rooms, one after the other.
You never come to an end, and that is how it should be.

Tomas Tranströmer, 'Romanesque Arches,'
For the Living and the Dead

Contents

PART II: THE ROAD TO SALAMANCA

PART III: THE PUPPET ON A STRING

PART I

THE CROOKED FINGER

The car accident

EARLY IN THE MORNING OF 16 DECEMBER 2013 EVA DROVE ME TO the Statoil depot in Kungsbacka, where I collected the car I had hired. I was going to drive to Vallåkra, just outside Landskrona, and back. The car was due to be returned that same evening. The following day I would be busy signing copies of my latest novel in bookshops in Gothenburg and Kungsbacka as part of the pre-Christmas publicity programme.

The wintry morning was freezing cold, but there was no rain or snow. The drive would take me three hours if I stopped for breakfast on the outskirts of Varberg, as was my wont.

The head of my theatre in Maputo – Manuela Soeiro, with whom I had now been working for thirty years – was visiting Sweden. This was to be the first real meeting concerning the production we were planning to stage the following autumn. Manuela was staying with Eyvind, who was going to direct the version of *Hamlet* I had been thinking about virtually all the years I had been working at the Teatro Avenida.

It had struck me very early on that *Hamlet* was ideal for adapting as a drama about an African king – the fact is that something very similar to the plot of *Hamlet* actually took place in a part of southern Africa in the nineteenth century. My idea was that at the end of the play when everybody is dead and Fortinbras comes onstage, he would be the white man who arrives to start colonising Africa on a serious scale. I therefore thought it would be logical to allow

Fortinbras to conclude the play with the 'To be or not to be' soliloquy.

If you are going to perform *Hamlet*, you must have an actor who can play the part in the way you envisage it – and now we had just the man. Jorginho would be able to do it. He had developed significantly over the last few years, and he was also then best of all the actors when it came to the way he approached the language. It was a case of now or never.

As I drove through Halland I found myself looking forward to the coming day. I was filled with great expectations.

The roads further south were dry, although it was very cloudy and overcast. I wasn't driving all that fast, unusually for me – I had given them an arrival time and I didn't want to get there too early.

Then suddenly it all happens very quickly. Just north of Laholm I pull out into the outside lane in order to overtake a slow-moving lorry. Somewhere on the road surface is a patch of something, possibly oil: I start skidding and lose control, the car crashes head-on into the central barrier and the airbags inflate. I black out for a second or two.

When I come to, I sit there in silence for a while. What has happened? I feel around to make sure I am still in one piece. I'm not injured, I'm not bleeding. Then I get out. Cars have stopped and people are running towards me. I tell them I'm OK, I'm not hurt.

I stand on the verge and telephone Eva. When she answers I make a point of trying to sound calm.

'You can hear that it's me,' I say. 'And that I'm all right.'

'What's happened?' she asks immediately.

I tell her about the accident. I play down the crash, and insist that all is well. I don't really know what's going to happen next, but I'm fine. I don't know if she believes me.

Then I telephone Vallåkra.

'I'm afraid I shan't be coming,' I say. 'I've crashed into the central barrier on the road just outside Laholm. I'm not injured. But the car's a total write-off.'

The police arrive. I blow into their bag but I'm completely sober. I describe the accident. While all this is happening the fire brigade tows away the car, presumably to the scrapheap. An ambulance driver asks if I want a lift to A & E just to be on the safe side. I say no as I am not in any pain at all.

The police drive me to the railway station in Laholm; half an hour later I'm on a train back to Gothenburg.

I still haven't been to Vallåkra, and I never did the book signings there.

Without really knowing why, I date my cancer to that very day: 16 December 2013. There is no logic in doing so, of course. My tumours and metastases must have been growing for some considerable time. Nor did I have any symptoms or other indications on that particular day.

It was more of a warning. Something was happening.

A week later, just before Christmas, Eva and I went to our little flat in Antibes, on the Mediterranean coast. In the morning of Christmas Eve I was woken up by pains in my neck and a general feeling of stiffness. I thought I must have been stupid enough to lie in an awkward position and given myself a twisted neck – what the doctors call torticollis.

But the pain didn't go away. Instead, it spread quickly down my right arm. I lost all feeling in the thumb of my right hand. And it hurt. In the end I rang an orthopaedic specialist in Stockholm I was lucky enough to get hold of despite the fact that almost everybody was on holiday for Christmas. I went back to Sweden and he examined me on 28 December. He thought it could well be early signs of a slipped disc at the top of my spine, but of course it was not possible to say without a scan, which we agreed I should have as soon as the Christmas holidays were over.

The 8th of January dawned. It was a cold morning, and snowing lightly. I thought it was high time to get the slipped disc diagnosis confirmed. I was still suffering severe neck pains. Strong painkillers helped, but that was only a stopgap measure. The slipped disc needed proper treatment.

Early in the morning I had two scans. Two hours later the torticollis and slipped disc theory had changed into a cancer diagnosis. I was shown a computer image of a cancerous tumour, three centimetres in diameter, in my left lung. And there was a metastasis in my neck. That was the cause of my pain.

The diagnosis was very clear: it was serious, possibly incurable. I asked hesitantly if that meant I should go home and wait for the end.

'Not long ago that would have been our advice,' said the doctor. 'But now we have treatment options.'

Eva was with me at the Sophiahem when I was informed of the situation. Afterwards, as we stood outside in the cold winter weather waiting for a taxi, we didn't have much to say. We probably didn't say anything at all, in fact.

But I saw a little girl jumping up and down in a snowdrift, full of joy and energy.

I saw myself, as a child, jumping around in the snow. Now I was sixty-five years old and had been diagnosed with cancer. I was not jumping around.

It was as if Eva had read my thoughts. She took a firm grip of my arm.

As we drove away in the taxi the little girl was still jumping up and down in her snowdrift.

Today, as I write this on 18 June, one could say that the time that has passed since then was both lengthy and short.

I am unable to write a full stop – neither after a fatal outcome nor a declaration that I am healthy again. I am in the middle of something. There is no conclusion as yet.

But this is what I have been through and what I have experienced. The story does not have an ending. It is ongoing.

That is what this book is about. My life. What has been, and what is.

2

People reluctantly on their way into the shadows

TWO DAYS AFTER THE CAR CRASH I PAID A VISIT TO SLÄP CHURCH, which is close to where I live on the coast, just north of Kungsbacka. I suddenly felt an urge to see a painting I had observed and admired many times. A painting like no other.

It is a family portrait. Years before photography was invented, people with sufficient means used to commission oil paintings. This picture depicts the vicar Gustaf Fredrik Hjortberg and his wife Anna Helena and their children – all fifteen of them. The picture was painted at the beginning of the 1770s when Gustaf Hjortberg was in his fifties. He died a few years later, in 1776.

It is possible that he was the person who introduced potatoes into Sweden on a serious scale.

What is striking and remarkable about the picture, and perhaps also frightening, is that it doesn't only depict the individuals who were alive when the artist Jonas Durchs started work on the project: he also painted the children who were already dead. Their brief visit to this earth was over, but it was felt they should be in the family portrait even so.

The picture is constructed in a way that was normal at the time: the boys – both the living and the dead – are gathered around their father on the left of the picture, while the girls are standing around their mother on the right.

Those who are alive are looking at the observer – there are quite a lot of modest, perhaps shy smiles. But the dead children's faces are half averted from the observer, or partly hidden behind the backs of the living. All that is visible of one of the dead boys is his forehead and one eye. He gives the impression of trying desperately to make his presence felt.

In a cradle beside the mother is a small child, half hidden. Girls are hovering vaguely in the background. There seem to be six dead children in all.

It is as if time has stood still in the painting. Just as is the case in a photograph.

Gustaf Hjortberg was one of Linnaeus's disciples, although he was never outstanding in any way. He made at least three voyages with the East India Company to China as the ship's chaplain. Also depicted in the painting is a globe of the world, and a lemur. Hjortberg is holding a sheet of paper in his hand, covered in writing. We are in the presence of an educated and sophisticated family. Gustaf Hjortberg lived and died in accordance with the ideals of the Age of Enlightenment. He also had a reputation of being well versed in medicine – people went on pilgrimages to Släp in order to receive advice and be healed.

It is about 250 years since these people lived and died. Eight or nine generations, no more. In many ways they are our contemporaries. And above all, they belong to the same civilisation as those of us who contemplate the painting.

Everybody in the picture is smiling. Some a little stiffly, others introspectively, a few are quite uninhibited and close to me as I scrutinise the picture.

But needless to say, what one remembers about the painting is the children who are half hidden or looking away. The dead. It is as if they are in motion, moving away from the observer and into the world of shadows.

What is so touching is the reluctance of the dead children to disappear.

I know of no other picture that depicts so vividly the stubborn determination of life to continue.

I hope this painting will survive into the future – a future so far distant that I am incapable of imagining it – as a greeting from our civilisation. It combines a belief in reason with the tragic conditions that are inherent in human life.

Everything is there.

3

The great discovery

IN THE EMOTIONAL CHAOS THAT ENVELOPED ME AFTER MY TORTI-
collis had metamorphosed into cancer, I noticed that my memory
often transported me back to my childhood.

But it wasn't long before I realised that my memory was trying
to help me to understand, to create a starting point that would enable
me to cope with the potentially fatal catastrophe with which I had
been stricken.

I quite simply had to start somewhere. I had to make a choice.
And I was becoming increasingly convinced that the beginning lay
somewhere in my early life.

I eventually chose a cold winter's day in 1957.

When I open my eyes that morning I am unaware that the day is
going to reveal a big secret.

Quite early I am on my way to school through the darkness. I am
nine years old. It so happens that my best friend Bosse is ill. I always
pick him up from his house, which is only a few minutes' walk from
the district courthouse where I live. His brother Göran answers the
door and says that Bosse has a sore throat and will be staying at
home. I will have to go the rest of the way to school on my own that
morning.

Sveg is quite a small town. None of the streets are very long.
Although fifty-seven years have passed since that winter's day I can
still remember everything in great detail. The few lights suspended
on cables across the streets are swaying gently in the gusty breeze.

The shade on the light outside the ironmonger's has cracked – it wasn't like that yesterday. Evidently it had happened during the night.

It must have been snowing while I was asleep. Somebody has already cleared away the snow from outside the furniture shop – that must have been Inga-Britt's dad. He owns the furniture shop. Inga-Britt is another classmate of mine, but she's a girl and we never go to school together. But she can run very fast. Nobody can ever keep up with her.

I can even remember what I had dreamt about that night. I'm standing on an ice floe on the River Ljusnan, which flows past the building where I live. The spring thaw has begun and the floe is floating southwards. Standing on one's own on an ice floe ought to be scary as it is very dangerous. Only a few months ago a boy just a few years older than I am drowned when an unexpected and treacherous hole in the ice opened up in a lake just outside Sveg. He was dragged down and his body has never been found, despite the best efforts of the fire brigade. His teacher drew a cross on his desk at school. It is still there. Everybody in his class is frightened of holes in the ice and accidents and ghosts. Everybody is scared of that unknown thing called Death. The cross on his desk is a source of terror.

But in my dream the ice floe is safe. I know I'm not going to fall into the water.

I cross the road just past the furniture shop and stop outside the community centre. There are two display panels outside. The cinema changes its programme twice a week, and the films are delivered in brown cardboard boxes from the goods depot at the local railway station. They come either from Orsa to the south or from Östersund. And they are still brought from the station by horse and cart. Engman, who is the caretaker at the community centre, lifts the boxes from the cart. I tried once, but failed miserably: they were too heavy for a nine-year-old. The cardboard boxes contained a bad cowboy film that I eventually watched. It was one of those B-movies where people talk and talk, with a brief gunfight at the end. Practically nothing else happens. And the colours are so peculiar. The people often have pink faces and the sky is more green than blue.

I see from the posters that Engman will be showing *The Hard Man*, which doesn't sound all that attractive, and a Swedish film starring Nils Poppe. The only advantage of the latter is that it is a U certificate and children are allowed in. That means I won't have to crawl in through the basement window that Bosse and I have a secret key for, so that we can always get in that way when the films are adults only.

As I stand there that freezing-cold morning fifty-seven years ago I experience one of those vital moments that will affect the rest of my life. I recall the situation in minute detail, as if the images have been branded into my memory. I am suddenly possessed by unexpected insight. It is as if somebody has given me a good shaking. The words come into my head of their own accord.

'I am myself and no one else. I am me.'

At that moment I find my identity. Until then my thoughts had been childish, as they were meant to be. Now the situation was entirely different. Identity is necessary in order to develop awareness. I am myself and nobody else. I cannot be exchanged for anybody else. Life has suddenly become a serious matter.

I don't know how long I stood there in the freezing-cold darkness, possessed by this new and bewildering understanding. All I remember is that I arrived late for school. Miss Prestjan, my teacher, was already playing the harmonium when I opened the outside door. I hung up my jacket and waited. It was strictly forbidden to go clomping into the classroom once morning prayers and hymns had begun.

It came to an end at last, there was a clattering of desks, and I knocked on the door and went it. As I was hardly ever late Miss Prestjan simply gave me a searching look and nodded. If she had suspected laziness, she would have said something.

'Bosse is ill,' I said. 'He has a sore throat and a temperature. He won't be coming to school today.'

Then I sat down at my desk. I looked around. Nobody had the slightest idea about the secret I was carrying with me. The secret I would keep for the next fifty-seven years.

4

Quicksand

IT SUDDENLY SEEMED AS IF MY LIFE HAD SHRUNK. THAT JANUARY morning when I received my cancer diagnosis, I had the feeling that my life was dwindling away. Very few thoughts came into my head; my mind seemed to be a sort of desert-like landscape.

Perhaps I didn't dare to think about the future – it was so uncertain, a veritable minefield. Instead, I kept returning again and again to my childhood.

When I was eight or nine years old I passed through a period in which I kept thinking about what kind of death frightened me most of all. That is nothing remarkable – people have such thoughts at that age. Life and death begin to be serious topics that one needs to come to terms with. Children are extremely serious creatures. Not least when they reach the age when they slowly take the step that changes them into conscious human beings – conscious of the fact that they have an identity that cannot be changed. Over the years what one looks like in a mirror changes, but behind that mirror image is always the real you.

Your identity is formed when you decide your attitude towards serious questions. That is something known to everybody who has not forgotten all about their childhood.

What frightened me more than anything else was falling through the ice on a lake or a river and being sucked underneath the ice sheet, unable to break through to the surface. To drown just underneath the ice through which you could see the sun shining. Suffocating in the cold water. Being overcome by panic from which no one could rescue you. Screaming without being heard. Screams that froze and turned into ice and death.

That kind of fear was not so strange; I grew up in the province of Härjedalen where the winters were long and severe.

Around that time, a girl about my age actually did fall through the all-too-thin ice on the Sandtjärn lake. I was there when they recovered her body. The word had spread very fast through Sveg. Everybody came running up. It was a Sunday. Her parents were standing next to the lake where the black water in the hole stood out among all the whiteness of the ice and snow. When the volunteer firemen had dragged out the girl with their grappling irons, her parents didn't react as they would have done in a film or a book. They didn't burst into tears. They were completely silent. It was others who wept. Her teacher, I recall. The vicar and the girl's closest friends.

Somebody vomited into the snow. It was very quiet. The white clouds of breath coming out of everybody's mouths were like incomprehensible smoke signals.

The drowned girl had not been in the water all that long. But she was completely stiff. Her woollen clothes crackled and creaked as they laid her down in the snow. Her face was absolutely white, as if it had been made up in that colour. Her blonde hair stuck out from under her red cap like yellow icicles.

But there was another kind of death that terrified me. I had read about it somewhere. Looking back, I have tried to remember where. Possibly in *Record Magazine*, which combined fictional tales about sport with thrillers and adventure stories. Or perhaps it was in some travelogue from Africa or the Arab countries. I have never managed to find it.

It was about quicksand. About how a man in a khaki uniform, with a rifle over his shoulder, dressed for an expedition, happens to tread on the treacherous sand and is immediately stuck fast. He is sucked inexorably further and further down, totally unable to break free until the sand begins to cover his mouth and his nose. The man is doomed. He suffocates and eventually the last glimpse of his hair-covered scalp disappears under the sand.

The quicksand was alive. The grains transmuted into ghastly tentacles that devoured a human being. A flesh-eating sand hole.

I was able to avoid treacherous ice floes, and there was not much in the way of sandy beaches by the lakes or the River Ljusnan. But many years later, when I was wandering around in the sand dunes at Skagen, or later still on African beaches, the memory of that quicksand cropped up inside my head.

When I was told I had cancer, that same feeling of terror burst out inside me again.

What I felt was precisely that fear of quicksand. I fought against being sucked down and swallowed up by it. By the totally paralysing realisation that I had been stricken by a serious, incurable disease. It took me ten days and nights, with very few hours of sleep, to keep myself afloat and not be incapacitated by the fear that threatened to overcome all my powers of resistance.

I can't remember being afflicted by desperation so great that I burst into tears. Nor that I screamed out loud in despair. It was a silent battle to overcome the quicksand.

And I wasn't sucked down totally. In the end I was able to crawl back out of the sand and begin to come to terms with what had happened. I no longer thought in terms of lying down and waiting for death to come. I would accept the treatment that was now available today. Even if I would never be completely cured, there was a possibility that I could live for quite a long while yet.

Being stricken by cancer is an extreme catastrophe. It is only after some time that you know if you are going to be able to handle it, to resist it. I am still not clear about what I thought and experienced during those ten days after I had received that catastrophic diagnosis. Perhaps I never shall be? Those ten days at the beginning of 2014, after Twelfth Night, are shadowy, as dark as the Swedish midwinter. I was occasionally subjected to attacks of the shivers – reminiscent of the occasions when I was stricken with malaria. I spent most of the time lying in bed with the covers pulled up to my chin.

The only thing I am quite clear about is being convinced that time had stood still. As if in a concentrated and condensed universe, everything had become a point in which there was no past or future: nothing but now. I was a human being clinging fast to the edge of a patch of death-bringing quicksand.

When I had finally conquered the urge to give up, to allow myself to be swallowed up into the abyss, I read some books about what quicksand actually is. And I discovered that the story of sand that can suck down and swallow up a human being is in fact a myth. All the stories describing it are inventions. Among other authorities, a university in Holland has conducted practical experiments to prove the point.

Nevertheless, the comparison with quicksand is still the one I acknowledge today. That is what the ten days that completely changed the circumstances of my life were like.

5

The future is hidden underground

THE FIRST TIME I HEARD THE WORD 'ONKALO' WAS IN THE autumn of 2012. At that time, of course, I had no idea that I would be diagnosed with cancer within a couple of years.

'Onkalo' is Finnish and means cavity or cavern. The word can also be used about something magically mysterious, as in 'the troll lives in the caverns of the mountains'.

By sheer coincidence, while travelling on a train from Gothenburg to Stockholm I found myself reading a newspaper article about work to dig tunnels and very deep caves in the Finnish mountains, in which nuclear waste would be stored more or less for ever – at the very least for 100,000 years. Even if the radioactive waste is at its most dangerous – most lethal – during the first thousand years, there must be a guarantee that it will be stored safely for 3,000 generations to come.

I have lived with atomic power for the whole of my life. Even from my childhood I have vague memories of protests and the fear of atomic weapons, and of a devastating war between the Soviet Union and the USA which were two wild animals, only just kept apart and only occasionally at peace with each other. Then came nuclear power, the accident at Three Mile Island, followed by Chernobyl and, most recently, by Fukushima. I am convinced that there is already a clock ticking down to the next nuclear disaster. I question the validity of nuclear power. Every accident, or report that a catastrophe has only narrowly been avoided, has made me more negatively disposed. Naturally I have been aware of how slowly the radioactivity breaks down, and how dangerous the waste is that we shall be forced to live with for thousands of years. But it was only on that autumn day two years ago that it actually dawned on me what the real significance of it all was.

The newspaper article was tucked away on an inside page. Other news – about the love life of a rock star, how to avoid paying tax without breaking the law or how to lose X kilos within a fortnight – seemed to be much more important.

I have no difficulty in understanding that, of course. Life is lived in the here and now. People are seldom able to extend their curiosity beyond the next few days, or months, or years. Or perhaps it would be truer to say they focus only on the next lottery draw, or some other game that they hope to win, in order to wave goodbye to all their obligations and emigrate to some paradise in the Caribbean or Asia.

Nowadays people in our part of the world no longer believe in God. They believe in scratch cards and other games of chance. There is no end to all the scratching and gambling. If you have the combined skill and good luck to win a large sum of money, you have killed the goose that lays the golden egg. You don't need to work any more, you don't need to worry about anything: you can treat society with arrogant contempt.

It seems to me typical that the kind of financial rewards available for winning these days demonstrates this attitude very clearly. In some games, you can win a fixed monthly wage – already taxed, of course – for twenty-five years, or even longer.

Nevertheless, tucked away in that newspaper was an article about a hiding place in the Finnish mountains called Onkalo where nuclear waste will be stored for vast lengths of time.

A few days after that train journey I wrote to Onkalo and asked for permission to visit them. I received a swift response saying that I would not be welcome. The letter informed me that they did not want their premises to be used as the location for a thriller. I sent an angry reply saying that such a project had never occurred to me. If I had an opinion about what they were doing, it was a philosophical one. How is it possible to store potentially lethal waste for 100,000 years, bearing in mind that the oldest buildings raised by humans that are still standing are 5,000 to 6,000 years old? How is it possible to guarantee something that nobody living today will be able to check?

I received another reply saying that they had decided not to accept visitors because they could not guarantee people's safety in the caves and tunnels. Needless to say, I found this frightening, but amusing at the same time – how could they not guarantee the safety of a single visitor and yet maintain that the waste would still be there in the incomprehensibly distant future, long after I and the director who replied to my letter had died and rotted away in our graves?

It was clear that I would never be able to visit Onkalo. But similar work was taking place in Sweden. Just outside the town of Oskarshamn.

I had visited that town several times when I was eighteen. That was long before any nuclear power stations at all had been built in Sweden, and long before the question of taking care of the waste had become a problem for the government and Swedish citizens.

I wrote to the nuclear power station in Oskarshamn, and was told that I would be welcome to visit them. A few months later I did so.

Now, when I am living with my cancer, I think I have acquired new and unexpected perspectives on the way in which we handle nuclear waste.

6

The bubble in the glass

VIKTOR SUNDSTRÖM WAS A SELF-TAUGHT ENGINEER WHO WAS married to my aunt. He became a friend of mine when I was a young man because, despite his age – he lived until he was about ninety-five – he was still a political rebel. He never tired of complaining about the terrible conditions in which the poor people in his home province of Värmland had been forced to live at the end of the nineteenth century.

He once tried to explain the universe to me. At that time, in the middle of the 1950s, the Big Bang theory had not been accepted by all scientists as an explanation of the origins of the universe. Viktor maintained that the universe had always existed. When I asked what had existed before that, his answer was that there was no 'before'.

That was impossible to understand, of course. The whole of my childish image of the world collapsed. I recall vaguely that Viktor realised he had made me insecure and perhaps also afraid when he robbed me of that 'before'.

'Nobody knows for certain,' he said by way of consolation. 'The universe is a mystery.'

He didn't believe in God. He approved of the fact that my father had forbidden us to go anywhere near any kind of Sunday school. He never went to church except when he felt obliged to attend a funeral. He was completely indifferent to what would happen to his own body after his death.

For me God was something big and frightening. An invisible being who slunk along by my side and could read my thoughts. I gathered that neither Viktor nor my father believed that this invisible God had created the earth and other planets and stars. For some years this resulted in a feeling of insecurity inside me. I found it unsatisfactory for a universe and all its stars glistening in the cold winter nights to be one vast mystery.

There had to be something else. There had to be a 'before'.

Even if I had tried I would have been unable in those days to imagine an expanse of time in the future 100,000 years long. I still can't do it. I can see the mathematics, I can count the generations, but even so I don't understand it. How is it possible for a human being to imagine a comprehensible world in such a distant future? How could I imagine a descendant of mine 3,000 generations ahead? The future gets lost in the same kind of mist as when we look back in time. We are surrounded by fog, or perhaps compact darkness, whichever way we turn. We can send out our thoughts in all directions and all dimensions of time, but the replies we receive are not worth much. We are unable to penetrate what not even science-fiction writers manage to depict all that satisfactorily.

Researchers can use mathematical models to calculate everything from when the universe was first created to the day when the sun will expand so much that it swallows up our earth, long after all the oceans have evaporated and all life has ceased to exist. In the end, the life-giving sun will be our death. Like a gigantic fire-breathing dragon it will swallow up the earth and then become one of the cold, dead dwarf stars. But the mathematical models do not make the passage of time any more comprehensible.

There are other ways of approaching the impossible task of trying to imagine a world hundreds of thousands of years ahead of our present day. This is one of them:

Several years ago I asked a good friend of mine who is a glass-blower by profession to make me a glass containing an air bubble. Such a glass would normally be a blunder by a competent and self-respecting glass-blower, and be thrown away without a second thought. But I was interested in the difference between truth and falsehood, between myth and reality. In the back of my mind was also the question of time and eternity.

There is a myth that says that a bubble trapped inside the transparent wall of a glass moves. This happens so slowly that it is impossible to detect movement simply by looking at it – even during the course of a long lifetime the bubble would not appear to have moved at all in any direction – it would take more than a million years for it to return to its starting point. In other words, the bubble has an orbit, just as the planets move in accordance with a set pattern and at set speeds.

Harry Martinson has written impressively about this in his outstanding space epic *Aniara*. However, if we postulate that this is not a myth but is actually fact, we are faced with another problem: how can we possibly check it? Nobody holding that glass in his or her hand today is going to exist in a million years' time. Thousands of generations of human beings cannot report on exact memories of what their eyes have seen during thousands of years. We cannot possibly know for sure if the movement of a bubble of air through glass is true or false, myth or verifiable truth.

Needless to say, scientists can create a model and conduct experiments, but that can only give us an indication of probability, never an indisputable truth.

Trying to see 100,000 years into the future is a compromise between what we can imagine on the basis of factual knowledge and what our fantasy and imagination aided by mystical experiences might indicate.

A human being is a creature that has been evolving for thousands of years, developing more and more appropriately practical abilities. We would hardly have been equipped with the enormous creative capacity that comes from fantasy and imagination had it not been for the need to survive, to protect our children and to find new ways of obtaining food when normal conditions become chaotic as a result of drought, floods, earthquakes or volcanic eruptions.

The history of mankind, like that of all other living beings on this earth, is based ultimately on the creation of survival strategies. Nothing else is of real importance. This ability enables us to reproduce, and to pass on to new generations ways of handling exactly the same problems of survival that we have faced up to ourselves.

Life is the art of surviving. Nothing else.

The glass containing the bubble of air is still standing on a shelf in my home. If nobody knocks it over so that it falls and shatters, it will still be there long after I have passed away.

And I believe that bubble will move. But I shall not see it doing so.

7

Last will and testament

ONE DAY, IN THE SPRING OF 2013, I WRITE MY LAST WILL AND testament. There are still seven months to go before I start feeling pain in my neck, and I have no physical or mental indications that such problems might be in store. I am not ill, and do not suspect that death might be already standing in the porch, waiting to come in.

The reason I write my will is quite different.

When my father died many years ago he had left detailed instructions about what should be done with his belongings after his death. This meant that my siblings and I never needed to worry about what he would have wanted. Which bundles of letters should be burnt? Which should be kept, and even read? What should happen to his furniture and books? Was there anybody who should receive a legacy? It was easy for us to sort and distribute his estate, and then devote ourselves to the much more important matter of mourning his passing.

Writing one's will is to acknowledge one's mortality. To some extent, of course, one does it for highly egotistical reasons – but mostly, I think, it is to make things easier for those left behind.

Once you are dead, you are dead. You can no longer influence earthly things. Being alive is being able to say yes or no. Being dead is to be surrounded by silence.

When did human beings start writing wills? When they began to own things that could be of value to those left behind, of course.

Owning things in accordance with the law brings with it the need for a written statement of what should happen to those items after the owner's death.

No doubt most people think they ought to write a will – but they never get round to it, apart perhaps from a few sketchy points in a notebook. They keep putting it off. In many cases it is probably due to a naive superstition: they are afraid that writing a will might entice death, and encourage him to come immediately and collect them. For others it may well be a feeling that there is no big rush: they are still young, after all. There's plenty of time left in which to do it.

People create the greatest of all illusions: *if* I die. Not *when* I die.

But suddenly they are killed in a road accident. Or they are stricken with aggressive cancer, and all thoughts of making a will simply disappear. Fighting to survive takes up all their energies.

Civilisation leaves no wills behind. That is something only individual human beings do. Neither the Mayans nor the Incas, the Egypt of the Pharaohs nor the Roman Empire, vanished at a stroke. The decline came slowly and stealthily, and was ignored for as long as possible. It was simply unthinkable for such a dominant civilisation to collapse. The gods were a guarantee for that. As long as you made sacrifices to them, followed the advice and demands of the priests or shamans, you belonged to a civilisation that would last for ever. That seems to be a characteristic common to all great and classical civilisations: they seemed immortal to those who lived in them.

A striking example of a culture that collapsed is the one that faded away on Easter Island. Today Rapa Nui, as it is called in Polynesian, is a remote island in the Pacific Ocean. It is completely without trees. Scattered around in the undulating grass-covered landscape are gigantic sculptures of the former civilisation's gods. Ever since Easter Island was discovered on Easter Day in 1722 by the crew of a Dutch ship commanded by Captain Jacob Roggeveen, people have been astonished by these sculptures. Some have fallen, others are still standing, precisely where they were once dragged into place and raised. But most remarkable of all are the quarries where the statues were originally carved out. There are several half-finished statues still lying there, including one that would have been bigger than all the rest.

It is an unfinished god, not sufficiently complete to be transported – with enormous effort and brilliant contemporary engineering skill – to the place where the priests had decided it should be raised.

The quarries on Easter Island are a sort of cemetery for dead gods that were never actually used. The quarry workers suddenly abandoned their half-finished works of art.

Did somebody compel them to stop work? Or did they do so of their own accord? Did they flee in a sudden attack of panic? Did their belief in what the gods represented suddenly fail them? Nobody knows for certain.

Nevertheless, today it is possible to establish with a fair degree of confidence what caused that rich culture to collapse. Or at least the alternatives can be reduced to a small number.

A significant number of researchers believe that the people who originally colonised the island brought with them – presumably unintentionally – rats, which had no natural enemies on the island. As a result the rats multiplied dramatically and were able to live on seeds from the palm trees that were widespread on the island at that time.

Easter Island had been populated by people from the Pacific Ocean archipelago, who undertook long voyages to the isolated island. The forests were presumably one of the assets that induced the sailors to stay on the island. Many researchers suggest that the ravaging of the forests eventually led to the collapse of the civilisation that developed on the island over some 400 years because the inhabitants were no longer able to support themselves. Without trees it was impossible to build boats to use for fishing or, towards the desperate end, to travel away from the island, perhaps back to the coasts from which they had originally come. The forests had been stripped bare in order to provide fuel, but also to create wooden rollers to transport the gods to the places where they would be raised and worshipped. The soil that had previously been used for growing food blew away without the tree roots to keep it in place on the rocky ground. And of course the rats ate all the seeds, so that the trees could not reproduce themselves.

We do not know what happened during the last years of the Easter Island civilisation. There are no written records. But wooden sculptures that have been discovered suggest that the inhabitants starved to death. The carved figures depict emaciated, hungry people. Their protruding rib bones are as significant as their facial expressions.

The struggle to find food might well have led to fights between various groups. It is not difficult to envisage the social chaos, the religious despair and the brutality into which people descend when there is only enough food for a minority.

Nobody wrote a will, of course. Neither a personal document nor one that could be a source of information enabling us to understand what was happening during that final period before Easter Island became as deserted as it had once been. What the last inhabitants left for us to interpret was a silent warning. The deserted island, the overturned or unfinished statues were the nearest they came to leaving a will. Confirmation that in the end, even the most advanced cultures decline and disappear.

There are no last wishes left behind by the cultures and civilisations that preceded our own time. By means of archaeology, palaeontology and other aspects of research, and with the aid of increasingly sophisticated technical aids such as microscopes and telescopes, we can dig deeper and further back in time and understand more about the past.

But two concepts sum up all that has been discovered, and probably all that will ever be discovered: survival and extinction.

By examining the world in a rear-view mirror, as it were, we can see what we are also heading towards. Naturally, nothing will be exactly the same – history never repeats itself as a mere imitation.

But in our case we can say that we have already established what will be the ultimate record of our civilisation.

Not Rubens. Not Rembrandt. Not Raphael.

Not even Shakespeare or Botticelli, Beethoven, Bach or the Beatles.

We are leaving something completely different behind. When every other aspect of our civilisation is dead and gone, two things will remain: the spaceship *Voyager* on its never-ending journey through space and the nuclear waste hidden away in the mountain caverns.

8

The man in the window

ONE EVENING I AM SITTING AT HOME, THINKING ABOUT HOW THE illness known as cancer entered my life.

When I was nine years old I developed a pain in my stomach that was so bad that I was taken into Sveg's little hospital. The doctors suspected that I had appendicitis and would need an operation. I didn't, in fact. The pain eased and the consultant, whose name was Stenholm and who frightened everybody he came into contact with, concluded that I had merely got a little fluid in my appendix that gradually dried up and disappeared of its own accord.

But I was kept in a general ward for three days. At the far end next to the window was a large man with thin hair and a pot belly. He had cancer. On the left side of his bulging stomach was a festering, purulent sore. The wound was dressed every morning and every evening, and the bloodstained, pus-soaked bandages were thrown into a tin bucket and taken away. I gathered from the patients in beds closest to him that the wound gave off a very unpleasant smell. Once, when he had gone to the toilet, I heard people whispering about the wound being cancerous: the whole of his stomach was being eaten away by tumours, and one had forced its way out of his stomach and through his skin.

Nobody said as much in so many words, but even a nine-year-old like me realised that the man was dying. He was a horse dealer and used to buy and sell Northern Swedish horses, and occasionally also Ardennes from Belgium. I think his name was Svante, and his surname might have been Wiberg – or was it Wallén? But I know for a fact that he bought and sold horses.

Nobody came to visit him during the days I spent on the ward. When he wasn't lying immobile in his bed, he used to stand in front of one of the tall windows. He would stand there in his ill-fitting nightshirt, his belly hanging awkwardly and his hands behind his back, staring out of the window like a policeman on patrol. It often seemed as if he stood there for hours on end.

The day I was discharged I went over to the window to see what it was he had been looking at.

The window overlooked the hospital mortuary – a small, white-washed building lying alongside a shed for storing rubbish and an old abandoned stable. Perhaps he once used to keep his horses there? By the time I left the hospital I knew that cancer was something with a nasty smell, and it produced bloodstained and pus-soaked bandages. It had absolutely nothing to do with my own life apart from being a distant threat hidden away in the general ward of an insignificant hospital in the north of Sweden.

I remain sitting there in my flat in the darkness. It is half past four in the morning. Another memory has just cropped up inside my head. Or perhaps it would be more accurate to say that I had taken it down from a shelf inside the archives of my memory. I start thinking about something that happened exactly twenty-one years ago.

I remember very clearly the last cigarette I ever smoked. I smoked it just outside the entrance doors to Johannesburg International Airport. In December 1992 it was still called the Jan Smuts Airport. A few years later, when the apartheid system had disappeared once and for all into the rubbish dump of history, it was renamed after the heroic freedom fighter Oliver Tambo.

I had been wandering around in Maputo for a month, feeling more and more out of sorts. For a long time I thought I was suffering from some persistent virus, or an attack of malaria that had not yet come to a head. I was busy rehearsing a new play at the theatre. Every afternoon when I got into my old Renault I had to force myself to start the engine. Tiredness was beginning to feel crippling, irrespective of how long I slept.

One day I pulled up outside the theatre and switched off the engine. But I didn't have the strength to get out of the car. I gave up. I shouted for the theatre's stage manager Alfredo, who was standing outside the entrance, putting up a poster.

'I don't feel well,' I said. 'Tell the actors they can have a reading day today.'

I drove back home and fell asleep as soon as I lay down on the bed. In the evening I went out to buy some food. In the shop I happened to bump into Elisabeth, a Swedish doctor and a friend of mine. She looked me up and down.

'You're all yellow,' she said.

'Am I?'

'Yellow all over. Come and see me tomorrow morning. Eight o'clock.'

The following day she sent me to a laboratory. They did a test on my liver, the result of which ought to have been 20 – my reading was 2,000. I don't recall what the test was called.

'This is not something I can deal with,' she said. 'Not here in Mozambique. I'll telephone a hospital in Johannesburg – you must get yourself there today.'

The South African Airways flight that evening from Maputo was not long, only forty-five minutes. I stood there outside the airport entrance and smoked a cigarette. When the car from the hospital in Sandton arrived I squashed the butt under my heel. I didn't realise at the time that it was the last cigarette I would ever smoke.

Within a few days they had established that I was suffering from a particularly aggressive form of jaundice. I suspected that I had been infected by dirty vegetables during a trip to the north of Mozambique where I had eaten in a few restaurants with somewhat unreliable levels of hygiene.

That was at Christmas in 1992. It was still by no means clear what was going to happen in South Africa now that the apartheid system was falling apart. During the nights, as I lay in my hospital bed, I occasionally heard gunfire somewhere out there in the darkness. Johannesburg was a city infected with criminality. Hatred between the races was widespread, as was fear.

On the morning of the third day a doctor I hadn't seen before came into my room.

'We have scrutinised the X-ray pictures we took yesterday,' he said, his broken English revealing the fact that he must have been a recent immigrant, probably from Eastern Europe. 'We have found a dark patch in one of your lungs. We don't yet know for sure what it is. But soon.'

He left the room. The door had barely closed behind him when a thought struck me: cancer. The fact that I had extinguished that cigarette outside the airport in Johannesburg was not going to help me. Smoking meant that I was now going to die.

A memory from Skellefteå in the beginning of the 1970s flashed through my mind. Old Dr Sigrid Nygren, an inveterate theatre enthusiast, had conducted a general medical check-up on me. I had just recently turned twenty.

'Do you smoke?' she asked.

'Yes.'

'You should stop. Otherwise you'll go down with cancer in what should be the best years of your life, when you're forty or forty-five.'

I was forty-four now. I lay there in hospital with my jaundice and waited for information about what the doctors had discovered in the X-ray. I couldn't get the thought of death out of my mind. I lay there conducting a pathetic but at the same time entirely natural bargaining exercise, promising to be an infinitely better person if only the diagnosis wasn't cancer.

Afterwards, when the doctor had informed me that it was just a deposit of fluid in my left lung and not a tumour, I realised that what had scared me most of all was my age. I would die eventually, of course, like everybody else: but I didn't want to die yet. Not before I had even reached the age of forty-five.

When I was diagnosed with an aggressive primary tumour in my left lung, one of my first reactions was one of disbelief. After all, I hadn't smoked at all for twenty years. So how could I have lung cancer? That was one of the few occasions when I came close to feeling sorry for myself. It felt unjust. But I didn't give in. It wasn't easy. Sometimes the only thing one can do is to complain.

I still feel the same. If you are a child, a teenager, young or middle-aged, then of course you will feel it is unfair if you are diagnosed with cancer. But if, like me, you have lived for approaching seventy years, longer than most people in the world could ever dream of, it is easier to become reconciled to the fact that an incurable disease has taken over your body.

That is only partly true, of course. It's not quite as easy as that. Death always comes as an uninvited guest and makes a mess of everything:

'It's time to leave now.'

Nobody wants to die, whether they are young or old. Dying is always difficult. Especially if you are on your own.

In the early 1960s, when I spent a few years following humanities courses at the Högre Allmänna Läroverket school in Borås, the much-despised morning assembly was compulsory. In those days it was dominated by some kind of Christian service. There were very few exceptions. On one occasion the remarkable actor Kolbjörn Knudsen delivered a short extract from *Peer Gynt*, which succeeded in waking up pupils who were dozing off or surreptitiously doing their homework. Sometimes there were poetry readings, mainly poems by Ferlin or Gullberg recited in a shaky voice by a nervous senior pupil.

But most often the assemblies were conducted by some clergyman or other. I particularly remember one hospital chaplain. He came to the school at regular intervals and told us about the final hours of young patients in his spiritual care at the hospital, dying from some fatal disease. His theme was always the same: even for very young people the horror of death can become tolerable if you commend your soul to God.

The sentimentality and duplicity were repulsive. He nearly always started crying himself as he told his tales. It seemed to me that he must have been typical of the most bigoted of Sunday-school preachers.

Later in life I came across the German writer Georg Büchner, who died in his early twenties. By then he had already written a shocking manifesto in Hessen, been deported and hunted by the secret police, written three masterpieces – especially *Danton's Death* and *Woyzeck* – as well as a doctoral thesis on the nervous system of fish.

When he died he was living in Spiegelgasse in Zürich. He had been stricken by typhus. I often used to wonder about how this gifted man reacted to the news that he was about to die when he had barely begun to live life. His desperation and despondency must have been hellish. Or did he simply ignore the facts that ought to have dominated every second of his life? Perhaps he did what seems to be the usual thing, and as death approached he began to draw up grandiose plans for the future that lay in store once he had risen from his sickbed.

A cold winter's morning was soon to break as I sat there in my red armchair and allowed my thoughts to wander. Perhaps I dozed off. The moonlight that had illuminated my bookcase had faded away. I must remember to ring Lars Eriksson and order at least another twenty metres of oak shelving. Oak from Latvia, I suddenly recalled. I had no idea why Swedish oak was evidently not good enough even for bookshelves.

I was sixty-six years old and had been stricken by cancer. Before long I would begin a course of chemotherapy. Neither I nor the doctors around me knew whether or not it would be successful.

I didn't dare to think about what would happen if the chemo-therapy was ineffective.

It didn't matter if I was sixty-six years old or a child in a hospital in Sveg facing up to the reality of death for the first time.

9

Hagar Qim

THE TEMPLE WAS BUILT BEFORE I WAS BORN. THE TEMPLE WILL still exist after I am dead.

Very early on in life I decided that there were two Mediterranean islands I really must visit. While sitting through boring lessons at school I would have my atlas open, studying Crete and Malta. I knew about Knossos and the dolphins depicted on the walls of the ruined palace there, but in those days Malta was little more than a name to me.

However, I longed to go there. I'm not sure exactly what it was that enticed me so. One winter, when I was about thirty, I took a train to Athens and then the ferry to Crete. I spent a month in Heraklion, reading up on local history, which I thought I knew too little about. It was a damp and chilly winter. I read and went for walks, ate at cheap restaurants and occasionally went to the cinema.

Malta was a different story altogether. I went there in 2012. It was about as hot as Africa – a silent wall of sheer sunlight. And when I went there, at long last I knew why.

On the south-west coast of Malta there is something that nowadays can probably be designated the world's oldest building that is still standing. On a stone plateau overlooking the sea is the temple known as Hagar Qim, which simply means 'raised stones'. There are, in fact, several buildings that have been joined together over a very long period of time. But it has been established that the oldest parts are between 5,000 and 6,000 years old. Around that time, or perhaps slightly earlier, Malta was inhabited by farmers who had arrived by boat from Sicily. That was the period known as the younger Stone Age.

The temple, nowadays regarded as one of the oldest in existence created by human hands and not reduced to ruins or fragments, is astonishingly skilfully built. The observer is astounded by the precision with which various gigantic blocks of stone have been joined together.

We know little more about the people who built the temple than I have already stated: they were farmers who came to this uninhabited island as colonisers. Archaeological investigations of burial sites have produced the remains of primitive tools, but nothing to suggest military equipment. The incomers had peaceful, not war-like, intentions.

We do not know who or what was worshipped in this temple. There are no inscriptions or legends to suggest who their gods were. It is evident from the remains that have been discovered that animals were sacrificed, but we have no idea about the religion of the colonists. Their gods have fallen silent for ever.

All that is left is the substantial stone building they raised. The efforts involved must have been immense. There must have been individuals who acted as architects, others who planned the building projects, and above all those who did the manual work. We can safely assume that it took a very long time, and that the temple was never actually finished but was constantly changed, made more attractive and more majestic. Perhaps their religion was quite simply the building of this temple? A wordless cult that expressed itself via the cutting, moving, lifting and joining together of stone? Nobody knows.

Many hundreds of years after these immigrants came to Malta from Sicily, other groups of people followed suit. These new arrivals were also peaceful and mingled happily with the inhabitants already ensconced there. But later on other, more war-like, immigrants arrived in Malta, took possession of the island and hence also the temple. New symbolic worlds were established and different gods came to be worshipped as the centuries passed. As in so many other places during the history of the world, the gods were hounded out of their temple and replaced by other tenants to whom prayers were said.

Six thousand years is a long time, no matter what you compare it with. If we reckon every human generation spans about thirty years, it corresponds to at least two hundred generations.

The temple complex was built at least a thousand years before the Cheops pyramid. The temples of the Aztecs and the Maya civilisation are even younger in comparison. The majestic cathedrals built by the stonemasons of Europe came into being less than a thousand years ago. In the long-term perspective they are barely teenagers.

Hagar Qim stands there as a solitary monolith inviting the same kind of reverence as a very old human being. The temple illustrates a fact that is both unexpected and crucial for what I am trying to say: even if it seems a very long time ago, 6,000 years is an insignificant period of time when we try nowadays to construct buildings that will keep nuclear waste safe for at least 100,000 years. The difference is staggering – 94,000 years. Nothing created by man will ever come close to the task we have before us – the task at which we must succeed.

Today we can board an aeroplane and a few hours later disembark at an airport just outside Valetta. Then we can travel by car southwards along the meandering roads, and come to the temple that is lying there in wait for us. The stone columns stare out silently over the sea, like hidden guards keeping watch on the horizon for boatloads of new immigrants.

Hagar Qim is indeed a very old building – but there are cave paintings and ivory sculptures reckoned to be 40,000 years old. Needless to say, both the animals depicted by the cave painters and the Hagar Qim temple are examples of the ability of human beings to create art.

But nothing in the human world was there to start with; everything has been created and developed.

That is made clear by the sculpture of the lion man that was discovered in south-eastern Germany a few days before the outbreak of war in September 1939.

10

The lion man

THE LATE SUMMER OF 1939 WAS VERY HOT THROUGHOUT EUROPE. The beaches and seaside resorts in Sweden were full of people. Many people still living could recall the suffocating heat that enveloped Europe during the summer of 1914, in the months before the outbreak of the First World War. Their unease increased as the Austrian corporal's demands regarding the borders of Germany became increasingly implacable. The key event that sparked the First World War was the assassination of the heir to the throne of the Austro-Hungarian Empire in Sarajevo; behind it lay both stupidity and arrogance, but also political dreams of expansion and colonial domination.

The risks of war were now increasing again. There were those who maintained, rightly, that the First World War had never actually ended. There had been a pause for just over twenty years. Now the curtain was about to rise on Act II if the European leaders failed to find a way of preventing Hitler from converting his threats into action. But his demands grew more ominous by the day. England's prime minister, Chamberlain, came back from a summit meeting with a document signed by the German chancellor; many people doubted the validity of this 'scrap of paper', and suspected that the words uttered by Chamberlain when he disembarked from the aeroplane about 'Peace in our time' were among the most misguided ever spoken by a politician.

But not everybody was lying on beaches and making the most of the heat, or going through agonies regarding the increasing threat of war. Some archaeologists were investigating a series of caves in Stadel in the Swabian Alps in deepest south-east Germany. The fact that Nazi soldiers had begun their advance into Poland was not important to them.

In fact, a few days before the outbreak of war on 1 September 1939 they made a discovery – or rather, a lot of small finds they made would turn out to be a major discovery. They found some two hundred fragments of ivory from the tusk of a mammoth, and collected them with the scrupulous care characteristic of conscientious and passionate archaeologists.

But that was that. War broke out and the bag containing the ivory remains was stowed away in a cupboard in a museum until 1970. Then at last experts began to link together the fragments that had been collected over thirty years previously. It soon became clear that it was possible to envisage how they fitted together into some form of sculpture, but that a lot of parts were missing. In 1989 another search was made of the cave, and more fragments were recovered. So far, about a thousand fragments have been found, many of them very tiny.

In 1939 it was clear that an astonishing discovery had been made – something that would dramatically change the history of how human beings began to create art. Now it became obvious that the sculpture slowly being pieced together was of a human being with the head of a lion.

There are simpler figures carved by human beings that can be assumed to be older than this lion. But the crucial and revolutionary aspect of this 30-centimetre-tall ivory sculpture is precisely the combination of human being and animal. Here an artist has been at work, someone who created something more than merely a carving of a figure out of a mammoth's tusk, something more than just a reproduction of an animal on a cave wall. The remarkable thing is that the artist has created something unexpected. He – or she – has imagined an abstraction, something that doesn't exist in the real world. In his or her mind's eye he or she has conjured up a mixture of a human being and a lion. We cannot possibly know why the artist decided to produce a concrete image of this vision. Is the sculpture supposed to suggest that a man can possess the power of a lion? Or that a predator can possess human traits? The artist has created something of which there is no model, something quite new, a combination of the fantastic and the real.

Has the artist imagined that the finished sculpture already exists inside the ivory? And that his or her task is simply to cut away everything unnecessary in order to release the sculpture of the lion man that was waiting to become alive?

The archaeologists who have researched the sculpture have concluded that it must have taken about two months to make, given the knives of flint to which the sculptor would have had access. Two months of work in daylight.

We can draw another conclusion from this. The man or woman who created the lion man must have lived together with other people who were able to ensure that he or she was supplied with sufficient food. The artist was looked after. And this leads to two more conclusions. There was some form of social organisation able to provide for someone who didn't go hunting or collecting plants. And this suggests that the sculptor must have had special significance for the group as a whole. Did this take the form of some kind of religious worship? Or were the people surrounding the artist impressed by what he or she was able to produce? Was the artist regarded as a kind of magician?

The fact that the artist was able to produce a symbolic figure makes specific demands on the capacity of the brain. What is known as the prefrontal cortex is not a part of the early stages of the development of the human mind. It comprises the front part of the frontal lobe and has to do with our ability to acknowledge or to ignore various external stimuli. These would include information that dictates an individual's actions.

And so, 40,000 years ago, a person sat with a piece of ivory in his or her hand. Perhaps he or she had previously carved out remarkable symbolic figures? Or was this the first sculpture made by the artist, which as a result of a marvellous coincidence has survived and in recent times been pieced together again, in almost complete form? We cannot know.

We don't know who the artist was. He or she has left behind no means of identification. Nor is it plausible that it was important for the man or the woman to explain to future civilisations that he or she was the person who had created this remarkable work of art.

The artist lived 1,300 generations ago. They belonged to what we now call the Aurignacian culture, named after the site of an archaeological find in Aurignac in France, which also produced many cave paintings.

One day in April 2013, I pay a visit to the British Museum in London where a replica of the lion man is being exhibited temporarily. It is a very special experience, standing in front of the little sculpture and gazing into the eyes of the ivory figure.

He can see me, I think. And I can see him.

Without knowing why, I suddenly get the feeling that I recognise him.

11

Ice

A FEW HUNDRED YEARS AGO NOBODY BELIEVED THERE HAD BEEN such things as ice ages.

One of the significant undertakings of the nineteenth century was establishing the timing of the very cold periods that had affected parts of the planet at fairly regular intervals. The layers of ice, which could be several kilometres thick, had compressed the earth's crust and transformed the landscape into a covering of gravel.

Among those who came to play an important role in our understanding of the history of the world and the recurrent ice ages was a scientist called Milutin Milankovitch. He was an interdisciplinary scientific team all by himself, as he possessed extensive expertise in a range of fields, including mathematics, engineering and astronomy.

The first scientist to argue seriously that there had been recurrent ice ages throughout our history was the glaciologist Louis Agassiz. Several others followed in his footsteps, but they were never able to explain satisfactorily the reasons why these ice ages occurred regularly but with different strengths and not always in the same places.

It was not until, in the middle of the First World War, Milankovitch decided to try to explain the cycles once and for all that a crucial step in our understanding of climate changes could be taken.

Milankovitch maintained that the explanation for the enormous temperature changes must have to do with the effect of the sun on the earth. That might seem to be blindingly obvious, but it didn't explain the big differences that occurred at intervals of thousands of years. Milankovitch used his comprehensive mathematical and astronomical expertise to calculate changes in the passage of the earth around the sun and the rotation around its own axis. He eventually realised that the earth was affected not only by the magnetic forces of the sun, but also by the gravitation from the moon and other planets in the solar system, especially Saturn and Jupiter. After a number of years' work he concluded that there were three factors affecting the differing movement patterns of the earth.

The first was that different forces contributed to changes in the rotation pattern of the earth around the sun. The second was that the angle between the axis of the earth and the rotation pattern kept changing. And the third depended on the direction of the earth's axis.

This means that the light of the sun illuminating the earth changed over slow cycles. When the beams were at their lowest level, the winter snow did not have time to melt away, especially in the northern hemisphere, and so the snow lay continuously from year to year, which in turn meant that the climate became even colder.

Today the earth's axis is pointing to somewhere close to the Pole Star – but this is not a permanent state of affairs. In about 10,000 to 12,000 years from now it will be pointing to somewhere near the star Vega. The change will continue to take place over many thousands of years until it is once again pointing at the Pole Star – but by then the Pole Star will also have moved because the universe is in a state of perpetual motion.

It is possible to measure the length of ice ages by investigating how much water at any given point is captured by the earth's covering of ice. It is possible nowadays to predict with a high degree of accuracy when the various ice ages will occur, how long they will last, and what the climate will be like between them. About 5,000 years from now the mountain chain that runs through Sweden and Norway will be covered by permanent ice. The crust of the earth will have been pressed down by about three hundred metres, which means in turn that sea level will have dropped by between five and fifty metres. Nearly all our archipelagos will disappear, and never return.

This ice age will be followed by a period characterised by a somewhat milder climate. But it is unlikely that many people will be living in Sweden then: it will simply be too cold.

Another ice age will reach its culmination in about 20,000 years. The ice will reach a thickness of about 1,500 metres. That ice age will be followed by a warmer period, which researchers predict will be quite similar to the climate of today's Greenland. The parts of Sweden that are not covered in ice will have constant frost in the ground, and agriculture will be impossible. Perhaps groups of hunters and fishermen will be able to roam around what is currently the southern and western coast of Sweden, but otherwise the country will be deserted.

The coldest ice age will reach its culmination about 60,000 years from now. By then the ice covering Stockholm could well be about 2,500 metres deep. When the ice eventually melts the sea will be about a hundred metres above what is currently high-water level.

Then it will gradually become warmer. In about 120,000 years' time the climate could well be similar to what it is today.

So eight or nine ice ages will come and go before what we have hidden away in our underground caverns is no longer dangerous.

A key question is, of course: how can the earth's crust be pressed down so deep without those underground caverns being damaged, collapsing or being crushed?

The answer is simple. A mountain that is pressed down retains its original form. The only thing that changes is the thickness of the heavy layer of ice, and the fact that what is currently the surface of the earth lies lower down.

Milutin Milankovitch died in 1958. He couldn't anticipate much of recent research into climate and ice ages, but he lived long enough to experience both atom bombs and hydrogen bombs. As the learned scientist he was, he must have wondered how nuclear power and its waste would be affected by the various cycles of climate change the earth would undergo.

There is a photograph of him, taken when he was about thirty years old. He is very well dressed, standing by a table. His face is sensitive and his smile suggests a mixture of shyness and self-confidence.

He is one of those scientists that nowadays only a few specialists know about, although his work enabling us to understand the past and to draw apart the veils concealing the future was outstanding in every way.

But do we now know everything about the ice ages lying in wait for us? Are all the secrets and riddles solved or answered?

No. Questions receive answers, but answers always lead to new questions.

This very morning an invisible bird is singing in our garden for the first time this spring. I naturally assume it is the same bird that sat in the bushes singing last year. I imagine that there is something in its trills that can only be produced by this bird, this year as well as last.

We live in a country of invisible birds and seasons. In a period of 100,000 years there are 400,000 seasons. Or let us say 380,000 seasons if we omit the ice ages when no seasons can be discerned.

The numbers are bewildering and cannot be grasped by our emotions or our intellect.

It is like looking into a mirror and being uncertain about whose face it really is you can see in the glass.

When everything becomes too complicated and difficult to comprehend, I generally look at a black-and-white photograph on my wall. It is of me as a nine-year-old, sitting at a desk in Sveg primary school. When I see that face, full of curiosity and confidence that everything is possible in life, I can feel the strength to understand coming back to me.

The short ice age inside myself is over. Everything is back to normal again. All truths continue to be provisional. Searching for an overview can begin once again.

I can't imagine that there is anything more important than that.

12

Turning time in a different direction

Let us imagine Sweden 40,000 years into the future.

Everything I imagine will be a guess. Archaeologists can embark on expeditions into the past in various ways, and nowadays we have an increasingly astonishing DNA analysis to help us understand what happened in the distant past.

But the future doesn't fascinate us in the same way as the past because there is nothing we can be sure about, nothing we can relate to via our own lives. Our imagination simply can't cope with what life will be like so far beyond our temporal horizons.

Nevertheless, there are some things we know for sure about what will happen thousands of years into the future. Quite a lot, in fact. But at the same time we have an unknown factor that did not affect earlier generations: how will climate changes brought about by humans affect various processes?

Forty thousand years from now dramatic events will have taken place – we can't say exactly when, only that they will happen. We are already heading there, even if the road is long. It is leading in a specific direction, towards an ice age that will take place somewhere between 10,000 and 50,000 years from now, and which will affect our part of the world.

When the ice age arrives, Sweden will be covered by a layer of ice almost a kilometre thick. All human buildings will be buried and destroyed underneath the ice. Houses, towns, bridges, and everything we have collected in museums, libraries and underground store-houses, or dug down into the earth as treasure.

After that ice age our climate will become gradually warmer. People – assuming there are any left – will be able to move into areas where the climate is tolerable. We shall once again be nomads, fishermen and hunter-gatherers. Humans will be back in square one, everything must begin all over again.

We cannot know if the brains of these people will have undergone some basic change compared with those in earlier historical epochs, but all the education that humans underwent throughout the ages will have disappeared. If a mobile phone or a computer survives the ice age, it will be a totally incomprehensible phenomenon. Perhaps something that fell down from some unknown planet in the universe? Something handed down by unknown gods?

When thunder rumbles there will be nothing to suggest that it is not due once again to a god riding around in his chariot with a hammer held in his raised hand. He probably won't be called Thor, but old myths are often recreated – not as imitations, but as something that never existed before, as there are no memories remaining from those times.

Time itself has lost its memory.

Can I envisage all this? As images I can conjure up in my mind? As logical consequences of convincing arguments produced by interdisciplinary scientific research? I don't know if I can. Sometimes I am convinced I can see what is coming, but just as often I am doubtful.

An iceberg almost three kilometres high that covers large areas including Sweden? One only needs to go for a three-kilometre walk and imagine the distance covered as a staircase leading up into the sky in order to understand the impossibility of seeing that future.

One day all the ice will melt again. If we had the possibility of glimpsing even for a few seconds the world revealed after the ice melted, we wouldn't recognise any of the landscape. We would be confronted by new mountains, new beaches, new bays. A whole new map would have been drawn by the ice, and we would find no trace of the past no matter how hard we searched: all we would see would be the silent gravel.

But what I have just said is not quite right. There will in fact be something left after the extinction of our civilisation.

One or more underground nuclear waste stations.

13

A journey into the nether regions

WE DROVE BY CAR FROM GOTHENBURG TO THE OTHER SIDE OF
Sweden, to Oskarshamn. In contrast with all the hostility I endured
in my attempts to visit Onkalo, I was well received in Oskarshamn.
There didn't appear to be any kind of secrecy attached to their activities, which is as it should be, of course. Here they are working to
assure future generations that everything possible is being done to
ensure that the poisonous nuclear waste is safely shut away in secure
stores.

I speak to a manager. She makes the only possible statement about
the nature of her work: 'It has nothing to do with my personal views
about nuclear power – but as it exists, somebody has to take care of
the waste.'

We travel down through a series of lift shafts bored into the rock
and come to a depth that should be too deep for the approaching
permafrost to reach, and to damage the copper capsules in which it
is now reckoned the nuclear waste will be stored, in caverns made
in rock that has not moved since time immemorial. When the waste
eventually becomes harmless, we will discover whether what is essentially a guess today is correct or not. The best-case scenario is that
the seal on the 100,000-year-old storage facility will not have been
broken.

But we are not able to pray to whatever gods we might believe in
for permission to make a visit into a future time when we will have
been dead for thousands of years. Nor do we know if there will be

any descendants of ours on the land exposed after the melting away of the ice, thinking that they are standing in a country that was once called Sweden.

It is not plausible. Not possible. Even the memories of humans are finite. Legends and myths will also die. If there is in fact a dream about a country that once existed and was called Sweden, it will be no more than a faint reflection of a legend that people will have no real reason for believing. Our reality, our rich memories of artistic and scientific triumphs and human defeats, will have been transformed into a mere saga. Atlantis and Sweden will then have something in common: nobody will be sure that either place really existed.

Nevertheless, we know what we hope for. We hope those people will have no idea that there is radioactive waste directly beneath their feet, a fatal clock that is still ticking away.

That is the memory that today's people plan to leave behind for future generations – that nobody will remember it.

The last thing we leave behind us is something we hide away so that nobody will be able to find it.

Not ever.

14

The young medical student

THE DOCTOR WHO GAVE ME THE NEWS ABOUT MY CANCER WAS called Mona. It was 'serious', and in addition it was probably 'incurable'. There was, in any case, no doubt about the implications for the rest of my life. The medics would set in motion the treatment they considered most appropriate. But nobody could give any guarantees.

Mona was a perfect example of what is meant by 'medical care'. She was well prepared, she spoke calmly and clearly, and she made time to listen to my questions. Time stood still in her consulting room. She must have had other patients waiting for her, but just now I was the one in there. She took her time and the consultation didn't end until she was certain that I didn't have any more questions.

Then I acquired Bengt Bergman as my consultant – although of course all the cancer specialists worked together. Every case of cancer is unique, but it is also a cooperative undertaking from which views and suggestions for action can be discussed and an agreed basis produced for continued treatment.

Needless to say, during that time I often thought about other doctors I had come into contact with during my life. Anyone who has lived for as long as I have will have come across quite a few, in various countries and in various more or less dramatic circumstances.

And new generations are appearing all the time.

Cecilia and Krister have a son, a young man who has just begun studying medicine at university in the northern Swedish town of Umeå. If I understand the situation correctly, he has already decided the subject in which he will eventually specialise: he wants to become a neurologist. I never ask him why, but I can guess his reasons.

'We live in a universe which we can only partially understand and map out. But inside us we all have another universe which we actually know just as little about. Our brains.'

I understand him. Assuming that is in fact the way he thinks. He doesn't just envisage himself as a highly specialised doctor at some point in the future: he wants to be one of those people who venture out into unexplored territory, just like those who in the past set out to find the source of the River Nile or a negotiable route to the North Pole. Or have more recently created the spaceships that are now on the way out of our solar system and into absolute silence and darkness.

I have never had a longing to venture out into the universe, but I can sometimes feel jealous of those who research into the human mind. And perhaps especially those who study the human memory. Why? I am hardly the researcher type – I wouldn't have enough patience. But I can well imagine that it must be a mind-blowing adventure to try to penetrate the human brain, where we all store a vast number of experiences, thoughts – memories, in fact. And perhaps one day to understand how this inner universe is constructed.

Can we possibly one day discover what is involved in thinking? Not just the chemical processes in which neutrons play a significant role, but what we could perhaps call the human soul.

Throughout history the memory has often been compared to a palace with an endless number of halls in which all our constantly growing collection of memories are placed on various levels or various shelves.

The first person we know of who made this comparison was the Greek poet Simonides, who lived in the fifth century BC according to our method of measuring time.

It is said that he once found himself present at a party in a palace. After he had gone home, the roof suddenly collapsed, killing all those he had just been talking and eating and drinking with. Living people who suddenly no longer existed. When he realised that he could still conjure up everything in his mind's eye, in the tiniest detail, exactly as it had been before the roof caved in, he began to think about the possibility that the palace existed equally as much in his own inner world as in the outside world. But the difference was that the ceiling hadn't collapsed inside his brain.

What is especially mysterious and inspirational about the image of a palace inside our minds is that we ourselves are the ones moving around from one of those endless halls to another –a sort of high priest or librarian, picking out memories from the past in accordance with our conscious desire.

During the night there are different librarians in action, more aggressive and anarchistic in their attitudes. I sometimes envisage them as a group of early surrealists or artists with tendencies towards Dadaism. They mix up memories and experiences in confusing combinations so that they are transformed into unrecognisable fragments of reality. These nocturnal figures conjure up absurdities, but also nightmares, often collected from the poison cupboard where they have been hidden away behind locked doors, which are broken open as the demon of the night rides past through the darkness.

What do these halls of forgetfulness look like? What happens as old age creeps up on us, bringing with it an increasingly bad memory, a furtive but growing senility which means that the contents of the palace are obliterated bit by bit? Or is everything in fact still there until our heart stops beating and the electric pulses that keep the brain alive have stopped circulating and providing the stream of constantly flowing energy we call life? Is it just a shadow that has enveloped the halls and rendered the contents invisible?

I imagine that forgetfulness has something to do with a sort of inner light – or rather, that the light is switched off in various halls and on various shelves. Bulbs are unscrewed by an invisible hand and never replaced.

Forgetfulness is darkness. We try to extinguish all the lamps of memory that can illuminate what we at some point buried – or hid away – so that future generations would know nothing about them, and would certainly not be able to track them down.

We locked up in underground rocky caverns a dangerous troll that would live for 100,000 years. But we didn't write a saga about it: instead we did everything possible to ensure that the troll would be forgotten. We tried to create a Song of Songs dedicated to forgetfulness. But is that possible? Can we trick future generations into believing that there is nothing hidden away down there in underground caverns? Will human curiosity and the never-ending search for new truths eventually expose the troll hidden down there in its cave?

We don't know. The most we can hope for is that it doesn't happen before the time has run out.

There is of course a paradox here. We have always lived in order to create good memories, not to forget. All culture has to do with preserving and searching for images from the past, while at the same time creating new ones. Art works both backwards and forwards – so that we don't forget what has happened in the past, but also to ensure that we tell stories about our own time for the benefit of those who will follow us.

The world of art often contains warnings about what has happened in order to ensure that it doesn't happen again. What are Goya's etchings about the horrific reality of war if not warnings to prevent the repetition of such barbarity?

It does happen again, of course, but his warnings also live on.

Memories are stories. Possibly cut up and reduced to fragments, but just as often whole stories. I envisage forgetfulness as a vacuum, our cold and empty inner universe. In forgetfulness humans become indifferent to themselves, to others, to what has been and what will come.

When we now try to deal with nuclear waste we are building a palace of forgetfulness. What is left after our civilisation will be forgetfulness and silence. And an insidious poison buried inside a cathedral blasted out of rock, into which no light will ever enter.

The first gods worshipped by human beings were almost always linked with the life-giving sun. The greatest miracle of all was that the sun reappeared each morning. In cultures that never had any contact with each other there are often similar stories about the origins of human beings. The sun was always involved. But in our civilisation, which has gone further than all previous highly developed civilisations, we are leaving behind us a final memory that comprises nothing but darkness.

15

A magician and an imposter

FROM A GALLERY IN THE PALACE THAT IS MY MEMORY I PRODUCE a painting by Hieronymus Bosch from about 1475, depicting a magician or illusionist in action. A little monkey that seems to be wearing some kind of mask can be glimpsed in a basket by his feet. He himself is standing behind a table on which are the traditional three beakers and several small balls. On the other side of the table is a group of spectators, and in front of them is a man leaning over towards the beakers. It is not possible to make out if he is simply astonished and impressed, or if he is sceptical.

And the magician is smiling – up his sleeve, as they say. He is not smiling to provoke his audience: he is smiling to himself, as if he were thinking that he has yet again achieved an illusion, or managed to fool the spectators.

Magicians usually operate on the basis of extraordinary manual dexterity. Not long ago there was an Israeli called Uri Geller who in my view used trickery rather than psychic powers as he claimed. He travelled around and performed on television in several countries during the early 1970s, and would bend spoons as he held them between his thumb and index finger, using what he maintained were spiritual powers. He could also reveal the content of images drawn by other people in other rooms, where he was unable to see them. There were lively discussions about whether he was a skilled charlatan, or whether he really did possess spiritual powers that were beyond the comprehension of ordinary people.

By pure chance I happened to be present once when he performed on the Norwegian television channel NRK. I was among the people who answered incoming telephone calls, some of which were very lively – Geller's performance was broadcast live, and the NRK telephone exchange was swamped with calls. People had been sitting in their cottages in remote areas of Norway and seen spoons beginning to bend in their kitchen drawers, or their wall clocks suddenly stopping. I recall particularly an old man who explained in a shaky voice that his wife had stumbled and broken her arm: was that also due to magic beams sent out by Uri Geller from their television screen?

I can't remember what I said to him, but I never believed in Uri Geller. There always seemed to be something calculating about him, something that had more to do with cynical speculation than artistic skill. I broke out into angry laughter when the conversation with the old man was over.

Over the years Uri Geller has spent time suing some of his critics. As far as I know he has rarely won any of his cases, but perhaps litigation is what he was really cut out for?

It is not all that big a step from stage magicians to all the cynical speculators who subject people suffering from cancer to various useless therapies. I can understand the despair that drives sufferers into the arms of charlatans, but I don't know how one can put a stop to it happening time after time.

On the other hand, of course, I am open to the argument that various homeopathic treatments should be respected and can be used alongside what we usually call 'Western medicine'. But you can never treat cancer on the basis of illusions. I am convinced of that on the basis of my six months of regular orthodox treatment, and my reading up on as many relevant areas of medicine as I have been able to manage.

I have come to recognise what a human triumph cancer research is. Even if it happens long after I am no longer alive, I am absolutely convinced that cancer will be defeated one of these days.

16

A dream about a muddy trench in Flanders

IT IS ABOUT A MONTH SINCE I WAS INFORMED THAT I WAS STRICKEN with cancer. I am undergoing a period of varying treatments, but will soon start on chemotherapy and also radiotherapy aimed at the metastases that have formed at the back of my neck. If my understanding of the skeleton's anatomy is correct, they are in the very vertebra that is broken when a person is hanged, in countries where 'the long drop' is still a legal punishment.

In my dreams I find myself actively involved in fighting during the First World War, at some point between 1914 and 1918 – at least thirty years before I was born. I am lying hunched up at the bottom of a wet and muddy trench. I don't know which country I'm fighting for. All around me are other soldiers, but nobody says anything. They are all silent. A grey, noiseless mist rolls over the deserted battlefields. In the distance I can make out a dead horse trapped in a dense thorn bush. It had been killed mid-jump, and one of its back legs has been torn off.

Silence reigns. There are no shots, no explosions. I turn to look at a soldier lying next to me. I notice that the nails on his fingers that are grasping the butt of his rifle are bitten away. I ask him what he thinks – when will the shells begin flying again?

He answers in a language I don't understand. His eyes are gaping wide, and he looks at me as if I were his enemy – which I might be. Everybody is everybody else's enemy in this waterlogged landscape.

In my dream I know that something is going to happen, but I

don't know what. Those of us lying there in the trench are waiting. We are waiting for death, if for nothing else.

The mist continues to creep over the brown muddy earth, which is full of craters caused by the exploding shells.

Suddenly the mist begins to change colour. It is no longer greyish-white. The change is slow at first, but becomes quicker and quicker. Now the mist is becoming a pale yellow colour. Too late those of us lying there in the trench realise that the mist is a new enemy creeping up on us. It is only when we breathe in the mist, which is comprised of poison gas, and feel the agony as our lungs and intestines are eaten away, that it dawns on us that the enemy is right next to us. And has even entered our bodies.

Then I wake up. For a brief moment I am totally confused. The pain has not stayed in the dream: it is still there in my memory.

Does it belong to the dream, or to my waking self?

Then I recall the bronchoscopy I had the day before. It was far from pleasant. After a local anaesthetic and sedative injected into my arm, a camera was thrust down my throat and into one of my lungs, where the primary tumour is located. It was followed by another thin tube which has a sort of knife attached to the end of it so that the surgeon can snip away at the tumour and extract pieces of tissue that can be extracted and sent for biopsy. Sister Marie says I will feel a little pain in my throat afterwards. She is right.

With all the tubes in my arm and in my woozy state, I am reminded of poison injections used to execute prisoners. But in my case it is a matter of attempting to save a life under threat by applying the best possible treatment.

In my dream the bronchoscopy has been transformed into mustard gas that seeps down like a yellowish mist into the unsuspecting soldiers' eyes and throats. Many of them die, others become blind for life.

As in a painting by Bruegel, they lead one another away from the battlefield and into the realm of the blind.

But in the darkness of night it dawns on me that it's not quite so straightforward as a real pain in my throat being transformed into a dream about a trench in Flanders. There is another dimension to it all. Now that I am awake I recall that mustard gas, so called because it could at times smell just like mustard, was not merely a ruthless weapon used in the First World War. The gas had not simply poisoned soldiers: it transpired later that it had a positive effect on soldiers suffering from leukaemia.

The deadly gas from the First World War, which was later forbidden by international conventions, also gave birth to a scientific development that eventually produced the cytotoxins used nowadays so effectively to fight cancer.

So that is why I had the dream. The thoughts and memories that raced through my sleeping brain were bearing a message for me. The trench was the waiting for the chemotherapy that I would soon be undergoing. The mustard gas would not kill or blind me, but would fight against my cancer. The yellow cloud would be transformed into a liquid that would drip slowly into one of my veins in the form of carefully selected cytotoxins, which with luck would attack my aggressive cancer cells.

Unfortunately my healthy cells will not be left in peace. In the worst-case scenario I could experience many side effects, of which the loss of hair from my head could be regarded as one of the least troublesome.

There will be periods when my immune defences are more or less totally ineffective, and my blood values could be so low that I shall need to be given blood transfusions.

My dream has become very clear. It has made me wide awake. I get up, despite the fact that it is only four o'clock, and go into the room where I keep my books. In one corner is the red armchair in which I often sit reading. I don't switch on any lights. The beam from an outside light illuminates one of the bookcases. It is crowded with books. Lars Eriksson made all my oak bookshelves to order, and I am reminded, once again, that he must now make some more for me. I don't have enough room for the piles of books that are growing higher and higher.

As long as I live those piles will carry on growing higher and higher.

17

The caves

THERE IS A BOOK ILLUSTRATION THAT I RECALL IN DETAIL, despite the fact that it is more than fifty years since I saw it for the first time. It occurs in Jules Verne's *The Mysterious Island*. The marooned engineers and their servants have been helped by an unknown benefactor when they most need it – among other things he has given them quinine when one of them was stricken by malaria.

In the end they manage to track down the mysterious man who has helped them; they descend into a cave where Captain Nemo is waiting for death in his submarine *Nautilus*. He is about to submerge it and turn it into his sarcophagus.

What has stuck in my memory above all else is the illustration of that cave.

One of my greatest obsessions when I was a child was looking for undiscovered caves. It started when I read about Captain Nemo's scuttled submarine. However, the chances of my finding caves in Härjedalen were not all that good. The land that had been covered by ice during the ice age was made up of broken stones, gravel and occasional high cliffs. The endless plains were covered in forests and heathland. The bedrock was of a type that made it unlikely there were caves carved out deep down below it. Nevertheless, searching for hidden entrances to secret rooms in the underworld, where the rock had been hollowed out by mysterious rivers flowing silently along vast distances underneath my feet, was something that never lost its appeal. You could never know. Nature could be capricious. At least, that's what I thought as a child.

Even now I sometimes feel, deep down inside myself, that I am still searching for caves. That there is an instinct – a lust – that I shall never be able to overcome. But nowadays actually finding that hidden rocky entrance is not so important. The most important thing is the lure, the searching.

In 1950, a few years after I was born, a group of boys discovered an opening in the Lummelunda Cave on the island of Gotland. The cave had been known about for several hundred years and people had been able to penetrate it for a short distance: but most of it was still unexplored. Three boys – Örjan Håkansson, Percy Nilsson and Lars Olsson – were convinced that there was another bigger cave system behind the opening section. Suddenly a large lump of rock shifted, and revealed an opening that had been hidden behind it. Now it would be possible to explore the whole cave system seriously. The boys must have been absolutely delighted by their discovery – I envy them that moment!

Nowadays that passage is called 'The Boys' Entrance'. And there are lots of similar boys' – or girls' – entrances. New caves are constantly being discovered, often by accident, despite the fact that *speleologists* – i.e. cave researchers – can now predict where the probabilities are greatest for finding cave systems that have remained hidden, or at least not been known about. Caves and hollowed-out caverns in rocky areas never occur by accident: there is always a cause, even if it can vary and be difficult to pin down.

Human beings found their way into caves in order to acquire shelter from the weather and protection from predators. Similarly, animals have also withdrawn into caves, not least in order to protect themselves from hunters.

It is inside caves that we find the earliest attempts by people to express the human desire to leave artistic statements for future generations.

It is also in one of these caves – the Chauvet Cave in southern

France – that we can find the signature of what we can safely call the first identifiable artist in the long history of mankind. He has decorated a large number of cave walls with pictures of animals. We know that he was a man because his signature indicates his sex. It is not written because there was no such thing as letters of the alphabet or a written language 30,000 years ago.

His signature is a number of strong imprints of his hands in among the animals. In similar fashion to the way we take fingerprints nowadays, he has coated his hands with pigments, the same coloured 'paints' that he used for the animal pictures. Then he has pressed them against the cave walls. He is not the only cave artist to do that, but what makes him unique, and also gives him a recognisable identity, is one of his fingers.

It is bent. We cannot know if it was an injury or if he was born like that, but doctors say it is very rare for a child to be born with a skeletal deformity affecting just one finger. So it is probably an injury he did to himself – or had done to him – later in life.

What is fascinating about this first identifiable artist is that his hand crops up in several different caves. All in the same part of France, to be sure; but it suggests that he might have been a peripatetic cave painter who was employed by various groups who lived peacefully side by side. When you examine the animal paintings he made, you can see that he was a great talent. His crooked finger did not prevent him from depicting animals and making them look uncannily true to life. Most impressive of all is his ability to depict their movement. You get the impression that the animals are actually jumping down from the cave wall. There is no doubt that an important element of his artistic talent is his ability to suggest that the four-legged animals are running away from or about to attack two-legged human beings.

Needless to say, we cannot know who this artist with the bent finger was. He was a member of one of the earliest, but hardly the first, waves of immigrants from the African continent. We cannot say what role he played in the group of 100 to 150 people to which he belonged – but as various groups have allowed him to decorate the walls of different caves, it is reasonable to guess that they saw in him the same things as we do: a man able to capture in a drawing the essence of a living creature and to reproduce it in a credible way.

Was he young or old? Did he have any assistants? Who prepared his paints for him? Was he married? Did he live with one woman, or was he a member of a group of polygamists? Did he have any children? Did he do anything else apart from painting the walls of caves? Did he go hunting with the rest of his group or did they supply him with food? Could he carve ivory or was he just a painter?

Did he have a name? Did anybody have a name at that time?

We don't know. In the Rift Valley footprints are preserved intact after early humans walked in volcanic ash that had not yet cooled down; in France there are these handprints with the bent finger. No archaeologist can work out who he was, how he lived and how he died. But my guess is that nobody forced him to depict those animals deep down in those caves. If there was any compulsion it came exclusively from inside himself. And the feeling in the group that he lived with that the paintings could be an invocation to improve their hunting success, if I am thinking along the right lines.

There is a common denominator in nearly all the cave paintings that exist, and it is also characteristic of our own rock carvings in Sweden: the animals depicted are created in great detail. Their eyes shine, their movements are reproduced dynamically. But when human beings are depicted they are mostly no more than unfinished sketches. Matchstick figures hastily produced, as if more detailed pictures were not necessary. One can speculate about the reason for that, of course, but in all probability it is simply because the animals were more important. Human beings lived by hunting and eating them.

Nowadays we no longer paint on the walls of caves. Instead we use explosives to create large cathedrals deep down in rocks that are billions of years old so that we can store and protect the waste produced by our civilisation.

Perhaps we shall post notices on the cave walls warning future generations to beware of the radioactive death that is lying there inside its copper containers and inviting investigation.

But how does one speak to people living 100,000 years in the future? After an ice age? People who know nothing about our history?

What should such a warning text look like?

The step from the cave painter with the bent finger to the people today who need to create symbols to warn people who might be living here many thousands of years hence is very long indeed.

Or is it?

18

The floating rubbish dump

JUST OUTSIDE SVEG, IN THE PROVINCE OF HÄRJEDALEN, THE SMALL
town with a population of about 2,000 where I grew up, there used
to be a communal rubbish dump. In the early 1950s, when Sweden's
most recent polio epidemic was at its height, it was forbidden to go
there. Only the rubbish collectors, who still used horses and carts,
were allowed to go there and disturb the many crows that were
always present. There was something frightening about the invisible
viruses or bacteria hidden away there. Sometimes when I woke up
in the mornings I hardly dared to straighten my legs, afraid that they
might have been paralysed during the night. And I wasn't the only
one with such fears.

The most horrific thing I could envisage was my breathing being
affected. If that happened to anyone they were placed in an iron lung
and might have to lie there motionless day and night until they died
many years later. Needless to say, the breathing machine saved a lot
of lives; but in pictures it looked as if bodies were being kept in a
shortened black locomotive.

I never heard any discussion about the need to enlarge the rubbish
dump. Rubbish didn't necessarily expand with increased consump-
tion. Most food was wrapped in materials that quickly disintegrated
after use. I have lived long enough to remember that a day's food
waste could be wrapped up in an old newspaper that was placed first
in a rubbish bin and then somewhere where the contents simply
decayed without any further action being necessary.

I grew up in the 'cardboard age'. It was some time before we entered the 'plastic age' in which we now live.

I have clear memories of how everything changed. I used to spend the summers a long way from the northern inland, in the archipelago of Östergötland in eastern Sweden, just south of Stockholm. Like all the other children I would run along beaches looking for objects that had floated ashore from passing ships. My most common finds were bits of cork from fishing nets and trawling equipment. Spending a day without finding any cork was unthinkable in the 1950s and 60s.

I occasionally struck lucky. Several logbooks had been thrown into the sea from a German freighter, registered in Hamburg. I never discovered if the skipper had been drunk or angry, depressed or desperate, when he threw the ship's most important documentation overboard, but the logbooks washed up onto the beach were like a visit from one of Jules Verne's books.

Almost imperceptibly at first, then more obviously, plastic floats started turning up among the pebbles on the beaches. Eventually the very last cork float was washed ashore, and after that they were all plastic. Then came plastic milk cartons and water bottles, but neither I nor anybody else collected those. Plastic felt dead in my hands, while cork always felt alive.

When I was young the sight of waste and rubbish was routine, nothing to get excited about. That was also the attitude of adults around me. Especially during the summer when we were holidaying on the east coast and most meals comprised the contents of tins, which were heated up on stoves. Traditionally a day came at the end of the summer when a rowing boat was filled with empty tin cans. It was rowed out into the bay, the cans were filled with water and then sank slowly down to the bottom.

They are still lying there today – hundreds of them from my family alone. Some of them will have rusted away, of course, others will not. It is unlikely that much in the way of dangerous substances harmful to the environment was used in the manufacture of the tin cans, and the attitude was straightforward: whatever sank to the bottom of the endless sea was done and finished with, and would never bother us again.

That has doubtless always been the attitude. When the English sailed to India in steamships during the nineteenth century, ladies accustomed to such voyages would discreetly advise their less experienced fellow travellers that it was a good idea to take with them old and perhaps worn-out underwear if they were not accompanied by servants who could wash the garments during the voyage. If you were travelling alone you could throw out used underwear through the cabin porthole. English underwear was always floating around in the wake of these ships. And when Thor Heyerdahl sailed on his *Kon-Tiki* around the islands of the Pacific Ocean and along the coast of South America, he and others on board saw worryingly large amounts of human waste and rubbish floating around. That was in the 1950s. And I recall from my time as a sailor in the Swedish merchant navy that all rubbish was thrown over the railings aft into the sea, the only special requirement being to ensure that the wind would not blow all the crap back on board.

I was fourteen years old when Rachel Carson's book *Silent Spring* came out, and started a necessary reassessment of our world, which was increasingly being used as a rubbish tip. I recall how sea eagles disappeared because their eggs were damaged by DDT and they didn't produce any young. But it was passive knowledge as far as I was concerned: I still regarded it as good fun to fill empty tin cans with water and watch them sink slowly down to the bottom of the sea.

Human beings have always produced rubbish. One of the most exciting and challenging kinds of research sites archaeologists can hope to find is thousand-year-old rubbish dumps piled on top of one another, layer upon layer. They find bones from various animals and fishes, but also burnt remnants of other substances in layers often a metre or more thick, which can reveal the eating habits of generations, and how they change. Rubbish dumps that are excavated and analysed can supply an astonishing amount of information about how those people lived.

But we don't only discover what people ate. We also learn about difficult times characterised by starvation and hardship. We can see how society was split up into classes with very different ways of life. We can see that some people lived much better, with access to more nutritious food, than people who might have lived only a few hundred metres away. One family or tribe ate well while others starved.

Our rubbish dumps nowadays look different, and also tell different stories.

The biggest rubbish dump in the world is not on land: it is in the Pacific Ocean. Between Hawaii and the Californian coast one can find millions of tons of rubbish floating around on the sea's surface. Sailors talk about hundreds of kilometres of rubbish that they are forced to sail through. Ninety per cent of this rubbish is plastic, which takes an incredibly long time to decompose. Most of it is small fragments, sometimes barely visible to the naked eye, which many fish eat. We can well imagine the consequences of that both now and in the future.

I have a photograph of a sea turtle that has found a plastic bag in the Pacific Ocean. The bag is partly full of air, and the turtle is in the process of sticking its head inside it. I don't know if it manages to do so, that is not clear from the picture; but if it does it might well suffocate inside the bag.

Needless to say, there are a lot of people working nowadays to reduce the ever-expanding amount of rubbish we produce. And we have a comprehensive system of recycling that didn't exist twenty years ago. The most damaging forms of packaging have been banned, and in many countries people are fined for fly-tipping. We also burn rubbish as part of a scheme to create new energy, especially for the heating of our homes.

But all this is not enough. Especially worrying is the fact that we still haven't found a way of disposing of the most dangerous rubbish of all, i.e. nuclear waste. The really big exploiters of nuclear power, such as China and the USA, have barely even begun to build temporary storage stations while waiting for eventual solutions to be discussed and decided upon.

What is happening – or rather, not happening – in a country like North Korea is something I would rather not think about. But I do.

Civilisations have always left rubbish behind. When a culture or an empire collapses, nobody tends to think about clearing up the mess they leave behind. However, neither the Egypt of the Pharaohs nor the Holy Roman Empire left behind dangerous or deadly rubbish.

But we are going to do so.

One of these days I myself will also be turned into waste matter – but my body is more reminiscent of cork than of plastic. It will start decaying as soon as normal bodily functions have come to an end.

Since I was diagnosed with cancer I have occasionally gritted my teeth and read about the decaying of human bodies. The knowledge I have acquired has given me a degree of calmness despite everything. Dying is the greatest of all human traditions. The actual moment of death varies, depending on one's age and illnesses, but then everything happens to everybody in the same way. The only difference is whether one has chosen to be cremated or to allow time and the earth to combine and transform one's body into new molecules which will always survive but in new combinations.

I assume that one day I shall be cremated. I have wondered whether it would be better for me to request more space, more cubic metres, so that my body can be sunk down into the ground in a coffin. To be buried in traditional style. But I don't think I shall. Even the smoke from the crematorium releases molecules that combine with others.

Eternity and its continuing cycle are everywhere.

19

Signs

IN THE 1980S I LIVED FOR A FEW YEARS IN ZAMBIA, CLOSE TO THAT country's border with Angola. It was 350 kilometres to the nearest shop, and during British colonial rule the place where I lived, Kabompo, had been used as a place of banishment for African rebel leaders who had been fighting for the destruction of the racial colonial system.

During my time in Kabompo there was a presidential election in Zambia. All the candidates were represented by drawings depicting animals – partly because that was the tradition, and partly because a large proportion of citizens were illiterate. The ruling president, Kenneth Kaunda, had a majestic African eagle as his symbol. His most dangerous opponent for the presidential post had been given a miserable-looking little rat as his symbol.

There was no doubt about what the outcome would be: Kaunda won, of course.

In today's society we are surrounded all the time by warning signs and indications that things are forbidden. The number of signs in public places instructing me how to behave has grown steadily during my lifetime. This is due to the fact that our society has become more and more complicated. In order to avoid chaos, for instance, the regulation of traffic has involved a steady stream of new signs.

On one occasion while I was in Africa I showed a good friend the standardised warning triangle that in Sweden indicates danger of radioactivity, and asked him what he thought it meant. He reflected for a while, then said that what the symbol reminded him of most was an electric fan. Or perhaps it was an aeroplane propeller in motion? He eventually decided it was a warning not to get too close to dangerous aeroplane propellers.

If I put one of my index fingers over my mouth, everybody will probably understand that it means they should be quiet. A sign depicting a finger over a mouth means the same thing. I have never come across anybody in Europe, Africa or North America who didn't understand that. Which is not surprising. A closed mouth means it is impossible to talk – that is a fact for all human beings. You don't need to wonder if this and many other symbols come from some ancient common language. The same signals are understood by everybody even if there has been no inter-cultural contact. No human beings have vocal cords in their ears or in their fingertips.

Signs and symbols are powerful tools. But who will understand the meaning of those symbols 100,000 years into our unknown future?

It is difficult, to say the least, for those working today to warn people a thousand years from now that nuclear waste is radioactive. Is it in fact impossible for anybody to understand what a warning sign should look like in order to be effective when they know nothing about future people's language, culture and understanding of what is dangerous? It is bound to be a mixture of a highly qualified guessing game and the most advanced thinking our brightest scientists can produce, combined with various elements of the experience and knowledge we possess.

The image of the rear-view mirror recurs. We need to be able to see backwards in order to see forwards.

There have been lots of suggestions for what these warning signs should look like. One was to write an appropriate text in every language spoken in our world – but that would result in an enormous mass of text. There is some hesitant agreement that the best solution would probably be a mixture of images, sounds and texts; but many wonder if there is any possible solution at all.

Another suggestion was to turn to the world of art. How would future human beings react to a copy of Edvard Munch's *The Scream* if it was reproduced in the primary rocks? Would the image of the screaming woman on the bridge make observers realise that they were being confronted by something horrific and dangerous? That is how those of us living today would interpret it.

I once showed a photograph of Munch's painting to a friend in Maputo. He immediately interpreted it as an expression of extreme angst. But we can only guess at the reactions of future human beings to Munch's picture.

What sound could we select to drive future people away from caves containing nuclear waste? Perhaps the kind of sound-bomb that produces noises that are unbearable for human ears, which the American military has developed and now has in its arsenal? Is that the way forward? But we know nothing about the nature of future people's hearing. Perhaps the inferno of noise would be ineffective? And who can guarantee that a solution based on present-day technology would still work 100,000 years from now?

So what do we do if there is no sure way of warning future generations? The only thing left to us is an illusion. To pretend that there is nothing there in the underground caverns.

The only tool we have available is man's capacity to forget – and that really isn't something we should rely on.

Forgetfulness of facts and lies often go hand in hand.

20

The raft of death

IT IS THE EARLY SUMMER OF 1816. NAPOLEON HAS FINALLY BEEN defeated and will eventually be poisoned to death with arsenic on St Helena, the windswept rocky island in the South Atlantic where he is being held captive.

France is ruled by a king belonging to the Bourbon family. Four ships from the French navy have been ordered to sail southwards. Their goal is Senegal on the west coast of Africa – as part of the transformation of Europe after the Congress of Vienna, the port of Saint-Louis will be handed over to the French by the English.

On 17 June, the little armada departs from Rochefort. Keeping a group of sailing ships together is an almost impossible task, and they soon lose contact with one another. But all of them know their ultimate destination.

One of the ships is the three-masted frigate *La Méduse*: there are almost four hundred people on board. Half of them are sailors, the other half are civil servants who will take over the administration once the *Tricolore* has been raised.

The captain of the ship is Hugues Duroy de Chaumareys.

He is inexperienced, and has hitherto spent most of his time working for the French customs authorities. Moreover, he has been an opponent of Napoleon. As most of the sailors on board were supporters of Napoleon, he is immediately disliked and despised by the crew.

Two weeks after leaving Rochefort, *La Méduse* runs aground off the coast of Africa. The area has many dangerous, shifting sandbanks that have never been properly mapped. *La Méduse* is stranded on a reef called Banc d'Arguin.

The vessel is well and truly stuck. On the captain's orders everything loose is thrown overboard in the hope of making the ship lighter so that it can glide away from the sandbank. But without success. Captain de Chaumareys then gives the order 'abandon ship'. As there are not enough lifeboats for the number of people on board, a large raft is constructed. The three tall masts are cut down in order to make the base of the raft in the shape of a square. The lifeboats will then tow the raft behind them as they head for the African coast, which is hidden in the mist to the east.

But the towing doesn't work; the hawsers are cut and the raft, with its 150 passengers, is abandoned – Captain de Chaumareys commits one of the most cowardly and dastardly acts of which human beings are capable.

The situation on board the raft soon shifts from restrained order to brutal chaos. The strongest throw the injured and weak overboard, food and water eventually run out and cannibalism begins. Survivors use cutlasses to carve up the dead bodies and eat the raw meat. The raft becomes a human slaughterhouse.

After fifteen days the raft is spotted by its sister ship, *The Argus*. Only fifteen of those on board have survived, and several of them die soon afterwards as a result of their trials and tribulations. In the end only three sailors from the raft survive and can return to France.

One of those survivors is the ship's doctor, Henri Savigny. When he gets back to France he hands in a report on what happened to the French Admiralty. Its contents leak out, and the incident becomes a major scandal.

The artist Théodore Géricault is about twenty-five years old when the catastrophe involving *La Méduse* takes place. In 1812 he had attracted a lot of attention when his painting of a cavalry officer on a bucking horse was exhibited at the Salon in Paris, and now he starts work on a big painting of the raft on which people lie dying after the shipwreck of *La Méduse*.

At first he concentrates on trying to create the atmosphere of horror on board: cannibalism, the throwing overboard of weak but still living sailors, the sea where there are no other vessels in sight, the hopelessness that is eventually the only remaining emotion.

He imagines a raft drifting around on a sea where no God displays any interest in the suffering of the castaways. When there is no hope, there is no God either.

The heavens are as empty as the sea.

Barely six kilometres away is the African coast, invisible because of the mist. But it cannot provide salvation; it might just as well be hell lying in wait for them.

Géricault starts to doubt. He makes an endless number of sketches but eventually begins to tone down the catastrophe. He seems to be asking himself the following question: what happens to human beings when they have lost all hope? When there is nothing left?

He provides no answer to that question. It is quite simply the wrong question to ask.

There is always something left.

The painting he eventually produces depicts the human hope that still exists even after everything seems to be finished. At the back of the painting, in the far distance, we can glimpse *The Argus*: but we can't make out whether the sailors on board the ship have noticed the raft.

The painting is on display at the Louvre in Paris. When I stand looking at it I get the feeling that it is a meeting place for the old and the new. Géricault studied both Rubens and Caravaggio when he was working on his raft; but with the same intensity he also studied dead and dying patients at the Beaujon hospital. It is said that he even took parts of dead bodies to his studio in order to examine the process of decay in more detail.

Most works of art are something one looks at or listens to. I myself sometimes find that I also sense a pleasant smell. Very occasionally

I have stood in front of a work of art and experienced an unusually nice taste.

Géricault has succeeded in doing something for me that few artists have managed to do. Munch and Bacon are other examples. And of course Caravaggio and Rembrandt. When I stand in front of Géricault's painting I can detect a stench of dying human bodies.

There is a remarkable contrast in the picture. Despite the fact that the people lying there are starving and half dead thanks to hunger and thirst, Géricault depicts them with almost athletic-looking bodies. He is bold enough to combine realism with the ideals that characterise classical art. By distancing himself from maintaining a purely realistic approach, he persuades those of us who view his painting to take our place on board the raft.

What really impresses me is Géricault's attempt to depict hope that doesn't really exist. I know of no other work of art that is as successful in expressing what one has to call a philosophical challenge.

After my visit to the Louvre I sit down in a nearby cafe. It is autumn, chilly, with a wind blowing in from the north-west. I have travelled to Paris in order to talk about my books.

I observe the people sitting at the other tables and think that all of them possess some kind of hope. The hope that something will succeed, that something will pass over, that something will be explained, that something painful will turn out to be a misconception.

All the time we need to ensure that our hopefulness is stronger than our hopelessness. Without hope it is basically impossible to survive. That applies to those of us who have cancer just as much as to others.

After I leave the cafe it starts drizzling. I walk towards the Père Lachaise Cemetery.

It takes me some time to find Géricault's mausoleum. He lived to be only thirty-two years old; on one occasion he injured himself so badly falling off one of his horses that it helped to shorten his life.

But he also suffered from tuberculosis. He knew early on that his days were numbered.

The monument attached to the grave itself was made by the now forgotten sculptor Antoine Étex. It is sentimental and shocking, depicting Géricault dying and slowly dropping the paintbrush he is holding in his hand.

The Raft of the Medusa depicts the hope that still exists when all other hope has vanished. We cling on to the rafts despite the fact that we have no strength left.

But hope is always there. Maybe as no more than a shadow. But still . . .

21

All this forgotten love

DEATH AND OBLIVION BELONG TOGETHER, IN THE SAME WAY AS cancer and existential fear.

Many years ago, during the 1960s, I was visiting an old house in Bastugatan in Stockholm that was undergoing renovation work. By pure chance my visit coincided with some of the men working on the house's foundations making a discovery. They found an empty Pilsner bottle containing a sealed message. Using a blunt carpenter's pencil, somebody had written: 'I sat here with my beloved one beautiful summer's evening in 1868.'

No names, no signatures; just this euphorically happy message to an unknown future.

Everybody I know has at some point carved their name onto a tree in the woods, or scratched their signature onto a cliff by the sea. Nobody wants to be forgotten. But nearly everybody is.

How many authors do we remember and still read today? I'm not only thinking about those who wrote hundreds of years ago, but also those whose books we bought and read in libraries who died maybe twenty or thirty years ago. How many of Ivar Lo-Johansson's remarkable novels are borrowed from libraries today? Strindberg is still going strong – but will he be a hundred years from now?

How many artists have disappeared altogether from our consciousness? How many scientists, engineers, inventors? And most important of all, how many 'ordinary' people?

Many people are not at all worried about this. Once you're dead, you're dead. While you remain in somebody's memory, you still have your identity. But eventually that fades away as well.

I admit that I am occasionally put out by the thought of being forgotten about altogether a few years from now. The feeling is just as much an expression of embarrassing vanity as it is a human craving. But I think I usually cope successfully with it.

How many of the 107 billion people who have lived on this earth hitherto do we remember today? Their names, their achievements? An increasingly small number. It is man's fate to be forgotten. Not even those people who have made themselves renowned in various ways will live on in people's memories for ever. How many people alive today will still be remembered five hundred years from now? Not many. Nowadays the human memory is if anything shorter that at any time in our history. We are constantly being bombarded with a never-ending flow of information, but we know and remember less and less. Our minds are being metaphorically blown apart. As new information comes storming in, earlier memories are consigned to mental rubbish dumps. If our memory palace was real, the level of water in the many halls would have been very high indeed as a result of this rainfall of data.

Those people who are working today on the storage of atomic waste know one thing for certain about their work: it will never be finished in their lifetime. In Sweden it will be another sixty years before the waste is buried in its capsules so that the rocky caverns can be sealed and never opened again. Vegetation will take over. Buildings will be demolished and a collective loss of memory will flourish. When the last of those involved in arranging the permanent storage of the waste dies, all direct memories will have vanished.

Demolishing the creations of human beings can also be a very rapid process. What happens to the world's highest bridges if they are not constantly maintained? They turn rusty and after a few years lose their ability to contribute to the safe transport of goods and people over inlets of the sea or ravines. Within ten or fifteen years the bridge will collapse. After another ten years there will be nothing left but the crumbling concrete foundations. And a few generations later the bridge will have disappeared forever from the human memory.

But in the primary rock selected for the storage of nuclear waste nothing will rust, nothing will decay. The only thing that will happen will be an invisible process – the gradual fading away of the radioactivity until it finally ceases to be dangerous for people and animals.

The people I have met who are devoting their lives to this work will never live to see it completed. Most of them are aware that they are part of a tradition. They belong to those who spent all their lives building something without seeing it in its finished state.

The Great Wall of China was started as a defensive construction by China's first emperor, Shi Huangdi, about 200 BC. Work was still taking place on the wall as late as the seventeenth century – so by then work on it had continued for 1,800 years. If you think of the work being handed down from father to son that means there were over sixty generations who never saw the end of the work they and their forefathers had been engaged on. The final stone was never put in place.

Nor did the master stonemasons who began work on Notre-Dame in Paris see the mighty cathedral in all its magnificence on the Île de la Cité. It was built between 1163 and 1345, and needed five generations to complete it.

Cologne Cathedral took even longer to complete: 653 years from the laying of the first foundation stone until the building was finished.

Many other monumental edifices got no further than the planning stage. When Hitler was resting, or at least taking time out after another bout of horrific murdering, he would contact the architect Albert Speer and pore over plans and models of what was to become the new Berlin, capital of the world. Hitler wanted to adorn his thousand-year Reich with a city that outclassed Paris, London and Rome. He wanted to build higher, bigger and longer than anything else in existence. But nothing came of it.

The people responsible for arranging the permanent storage of nuclear waste in Sweden are certainly not sentimental or unrealistic individuals. They are also well aware of the true humanity in working for the future, even though they might not complete the task on which they have embarked. They are forging their link in the long chain of human history.

But even so, I wonder. What do those with the responsibilities actually think? The ones who create the final links in the chain and are present when the tunnel opening is closed – and all being well will never again be opened. Have we done everything we could? Have we overlooked anything? Is there a dimension in this whole business that we have not been aware of?

What is involved in living with questions that simply don't have any answers? How can one calculate something that is impossible to calculate?

A few years ago a 45-metre-long asteroid raced past the earth at very high speed. It was 30,000 kilometres away from the earth and was never sucked into its gravitational field, but only a few days ago a meteor exploded inside the earth's atmosphere and bits of it were scattered over a Russian village, injuring many people.

Contemporary science has discovered about 10,000 asteroids whirling around in the section of the universe that we can observe, but there are millions out there. If one of them, perhaps several kilometres in diameter, were to crash into the earth within the next few thousand years, we cannot possibly know what the consequences would be. This is just one of the kind of things that we usually see in the doomsday films that are being made all the time because they sell so many tickets.

The truth about our environment is always provisional. What we knew yesterday is changed and replaced by what we know today. For most people life is something that is constantly developing.

I once had a good friend who was a farmer. He died many years ago. In the beginning of our long friendship he showed me his photograph album: he had collected pictures of his harvests and his livestock for each year he had worked on his farm. He never thought about an ultimate goal: as far as he was concerned farming was a continuous activity.

Perhaps nuclear power and the waste it produces is something that breaks all existing fundamental patterns? There has been nothing like it throughout the history of mankind.

22

Timbuktu

I SPENT OVER FIFTY YEARS DREAMING ABOUT ONE DAY VISITING the desert town of Timbuktu about which so many sagas are told. Nowadays it is in the country of Mali. I can't have been more than ten years old when I first came upon the name in a travelogue, and immediately had the feeling that it must be a town at the very end of the world. For me, being a child meant that I was always looking for something that had a specific beginning and an end. I imagined that there was a place beyond which it was impossible to go.

The road always came to an end somewhere. Just as one's life always ended in death.

The end of the world existed. And it was in Timbuktu.

I spent a lot of time drawing archipelagos when I was a child. I spent every summer on an island in the Östergötland archipelago, a long way away from inland Norrland where I was at home. The island was surrounded by an apparently endless mass of other islands, so drawing them was a natural thing to do. It was a flippant but fantasy-invoking journey into my creative instincts. I used to draw islands with strange shapes, secret inlets, narrow but very deep creeks, treacherous underwater sandbanks, and not least systems of caves which connected the islands by underwater passages.

Even today, when I am taking part in a boring telephone conversation or even simply sitting in a chair and thinking about nothing in particular, I discover afterwards that I have filled a sheet of paper with a new variation of the archipelago I used to create as a child.

Anyway, I did get to Timbuktu in the end. It was between forty and fifty degrees when the car I was travelling in crossed the River Niger by ferry, and the town lay stretched out in front of me in the heat haze, dusty, parched, and with sand constantly being blown along the streets.

I had gone to Timbuktu for two reasons: partly just to see it and to realise that the end of the world did not exist, even though Timbuktu did. In other words, I hadn't been completely wrong.

The other reason – the most important one now that I was an adult – was to view the treasure-filled archives overflowing with old manuscripts. At other times of unrest, the people of Timbuktu had hidden the manuscripts under the sand. Thanks to the hot and dry desert climate the thousand-year-old documents had survived. They were now kept in archives and libraries overseen with pride by the locals. Many manuscripts were still privately owned by people in Timbuktu, but they seemed to be regarded with such reverence that nobody sold them, despite the fact that cynical speculators were prepared to pay huge sums for the most attractive ones.

The two days I spent in those archives felt like the culmination of a fifty-year-long pilgrimage. Not only did I see proof of what I had always believed, namely that claims to the effect that the African continent had no written history were completely false, but I could even hold these manuscripts in my hands and think how, a thousand years ago, this desert town had been one of the world's most important intellectual centres. People had travelled long distances to get here – Arabs, Africans, Europeans – long before such places as the Sorbonne in Paris had even been thought of. For centuries learned discussions had taken place here, not only about theological texts – mainly Muslim, of course – but also in such widely differing fields as geography, astronomy and medicine. For the first time I understood properly the intrinsic importance an archive could have. Here was a place recording thoughts emanating from discussions and disagreements that led to the culmination of human learning.

It was as if Timbuktu was a town in which the Enlightenment was still alive.

Today, just a few years after my visit to Timbuktu, we know that for a time the town was occupied by Islamic jihadis who burnt a lot of manuscripts because they considered them to be blasphemous.

I was extremely angry when I realised what had happened; but I also discovered that a lot of manuscripts had been rescued and once again buried in the dry desert sand, despite the fact that doing so could cost people their lives. Most documents seem to have been preserved. But I hardly need to express my opinion of the people who destroy human scholarship in the name of their god.

The first archive I can recall seeing was in a basement room in the office attached to the courthouse in Sveg. I wasn't actually allowed to go there – needless to say, I went even so. There were long rows of shelving containing old legal documents, but more interesting of course were the cardboard boxes containing items of evidence from assault cases, each of them with a handwritten note explaining when and where this object had been lying on the courtroom table. Most of them were knives. But there were also knuckledusters and lead bludgeons. I also seem to recall an axe with a worm-eaten handle. I can still remember very clearly a question I used to ask myself: why keep all these objects when people have already been punished for their crimes? Why should all those knives and the other things still be kept down here?

Today I know the answer. Archives exist to make sure we don't forget our history. Not just what happened and how it happened; above all we should be able to see how we reacted to various events.

One of the world's oldest archives is the Vatican Archive in Rome. It contains the annals of the Catholic Church stretching over a thousand years back in time. One can take out documents that describe in detail historical events most of us know nothing about. There are trial records of the prosecution of Galilei, and the letters written by Henry VIII to the Pope requesting a divorce from one of his wives. There are minutes of the Inquisition's interrogation of alleged heretics who were later burnt at the stake. Giordano Bruno was one of them.

But not everything is about the brutal treatment by the Church of people who maintained that the world was not the centre of the universe. There are also touching letters from Michelangelo, for instance, in which he complains about not having been paid for his work.

Until the end of the nineteenth century this archive was hermetically sealed to everyone apart from a small number of the most powerful members of the Roman Catholic hierarchy. Nowadays it is more accessible, although there are still 'poison cupboards' whose doors are locked to outsiders. But the Vatican Archive belongs to the whole human race. Even those who are not believers, or adherents of other religions, should be prepared to defend this archive because what is preserved there is basically the history of mankind.

I can well imagine that the Vatican Archive could play an important role in the way we ensure that future generations will understand that what is inside those copper containers in the underground caverns is dangerous. Perhaps we should gather together all the discussions, all the various suggestions, and produce a sort of comic strip carved into the cave walls explaining how difficult it is for us to imagine how we can pass on a message that remains understandable for 100,000 years. An archive that doesn't contain any locked poison cupboards might be one step along the way.

If it is a genuine step, or one that leads us astray, is of course something that we cannot know.

Just as we cannot really know anything.

23

A different archive

THERE ARE ALSO DIFFERENT KINDS OF ARCHIVES.

There was once a man who was confined to Säter mental hospital: he spent most of his life there. I don't know what type of mental illness he suffered from, but I think he was plagued by powerful hallucinations that affected all his senses.

He was taken into hospital as early as 1912, and was still there when he died in the 1960s. He devoted his life to an activity that he was probably alone in pursuing.

There is a small museum at Säter mental hospital illustrating the way mentally ill patients used to be regarded, and what treatment they were given over the years.

A number of old books are kept inside a wooden chest. If you open any of these, here and there – and especially towards the end – you find that things have been written between the lines in pencil, a microscopic text. If you examine the handwritten text with the aid of a magnifying glass and a lot of patience, you discover that the writer has 'improved' what is printed in the book. Perhaps he has made the plot more cheerful, or more gloomy? In any case, he has transformed the books into his own creations.

Who would not like to do that?

The philosopher and alchemist Paracelsus left behind many writings on a very wide range of subjects. Among other things he wrote with great seriousness about his lifelong efforts to create gold – which of course has always been the ultimate aim of alchemists.

His texts have continued to be read for many centuries, and occasionally he has been translated into new languages.

Sometimes mistakes have been made, however. It is said that a keen alchemist in Paris as recently as around the First World War dug out one of Paracelsus's books, in which it stated that a certain metal should be kept in glowing embers in an oven for forty days in order to change it into gold – at least, that was what the author had originally written. But a mistake was made in the translation: it said the metal should be kept in the embers for forty years. The alchemist was an old man. He realised that he would have to live to be 120 years old in order to follow the advice of the Master.

He collected all his notes from a long life devoted to finding a way of creating gold, and left everything to an archive – nobody really knows which one – before disappearing from Paris without trace.

24

The courage to be afraid

AT ABOUT THE SAME TIME AS I LEFT THE QUICKSAND BEHIND ME
and slowly came to terms with my illness, I received a letter from
one of my oldest friends. I had got to know him in 1964, after I left
grammar school one January day at the age of sixteen and decided
to go to Paris. I had never met him before, but he was a jazz musician
in the French capital, and his parents had a little bakery in Borås. I
went to their home and got his address.

Now, fifty years later, I received a letter from Göran. He had read
about my illness.

He had left France many years before, although he occasionally
returned to play with his old band. He had married, had children
and amassed a unique collection of 78-rpm records. And he still
played, with various groups.

'What on earth can you write to somebody who's got cancer?' he
wondered.

He was right, of course. What can one say? And what does the
sufferer say to himself?

One of the first things that happened after I had shaken myself
out of the quicksand was that I started formulating questions about
courage and fear. Is it possible to be courageous without acknowledging one's fear? I don't think it is. In this context, fear is much
more than the primitive and fundamental dread of dying. The predator sees you, but you don't see the predator. Death always sees you
as fair game: but being afraid in this sense is just as much a matter

of being frightened of a pain that cannot be suppressed, or of no longer being able to experience what is going to happen the next day, and the day after that. The fear of dying is a mixture of rational reasons and the opposite: imagination and biological necessity. The foundation of life.

Fear is natural and based on the simple truth that what distinguishes us humans from other species is that we know we are going to die. The cats I have owned during my life have never been aware of their own death. They haven't even been aware that they were alive. They have simply been there, day after day – hunting, lying around, miaowing. Acknowledging one's fear of the unknown is realising what it means to be a person. Our existence is basically a tragedy. Throughout our lives we strive to increase our knowledge, our abilities, our experiences. But the bottom line is that all of that will be lost in oblivion.

I respect those who believe in a life after this one. But I don't understand them. It seems to me that religion is no more than an excuse for not accepting the conditions of life. The here and now, nothing more than that. That is also the unique aspect of our life, the wonderful part of being alive.

In the first book I wrote, back in 1973, is a sentence to the effect that a human being can spit into the sea, and by doing so can conquer all the eternity one needs. I still believe that, over forty years later.

I left behind the quicksand and began to accumulate courage, which in turn was based on the knowledge that I would never completely rid myself of my fear. But I was forced to be the strongest: I have to control my fear and never allow it to take control over me.

Nowadays I often think about frightened people I have met during my life. There are a lot of them. People can be afraid of almost anything. I don't think anybody is without some form of hypochondria, at least at times. Who doesn't recall one's teenage years when one was afraid of having been afflicted with STIs, without ever having had any symptoms at all, or the slightest reason for being afraid of having caught it! I have met several people who were afraid of having metre-long worms in their stomach, or afraid of going round a corner in the street in case there was somebody standing there with a knife at the ready despite the fact that it was broad daylight and there were lots of people around. I have met people who were convinced every single moment that their next heartbeat would be their last.

Personally, I am afraid of the dark. If I sleep alone I always make sure that a lamp will remain lit all night. Whether I am at home or in a hotel. But being afraid of the dark is something I understand. There is a very obvious reason for darkness scaring me.

It was December 1958. In the summer of that year Sweden had won a silver medal in the final of the football World Cup played at the Råsunda Stadium in Stockholm – they lost to Brazil 5–2. A seventeen-year-old by the name of Pelé had been on show to the whole world for the first time, and the Swedish fullback Sven Axbom had been unable to cope with the Brazilian right-winger, Garrincha.

But now I am at home in Norrland, and it is winter. When it is really cold the wooden beams inside the house walls twist and creak, as if they are trying to break free. I am asleep. It is two in the morning, but I am not aware of that: I'm asleep, after all. I don't need to get up at seven to get ready for school as tomorrow is Sunday. But I don't know about that either. Everything has come to a standstill while I am asleep: time and space simply don't exist as far as the sleeping child is concerned.

But something from the outside world forces its way into my slumbers. Something disturbing, worrying. Reluctantly I rise from the depths. Somebody is trying to wake me, but I don't want to wake up. I want to carry on sleeping. Maybe I turn over, pull the covers over my head. But the voice calling to me doesn't give up. Deep down there in my sleep I seem to recognise it, but I'm not sure.

In the end I wake up and open my eyes in the darkness. The curtains are drawn. No light comes in from the street. Everything is pitch black. Then I hear the weak voice again, calling to me. It's ng towards me out of the darkness. Now I know who it belongs to. It's my father. He is there in the darkness.

I'm still too sleepy to be afraid. I don't detect the danger. I ought to have done so. Why is he waking me up in the middle of the night? And why isn't the light switched on if he wants to talk to me?

I sit up in bed and fumble in the darkness for the reading lamp that is fixed to the wall above the head of the bed. I'm still not aware of any danger. I switch the light on and that light changes my life.

Lying on the floor just inside the doorway is my father. His dark blue pyjamas are covered in blood. His face is very white, his hair soaked in sweat with strands clinging to his face.

I can't remember what I thought at that moment. I can't recall the words that formed inside my head, but I know they had to do with my fear of being abandoned yet again. First my mother had left us when I was very small. Being rejected by your mother is of course practically unbearable for a child. And now, seeing my father lying there on the floor, I had the feeling that he was about to leave me as well. I wouldn't be allowed to keep him either.

It wasn't in fact blood on his pyjamas, but the remains of vomit. He had suffered a cerebral haemorrhage, but he survived. Nevertheless, from that night onwards I have always been terrified of what unexpected revelation darkness might have in store for me.

Of course I don't mention any of that when I eventually get round to answering Göran's letter. Instead, I remind him how beautifully he used to play Duke Ellington's 'Solitude'.

Courage and fear are always intertwined. It requires courage to live and courage to die.

But I have no intention of dying, I write at the end of my letter. Not yet, at least. I have far too much still to do.

I continue to prepare myself for the chemotherapy that is in store.

25

Paris

WHAT HAPPENED WHEN I WENT TO PARIS ON THAT OCCASION?

My resolve to leave school seemed to come suddenly. But it didn't really. In my subconscious and my imagination I had long been preparing for a clean break. Not because I was finding school difficult. I just thought it was boring to sit through all those sleep-inducing lessons when I had already made up my mind to become a writer. Learning and reading were things I could do in more effective circumstances than being shut up inside a classroom.

It was a Saturday afternoon. Because of a timetabling cock-up my class had been landed with a double period of Latin at the very end of the school day. My Latin teacher, Eva Jönsson, was brilliant, however; and she was also a talented pianist to whom one could listen in secret during the evenings when she was practising in one of the music rooms. Normally I had nothing against puzzling my way through Latin translations, but as I sat there listening to the bovine mumbling of one of my classmates trying to translate an extract from *De Bello Gallico*, it suddenly struck me that my time was up. When the bell rang I gathered together all my books, and without mentioning my decision to anybody I left the classroom never to return. I was not going to change my mind – that was something I had learnt from Hemingway.

In a way it was a bold decision, and of course also a foolhardy one. What would I do in Paris? I knew hardly any French, had no money and only the address of a jazz musician I didn't know. The whole idea was preposterous, and thoroughly romantic. The first part of the decision – leaving school – was correct. But the trip to Paris had neither rhyme nor reason. I didn't even have a passport.

I spent a few days thinking things over. I travelled by train to Gothenburg without a ticket, struggled against a strong headwind as far as Götaplatsen and then back to the Central Station. Before taking the train back home I would have made my decision: Paris or not. It was do or die.

The last thing I did before catching the train back home was to visit a shop on Stampgatan and steal a transistor radio.

That evening I told my father about my decision. He stared at me as if I had gone mad. After I had finished my brief and doubtless rather hesitant explanation as to why I was going to leave school and go to Paris, he sat there in silence. Eventually he asked me to repeat what I had just said. As I recall it now, fifty years later, my second version was even shorter.

'So you think this is going to work, do you? Where are you going to live? What are you going to live on? Nobody has ever heard of an author who is sixteen years old. What are you going to write about? What's the name of that musician whose address you have?'

'Göran Eriksson.'

He said no more. But during the night I heard him pacing around in his bedroom. I wondered how anybody would choose to be a parent.

I got myself a passport, bought a ticket, sold a collection of records and some books, gathered together all my belongings and packed a suitcase. I bought the suitcase with the money I received from a pawnshop for the transistor radio I had stolen in Gothenburg.

That theft still plays on my conscience.

I had a girlfriend by the name of Monika. She had blonde hair and a fringe. And beautiful, slightly dangerous eyes. I hadn't told her much about my plans for the future, but now that I had left school I told her what I intended doing. She thought I was out of my mind, and put an end to our relationship immediately. But later, when I had actually settled down in the French capital, she started writing letters to me and said that we did, in fact, belong together. She planned to come and join me in the summer. Or at least she hoped to do so. After all, it was rather unusual to have a boyfriend in Paris.

My birthday is on 3 February. Two days earlier, on 1 February 1965, the train from Copenhagen and Hamburg pulled into Gare du Nord. On the train I had been talking to a Swedish girl who was reading Blaise Pascal. I had no idea who he was. She lent me a book, and I read it without understanding it. I had with me my half-empty suitcase containing a pair of shoes, a few shirts and some underwear. In an inside pocket where I kept my passport I had two hundred French francs, which in those days were roughly equivalent to the same amount in Swedish kronor. Not a lot even then. In addition, which was much worse, I had an agonising toothache that started more or less as the train crossed the Belgian border.

I sat there motionless until the train came to a halt, and imagined that I was back at my school desk. Then I stood up and left the train. From that moment on I never again thought about going back to school.

It was cold in Paris. People were freezing, and so was I. I sat in a cafe at the station, ordered a coffee and a cognac, and hoped the toothache would go away. It didn't.

Anyway, I had an address in Paris. A name. Göran Eriksson, a Swedish jazz musician I had never met. His house was about as far away from Gare du Nord as you could get, down by the end of the longest street in Paris, Rue de Vaugirard, just before the Porte de Versailles. The taxi driver eyed me up and down sceptically, and demanded part payment in advance. He got it. When I came to the house and *la concierge* reluctantly let me in, Göran opened a door with a clarinet in his hand. As if it were the most natural thing in the world, he offered me a mattress. That night I slept off the toothache. When I woke up the next morning it dawned on me that I had in fact arrived in Paris.

I stayed there until the summer was over. More than six months. After some dubious negotiating I managed to get an unofficial job in a little workshop that cleaned and repaired clarinets and saxophones. I think I could still dismantle a clarinet and then put it back together again. Blindfolded.

Surviving was always a problem. Göran had no money. We had to help each other out. I spent much of my free time in jazz clubs. Caveau de la Huchette, Le Tabou and other establishments. I ate at the cheapest places I could find.

But I was in a university. I learnt the most important thing you have to know: how to look after yourself. To stand by your own decisions. I didn't become an author during my time in Paris, but that wasn't important. I took the first step towards becoming a human being with self-awareness. The big step forward after that discovery I had made – that I am myself and nobody else – while standing outside the community centre in Sveg.

Eventually I felt I'd had enough of Paris. Göran and I shook hands. Then I hitchhiked my way back to Sweden. My former classmates had already begun a new school year. I went up to the red-brick school building, but didn't go inside and had the feeling that I would never regret my decision.

And I never have. What I remember most vividly from my time in Paris is becoming aware of what it is like to belong to the dregs of society. In my case I was working in the black economy, wearing worn-out clothes, frequently hungry. People have no difficulty in identifying poverty – probably because they are so scared of becoming poverty-stricken themselves.

But of course I was only on a brief visit to that world. I could have given up and travelled back to Sweden, returned to grammar school and studied Latin until it was time for my school-leaving examinations.

But I didn't. Even a short-lived visit to the bottom level of society

means that one is faced with one of the most important decis
one has to make in life: what type of society do you want to help
to create?

That is the question that has come to dominate my whole life.

26

The hippos

THOSE SIX MONTHS IN PARIS TAUGHT ME THAT ONE HAS TO MAKE choices. Every day I had to decide if I was going to smoke or treat myself to a meal slightly more filling than the one I'd had the previous day. I had to decide which museums to visit, or whether I was simply going to wander around, observing people and considering what I was going to write about – not right away but at some time in the future.

Making decisions meant taking life seriously. Paris, where people were still affected by the recently ended colonial war in Algeria, taught me that. It was also shortly before the protests against the Vietnam War reached their maximum intensity. I myself was the teacher, but so were all the other people hurrying past me along the pavements or rushing down to the metro stations.

Even if, later in my life, I have occasionally made wrong choices, I still believe that not making any choices at all is a grave mistake. I am often intrigued by people who just drift along with the mainstream, never questioning aspects of their environment or trying to change things. People are different, and of course that in itself leads to different views about society. But choices that go deeper than that and are about what you intend to do with your life are the most important decisions you will ever have to make – and you must make them.

There is a little grocer's shop in Antibes I generally go to when I am staying in the town. A man sits behind the counter from seven o'clock in the morning until the shop closes twelve hours later. He has a little television set that he watches. I have never entered his shop when he hasn't been staring at the flickering screen. He seems to watch absolutely everything. More or less reluctantly he interrupts his viewing to accept payment for goods sold. Before I leave the shop he has always returned to his telly.

He is very friendly. He seems contented enough. But his life horrifies me. Has he really chosen to stare at that television screen and made it the meaning of his life?

For most people life comprises a series of circumstances that affect us and our ability to make conscious decisions as to how to deal with those situations.

One day I wandered round a street corner and happened to bump into the woman I eventually married. I couldn't know that she would be walking just there at that particular time; but I – or we – were then able to choose to react positively to that chance encounter, and we got married.

The most difficult decisions I have ever had to make in my life concerned abortion. On two different occasions I put pressure on a woman to have an abortion. Each time it was her choice, her decision, that is clear. But looking back, I feel that the pressure I put on these two women was too great. In several ways I made it into my decision, despite the fact that it should always be the woman who decides what to do with her own body.

I also feel that I have made choices and decisions that have required a certain degree of both courage and unselfishness. They have often also required me to display financial generosity that I couldn't afford in my earlier days.

The choices a human being has to make also involve deciding where one stands in an unjust society: we are all political beings, whether we like it or not. We live in a fundamentally political society, where we have a sort of contract with everybody else who lives alongside us. But it is also a contract that affects those who are not yet born.

On what grounds do we make our decisions? On what basis do we choose what we do or think or find offensive? What do we choose to do, and what do we refuse to go along with?

Having the possibility to make decisions about what to do with one's life is a great privilege. As far as most people on this planet are concerned, life is simply about survival.

That has always been the case for humans. To eat or be eaten, to be able to defend oneself against predators, enemies and illnesses. To make sure that our offspring survive and are as well equipped as possible to cope with what is in store for them. Through the ages only very few people have been able to devote themselves to anything apart from simply surviving. Admittedly never so many as today – but even so, at least half of mankind now live with no ability to make choices.

During all the years I have spent in Africa I have observed this struggle to survive, which never seems to ease off even for a single day. Every evening the worries start all over again.

A few years ago I visited Jaipur and New Delhi in India. Late one evening I took a train from Jaipur. Along the sides of the tracks was an endless, unbroken line of lights from the people who lived there, only a few centimetres from the rails. I travelled through the masses of ramshackle hovels that represented their existence, as people with empty eyes sat watching the train edging its way slowly and carefully towards New Delhi. I felt like Marlow in Conrad's *Heart of Darkness* as he travelled along a dark and threatening river. There was no water flowing around my railway line, but even so I had the feeling of being transported along the black river to some kind of destruction.

In the 1980s, just outside Lusaka, the capital of Gambia, I saw women and children sitting by the side of the road and hacking at lumps of stone, reducing them to macadam. It was unbearably hot and the air was thick with powdery stone. Somebody in the party I was with said these women were so tired that they were unable to think any other thoughts apart from the fact that breaking up these stones would provide themselves and their children with money for food. They were too exhausted for anything apart from surviving.

People living on the outermost edge of society have no choice.

Lying down on the road and dying is not a valid choice. Starving to death is not an alternative either. Nowadays we have the resources necessary to do away with such absolute poverty and lift all living people above starvation level. And yet we choose not to do so. It is a choice I cannot see as anything but criminal. But there is no court that can take action on a global scale and prosecute the criminals responsible for failing to tackle poverty and starvation with all available means. And that should force all of us to become involved and accept responsibility.

Today, so many years after I walked openly around the streets of Paris picking up cigarette butts from the pavements, I can see more clearly than ever what a privilege it is to have the possibility to choose. I have always been on the right side of the borderline, with the time and strength and enough food in my belly, to be able to choose between various alternatives.

I have often chosen wrongly and had good cause to regret my actions, but have not been able to go back and change the decision. More important, though, is the fact that I have never drifted along with the mainstream without offering some resistance or stating my point of view.

Actually, that is not quite true.

Once, nearly thirty years ago, I was forced to drift along with the current. It was in Zambia, on one of the tributaries of the great River Zambezi high up in the north-west part of the country, in the Mwinilunga district. I was in a little plastic boat with an outboard motor. There were four of us crammed into the all-too-unsteady boat. We had travelled upstream, then switched off the engine and drifted back downstream, fishing for tigerfish. At one point there was a fork in the river, and we were supposed to follow the branch leading to the spot where we had tents and a car waiting for us. It was important that we started the engine in time because close by was a regular haunt of hippos. They had recently produced young and were extremely aggressive. Not many people know that despite its apparently slow-moving sleepiness, the hippopotamus is one of the African animals that kill most human beings every year.

Needless to say, the engine didn't start when we pulled the cord. At first we regarded it as a bit of a joke, but we were rapidly approaching the place where the hippos' heads could be made out over the surface of the water. There was no chance of our rowing away from the animals, and if we ended up in among them it would all be over. They would overturn the boat and kill us.

It was ominously quiet in that boat, although the one person sitting next to the engine was frantically tugging away at the starting cord. There was nothing we could say. We all knew what would happen in a few minutes' time if we couldn't start the engine. Jumping into the river and trying to swim to the nearest bank was not a practical solution: the river was full of crocodiles. None of us would reach dry land.

Thank the Lord the engine started at last, and we managed to escape.

That evening, at our camp site, it was unusually quiet. The fire crackled away and the dancing flames were reflected in our faces.

Many years later I spoke about it to one of those who had been present. I asked what he had been thinking as the hippos got closer and closer. He replied immediately – he had already thought about it often enough.

'I was trying to think of an alternative course of action,' he said. 'But there wasn't one. It's the only time in my life that I gave up. When the engine started I thought for a moment that there must be a God after all. What happened wasn't something within the range of possibility for human beings.'

'The spark plugs had become damp,' I said. 'The person trying to start the engine had flooded them. It had very little to do with religion.'

My friend said nothing. For him God was a better explanation than a few wet spark plugs.

That was his choice. Not mine. God or a couple of spark plugs. We made different choices.

27

A cathedral and a cloud of dust

TWO WOMEN I MET BY ACCIDENT HAVE GIVEN ME INSIGHT INTO what can be enormous happiness, and also the opposite, equally incomprehensible sorrow. For me those two things represent life's extremities. In all probability no person can live life to the full without having experienced extreme sorrow. Nobody wants to be affected by tragedy, but it is an inescapable fact of life.

In 1972 I visited Vienna. I was on my way to Hungary and Budapest, but at the Hungarian border station my Swedish passport, which was valid but worn and badly looked after, was rejected. I had to wait in a freezing-cold station with a police guard before I was put onto a train to Austria. I never made it to Budapest on that occasion. I wandered around Vienna, unsure what to do as a result of my thwarted journey.

While walking around without consulting a street map but following my impulses, I suddenly found myself standing outside the majestic Stephansdom cathedral. I went inside and observed the enormous and impressive space. It was the middle of the day, and there were not many people there. The thick stone walls shut out all sound from the outside. The atmosphere was timeless. In that respect all religious buildings are similar, irrespective of what they look like or which religion they are dedicated to.

I sat down in a pew and contemplated the vast space on all sides. I don't know of any cathedral that hasn't made me think about the workmen who built it. They worked for many generations before the final stone was put in place, the last lead-framed stained-glass window eased into position and the meticulously planned sculptures duly carved.

As I gazed around I noticed a woman sitting alone in a pew, with her head bowed. I was diagonally behind her, but nevertheless had the distinct impression from her hunched back that she was in distress, afflicted by some deep sorrow. She was sitting there motionless, shut up inside herself in this enormous cathedral.

When we are faced with sorrow and tragedy we often become worryingly curious. We stop if we happen to come upon a road accident that has just taken place. We peer into the damaged car as we crawl past it. If an ambulance races down a street, its lights flashing and siren screaming, lots of other passers-by come to a halt when the vehicle pulls up outside a house and the siren falls silent. The most extremely curious among us wait until the victim is carried out of the house on a stretcher.

We stop because we want to make absolutely certain that we are not the person lying on the stretcher.

I stood up and walked along one of the side aisles until I came to the opening in front of the altar. Then I turned round. The lone woman had buried her face in her hands, but even so I could see from her hair and dark forehead that she was of African origin.

There she sat, surrounded by nobody. Her hands were tightly clasped. I tried to imagine what must have happened. Had she received heartbreaking news? Was it about her or about somebody else? A priest walking down the central aisle gave her a searching look, but didn't stop. I remained standing in the shadows next to an arched column, and continued observing her. I felt guilty about being curious, but at the same time found it impossible to tear myself away.

It was not until I had been standing there for a while, five minutes perhaps, that it occurred to me that there was something that I could do, indeed that I ought to do. I hesitated, but then walked over to the woman's pew and sat down beside her. She looked up immediately, as if I had startled her or intruded into a space she considered to be her own. First in German, then in French and finally in English, I asked if there was anything I could do. She didn't understand what I said. I had the impression that she spoke some form of Arabic, even if she didn't look as if she came from North Africa. My presence didn't make her feel any less alone. On the contrary, she seemed to become even more worried. She suddenly stood up and left. I turned round and watched her hurrying out into the sunshine that glistened brightly when the cathedral door was opened.

I never saw her again. But although it is now forty years since I entered the Stephansdom and met her, I still have no doubt that she was struggling with devastating sorrow. I don't know where she came from nor where she went to; I don't even know if she is still alive: but I still think about her often. Her image is nailed up on one of my inner walls as a sort of Icon of Sorrow. And she reminds me of what everybody ought to be aware of: that sorrow has to dwell inside a person in order for its opposite to become visible. The tale *Prins Sorgfri* ('Prince Sorrowless', a nineteenth-century saga turned into a play for children in 1977) is a story that appeals to all generations. There are no princes, and no ordinary people come to that, who can hide themselves away from sorrow and think that they have the privilege of never being affected by it.

And what about overwhelming happiness? That was another woman, another continent, another time – almost exactly twenty years after I had entered Stephansdom cathedral. And she was also African. I met her in Mozambique at an assembly camp for refugees returning home from Zimbabwe and South Africa after the brutal civil war had come to an end at the beginning of the 1990s. Worried people were standing around, with no idea of whether relatives and friends were going to return after many years of silence, whether they would be on the packed platform on the back of one of the lorries that kept appearing in clouds of dust on their way from the border. Children were looking for parents, parents were looking for children, friends for friends, relatives for relatives, villagers for fellow villagers. Whenever a convoy of lorries came to a halt, chaos broke out. People were lifted down with their bundles and plastic bags of belongings. The noise, like that from a swarm of disturbed bees, filled the air.

I suddenly heard a yell. But it was not an order to begin fighting; the yell was filled with astonishing and overwhelming joy. It sliced through the mass of seething humanity surrounding the lorries, and silence fell. Not a sound was to be heard apart from this repeated yell. I could see that it was coming from a girl aged about eighteen. In the middle of all those people, those who had arrived on the lorries and those who had been waiting in the scorching sunshine, a gap had appeared like the ring in a circus tent. In the middle of the ring were an old man and woman, and the young girl, shouting out in sheer joy, was dancing around the old pair, pulling at her clothes and her hair as she did so.

It was some time before it dawned on me that it was her parents who had been riding on one of the lorries. I discovered later that she had been separated from them when she was no more than seven or eight years old. She had no idea what had become of them. She had gone to the assembly camps in the vague hope of seeing them, but it was pure chance that they came there – there were lots of assembly camps and nobody knew who was going where. Nobody knew the right place to wait. And many of the missing persons never turned up at all. Many were dead.

In its way it was a miracle. They had found one another again. The young girl could only express her joy by dancing and tugging at her clothes. Her aged parents simply stood there, without moving a muscle.

I watched as the girl took her father by the hand and greeted him with a curtsy. Then she and her mother ran their fingertips cautiously over each other's faces.

The last I saw of them was when all three clambered up onto a different lorry which then drove off in a cloud of dust.

Somehow or other the Stephansdom and the cloud of dust in Africa are linked together in my life.

Irrespective of whether or not I am now ill.

PART II

THE ROAD TO SALAMANCA

28

Shadows

THERE ARE SOME THINGS I KNOW FOR CERTAIN ABOUT CANCER. The first is that illnesses caused by tumours have always affected human lives. There are certain forms of cancer that have increased in our society and our time. What we eat and the environment in which we live have created the circumstances in which some forms increase and others decrease. But tumours have been discovered in the skeletal remains of dinosaurs. Early human beings have also been affected – Neanderthal and Cro-Magnon people as well as *Homo habilis*.

That is not especially surprising. The basis of life is the splitting up of cells, a process that continues from the foetus stage to the day we die. Our cells are renewed millions of times. The fact that division sometimes goes wrong and starts a process that leads to the formation of benign or malignant tumours is understandable. In fact, one might well say it would be odd if that were not the case. One has to be rather cautious when one talks about nature being perfect.

The second thing we know about cancer is that no human being can be guaranteed to avoid it. The longer one lives, the greater the risk of being afflicted. The risk is slightly higher for men than for women.

It is also true that certain families are more likely to produce a genetically inherited form of cancer. And that some families are more prone to cancer in general than others. There is no plausible explanation for this.

As far as I know there have been virtually no deaths in my family for three generations due to illnesses caused by tumours, but on the other hand practically every male and female has died of heart disease or vascular disorder. For example, both my siblings and I suffer from high blood pressure.

I admit to being somewhat arrogant in this connection; I have often said that I didn't expect to be struck down by cancer, but my death would be caused one day by a short circuit inside my head.

I was obviously wrong.

The third thing we know for certain about cancer is that it isn't infectious. I can be surrounded by cancer sufferers without needing to worry. Cancer does not infect others by means of breath, bodily fluids or handshakes.

Nevertheless, some people behave as if the illness was infectious even so – they are not in the majority, but they do exist. When I say that I have it, they take an invisible step backwards so as not to come too near.

That is not especially surprising. It is not many years since a cancer diagnosis was more or less equivalent to a death sentence. The doctors were usually powerless and the disease was not only fatal, it was often also an extremely painful way of dying.

When I received my diagnosis it never occurred to me to keep it secret. Why should it? I don't know of course how I would have reacted if I'd been told I had syphilis. That can be avoided. It is infectious. But there are only limited ways in which one can avoid developing cancer. Don't breathe in too many petrol fumes and succumb to the type of cancer that is common among lorry drivers. Don't eat too much red meat and find you have developed tumours in your bowels. Don't soak your liver in alcohol. And of course, don't smoke.

But I haven't smoked for over twenty-five years and yet, nevertheless, I get a tumour in one of my lungs. If I place bets on all the roulette numbers apart from 1, I can't be sure that the ball won't stop on that one. Cancer makes no promises.

The past still casts a shadow over the illness today. In spite of the fact that possible treatments and subsequent results are increasing and improving all the time, it is hardly likely that cancer will ever be eliminated altogether, like smallpox and, one hopes, malaria. But the death rates will continue to decline. Nowadays two-thirds of cancer sufferers are long-term survivors. And that number will increase.

But the shadow is still there. I notice it especially in the way various people react when I tell them about my illness.

When I told people I had torticollis, an extreme form of a stiff neck, some of them seemed to regard it as a sort of joke. It was like when people are hard of hearing and misunderstand what one says. But when I told them the pain was not due to a stiff neck or a slipped disc, but a metastasis in a vertebra at the back of my neck, it was no longer a joke. Some reacted as one would expect: with sympathy, worry and friendly understanding. Others simply disappeared. Ceased to get in touch. They hid away in the shadow of cancer.

During this time I have often thought about what Selma Lagerlöf wrote in *Thy Soul Shall Bear Witness!*: 'God, let my soul reach maturity before you harvest it.'

There is no need to worry about the religious undertone. The truth is universal without anyone needing to burden it with Christian beliefs. People who have achieved some sort of spiritual maturity don't need to hide themselves away in the shadows. They continue to make themselves heard. I am still completely alive, not somebody sitting by the side of my grave, dangling my legs over the edge.

I admit that I have been surprised during recent times. People I thought might well flee into the shadows have proved to be strong enough to remain in constant touch, while others of whom I expected more have disappeared over the horizon.

But I don't pass judgement on anybody. People are who they are. One doesn't need to have many friends – but one should be able to rely on those one has.

Cancer is a terrible disease. It is also something one has to deal with alone, despite being surrounded by doctors, nurses, family members and friends. There are seldom outward and visible signs that one is suffering with it. No one who doesn't know the facts can tell by looking at me that I am seriously ill, since I have lost neither weight nor hair. I look like I always do, and behave as usual. The fact that I am very tired need not mean that I am ill. I might just as well have completed a book, or come to the end of a run at the theatre.

But what about me, how do I behave? Do I hide in the shadows too? Am I also heading for the shelter of thick bushes? Like the wounded animal I am, in fact?

In Zambia many years ago I once took part in the search for a male lion that had been shot and badly injured. There were four of us, each armed with a rifle. We were walking in line, fifteen metres apart. Paul was ahead of the rest of us, when he suddenly stopped and raised a hand. He was an African ranger and hunter, and impressed all of us. His raised hand meant not only that we should stop, but also that we should load our guns. Until now Paul had been the only one with a cartridge at the ready. He pointed at a thicket some fifty metres ahead of us. If Paul indicated that the lion was in there, there was no doubt that he was right.

The wounded lion would try to lie there, silent and motionless, for as long as possible. But if we came too close, he would attack in a last desperate effort to get away from both us and the pain that the wound was causing him.

When he came bounding towards us, it was Paul who shot him with a well-aimed bullet.

In which thicket am I lying hidden? What form will my final but vain attempt to flee take?

Things have not gone so far that I have tried to convince myself that I am not in fact seriously ill. Nor have I felt that I have been unjustly afflicted. That thought is totally alien to me. If cancer had been an infectious disease I could have made sure I avoided taking unnecessary risks. It is not difficult to avoid being infected with

HIV, for instance. One can successfully take a minimum of precautionary measures.

It sometimes happens that at night I dream about being healthy. That it is somebody else who has fallen ill. I stand looking at people I know, but somehow don't recognise, and express sympathy at their fate.

The truth is that like everybody else no doubt I dream about being the exception. That one day I shall shake off this serious illness and be able to say that by some miraculous means I no longer have any symptoms.

But I know of course that it is not true. The illness is incurable. Even if I live long enough to die of something else, or at least become old enough for continuing to live not to seem all that important.

Facing up to cancer is a battle conducted on many fronts. The important thing is not to waste too much strength fighting against one's own illusions. I need all my strength in order to increase my powers of resistance in confronting the enemy that has invaded me.

Not tilting at windmills that have taken on the form of shadows.

29

Luminous teeth

I RECEIVED MY FIRST WATCH WITH A LUMINOUS FACE AT SOME time towards the end of the 1950s. I remember it as a remarkable, even magical, experience.

I can still recall the green shimmer in my mind's eye, from the first time I saw it when I was standing in a closed wardrobe.

In 1895 the German physics professor Wilhelm Röntgen discovered that certain beams could pass through various materials, but then adhere to photographic plates. Nowadays we are well aware of the importance this discovery had – and still has – for medical processes: the English expression is 'X-rays', but in many Continental languages they are called 'röntgen images' after their discoverer. A simple break in a wrist or a complicated fracture in a shin can be analysed with the aid of X-rays and the appropriate measures taken. X-rays can also be used to trace irregularities in people's lungs that are difficult to find using other methods. But X-rays are not just used to discover illnesses: they are of equal importance when it comes to curing some diseases, especially those coming from tumours, since the rays can be directed to attack the damaged cells.

What was not known at first is that there are horrific side effects from X-rays. With hindsight one can say that the pioneers were not careful enough when they developed treatments without knowing about those side effects. And they affected many people who had no idea what was involved in being exposed to the invisible rays.

In 1915 an American invented a luminescent paint, which he called 'undark'. His name was Sabin Arnold von Sochocky, and his aims were not scientific. He wanted to earn money. In the company he founded, his employees – who were often illiterate, uneducated girls as young as twelve – had to paint luminescent crucifixes or hands on clocks that would glow in the dark. In order to paint extremely fine surfaces, the girls needed to press the brush hairs together with their lips.

For amusement they often also painted their teeth and nails with the luminescent paint. Then they would go into dark rooms and show one another their glowing features.

Needless to say, nobody had warned them that the paint produced radioactive beams and could be dangerous. In addition, the medical journal *Röntgen*, which was published in America in 1916, announced that 'X-rays have absolutely no poisonous side effects. X-rays are for human beings what sunlight is for plants.'

During the First World War the desirability and indeed necessity grew for instruments that were luminous in the dark. A few years after the end of the war it was calculated that there were about 2,000 full-time employees working with the paint.

But now some of the people who had worked with the paint started to die. Their illnesses varied.

Nobody told the truth about why this was happening. A dentist by the name of Theodore Blum did report that one of his patients had seriously damaged gums and that he suspected the cause was the patient's work painting luminescent hands on clocks. The patient died soon afterwards. But no action was taken and clocks with luminescent hands continued to tick.

It was 1925 before the revelation that it was dangerous to work with X-rays broke through the wall of silence. And it was Sochocky, the man who had started the company, who made the biggest noise and warned about the horrific things that could happen to those working with the luminescent paints. By then he had left the firm he had set up. His own breath was now radioactive.

An investigation into the company disclosed how horrendous

things really were. The girls working in the factory were sent into a dark room one by one, and doctors were able to establish that the women were more or less completely luminescent. Their faces, arms and legs, and their clothes, were all glowing as a result of the paint.

Nearly all of them were also ill. Their blood values showed that in various ways they had been poisoned by the radioactivity to which they had been exposed.

The truth that emerged was very simple: the people who thought that the radioactive rays passed harmlessly through the body had been wrong. The radioactivity remained inside the skeleton and in the end, if the amount of beams affecting an individual were too much and long-lasting, that person was smitten with cancer and most often suffered a painful death.

It became clear that the medics and others who examined the patients who had been working with radioactive paints were also exposed to serious risks. A chemist by the name of Edwin Lehman, who worked on the radioactivity, was healthy to start with but died a month later. He was attacked by a blood disease that killed him within a few weeks.

In 1927 five sick factory workers sued the company they had been working for – the firm that Sochocky had started and that he was now working intensively to shut down. There is a lot of evidence of the great despair and feelings of guilt he suffered when he realised the price his young workers had been forced to pay.

The newspapers dubbed the case 'The five women who are doomed to die'. They claimed compensation for the injuries and suffering they had been caused. One of them had undergone twenty gum operations and the whole of her lower body was paralysed. She was carried into the courtroom on a stretcher along with two of the other women who were also unable to stand. One of them couldn't even raise her hand to swear the oath when she gave evidence.

The five women lost their first case. The company's lawyers succeeded in arguing that the injuries had been incurred so long ago that time had run out for any compensation claims. But the women didn't give up, despite the fact that they became increasingly ill. Several of them were close to death when they appeared in the law courts.

They received support and encouragement from many people who were upset by their suffering. Marie Curie, who had discovered the basic substances that cause X-rays, sent a remarkable message: she recommended that the sick women should eat calf's liver.

She herself would die within a few years as a result of a blood disease caused by her being in contact with so much radioactivity.

After many more years, by which time two of those belonging to 'The five women who are doomed to die' had actually done so, a mediator succeeded in achieving a result in the long struggle. Each of the women was awarded only a fraction of the amount they had originally claimed, but they didn't have the strength to continue the struggle any longer. Much later it was discovered that even their graves were radioactive.

Six months after the judgement Sochocky himself died as a consequence of the radioactive beams. Cancer had caused his hands, mouth and gums to rot away. But he never ceased to fight for compensation to be paid to those who had been infected, and for conditions for those still working with radioactive paints to be changed radically so that they were issued with adequate protective clothing and equipment.

With hindsight it seems clear that this helped to ensure that those who eventually worked on the Manhattan Project could be confident that their protective clothing and equipment saved them from falling ill in the same way that the women working in the paint factories had done. None of the engineers, physics experts and technicians who created the atom bomb that was dropped on Hiroshima and Nagasaki was at risk of their jaws rotting away.

Similar stories can also be told about the injuries and the suffering caused by working with asbestos. Even today the Western world exports ships to India that are to be scrapped, for instance. The ships are crammed full of asbestos. And the workers who are compelled to do the necessary work are often not even issued with simple face masks. Many of them die from asbestos poisoning in which the microscopic fibres that are secreted by the asbestos are sucked into their lungs and eventually form a thick layer that prevents normal breathing. Many workers who are affected slowly choke to death. A worker at the Wittenoom mine in Australia compared the illness to 'having your lungs filled with wet cement'.

It happens time after time, and will no doubt happen again. People start on new projects without first trying to establish if there are hidden negative aspects.

There is always a risk. And when it happens, a hideous catastrophe can ensue.

The young women working in those factories who decorated their teeth and nails with phosphorescent paint, and laughed at each other's appearance, were sacrificed at the altar of our constantly inadequate patience.

It is so incredibly easy to take risks with the lives of other people.

30

Photographs

I HAVE SEEN A LOT OF PHOTOGRAPHS OVER THE YEARS THAT I
remember and keep looking at again. Images that capture a moment
which, just as in dreams, says something about myself even though
I am not actually in the picture.

But there are photographs that I know I shall never forget. Black-
and-white images that never fade and disappear.

Remembering and never forgetting are not really the same thing.

The first picture is black and white, somewhat grainy, taken in
either 1919 or 1920. The photographer is unknown. The copy I have
seen gives a vague, almost blurred impression – as if the photographer
recoiled at the sight of his subject.

It is an outdoor shot: in the background is what seems to be a
garden wall or some trees. The subject matter is a number of men,
ex-soldiers. They are French. They have chosen to live alone because
of the injuries they suffered during the First World War. Their faces
are badly deformed as a result of shrapnel or direct hits from bullets,
and some of them have other injuries as well – a missing leg, or arm,
or hand.

You don't need to look at the photograph for long in order to
realise that people meeting these men in the street would have felt
obliged to turn aside out of nausea and disgust at the sight of the
injuries. Their faces are not merely deformed: it is as if the brutal
insanity of war is ingrained in them. Some have no jaw, others no
nose or mouth, no ears or eyes, and parts of foreheads are missing.

But these men of varying age are posing in front of a camera. They are all neatly dressed, serious. They are looking directly at the camera. None of them seems to be trying to conceal his injuries.

I sometimes wonder why the picture was taken. Who paid the photographer? The men themselves, or somebody else? It is most certainly not a picture for sending home as a Christmas greeting. Was it a serious attempt to demonstrate the devastation that war imposed on the soldiers who fought in it without actually dying in the trenches or during the pointless attacks to regain a hundred metres of a battered field?

Despite the distorted faces one can still make out what were once men with lively personalities, who now live in isolation in a large stone-built villa behind a high wall. I don't know what they did there. I have no idea how some of them could manage to eat despite their shot-away jaws and mouths. Nevertheless, the important message given by this photograph is that these people are still alive. The picture says: Here we are. Despite everything. Despite everything we are still alive. Despite everything we are prepared to show ourselves well dressed and serious in front of a camera that captures the moment and spreads it all over the world.

I believe there is an invisible link between the factory girls who painted their faces and the soldiers facing the camera. Although there is no direct connection apart from their immense suffering.

And there is also something that connects these people with the painting in Släp Church in which Gustaf Hjortberg's dead children look away from the artist.

The second picture I shall never forget is in fact a whole series of photographs taken within a few minutes of each other. A military patrol somewhere in Yugoslavia during the Second World War has captured partisans who are suspected of having ambushed German troops. Now the partisans are to be executed without a proper trial. Most of them are very young, about the same age as the German soldiers.

They are assembled in a field. As drying racks covered in hay have been set up in the background we can be confident that the time is summer or early autumn, and it is clearly hot. The German soldiers are wearing thick uniforms, with their tunics buttoned up to their necks as discipline demands, while the men waiting to die are wearing only trousers and thin unbuttoned shirts.

The German soldiers have a photographer with them. It is not clear in this case who the photographer is: a German war reporter or a Yugoslav collaborator.

Those who are about to be shot are lined up in front of some of the hay racks, and the soldiers prepare their weapons.

Then something remarkable happens. One of the German soldiers throws down his gun, tears open his uniform tunic and joins the men waiting to be shot. One cannot tell from the pictures if he is calm or agitated; he has simply left the firing squad and changed sides – instead of doing the shooting he has chosen to be shot.

There is nothing in the photographs to suggest any animated dialogue between the soldiers and their comrade who has thrown down his rifle. No indication that the soldiers are trying to persuade him to come back, by means of arguments or orders or a physical attempt to separate him from the Yugoslavian partisans.

That is really the most disturbing thing about the series of pictures. Everything seems to be proceeding as planned, the soldiers continue with what they have started, and military discipline is upheld.

In the last of the photographs the partisans are lying dead, together with the German soldier. As he has thrown away his tunic and his steel helmet he is no longer distinguishable from the others.

In this last picture the soldiers have left. The photographer must have stayed on for a few minutes. There is no sign of the German soldiers having taken care of their dead comrade. As soon as he changed sides, he ceased to exist. He was simply one of those to be executed.

Naturally, these pictures raise many questions and create many emotions. What made the German soldier sacrifice his own life, despite the fact that doing so was of no help to those who died around him? What was it that in the end made the situation so unbearable for him that he chose not to live any longer? Did he see himself reflected so strongly in the partisans that he knew the rest of his life would be impossible if he took part in the summary executions?

We cannot know. Just as we cannot know what his comrades thought. It must have come as a complete surprise to them, but without questioning the order they were given they aimed their guns at the man with whom they had just smoked a cigarette.

Two pictures that feature war and the victims of war. Both of them are also about courage. About making the most important and difficult decision an individual can possibly make. Choosing to die rather than to live. To offer your life for completely unknown people, who have also committed hostile actions against your comrades.

Can I say that I understand the German soldier?

In order to answer that question I must know how I would have reacted in the same situation.

I can't do that. All I can do is to keep looking at the pictures and never give up my attempt to understand.

31

The way out

JUST AS EVERYTHING IN MY LIFE HAS CHANGED, EVERY NEW morning brings with it a fresh challenge. I have to think about something other than my illness. Every morning I spend a certain amount of time asking myself how I feel, if I have any new side effects, or if it looks like being a good day. But if I am unable to thrust aside such thoughts with a real ice-hockey tackle of an effort, the battle is lost before it has even begun. Then there is a risk that resignation, suffering and fear will gain the upper hand. What course is open to me in that case? To lie down and turn my face to the wall?

When I managed to drag myself up out of the quicksand about three weeks after the cancer diagnosis and found myself in a position where I was able to start fighting, the most effective way of doing so was obvious: books. At difficult times whenever I have needed to give myself relief or consolation, or perhaps a breathing space, my instinct has been to pick up a book and immerse myself in its text. I have turned to books when love affairs have come to an end. When a theatre production went wrong, or I failed to meet a deadline, my books have always been there. As a sort of liniment. But even more as a means of diverting my thoughts in a different direction, in order to gather strength.

And that was the case now as well. On my desk are all the books I haven't yet read – but on this occasion something happened that was new for me. I found myself unable to devote myself to new, unread books, even if they were by authors I always used to approach with great interest. I was unable to deal with the new, the unknown. Reading a new book is to journey into the text as if one were on an expedition, but I found that I was going round in circles. I read a page, but was unable properly to grasp what it said. The words were like shut and bolted doors, and I didn't have a key.

For a brief moment that made me afraid. Were books beginning to let me down, just when I needed them more than at any other time in my life so far?

But that was not the case. When I picked up a book that I had read many times before, the words opened themselves up again. What I was unable to cope with was the new and the unknown; but what I had read before, perhaps on several occasions, had the same effect as ever. I read and was able to stop thinking about my illness.

The first book I opened was one of the many versions of Defoe's *Robinson Crusoe* I have collected over the years. The edition I picked out of the bookcase at random was published by Torsten Hedlunds förlag in Gothenburg in 1892. Professor Karl Warburg has written an introduction, which is a description of the life of Daniel Defoe. Jean Rossander's translation from English is somewhat ponderous, but quite close in meaning to the original. And the book also contains Walter Paget's classic illustrations.

I know of no better novel than *Robinson Crusoe*. It reveals the secret behind the difference between a good and a bad story.

Robinson Crusoe is about a shipwrecked sailor who spends many years alone on a desert island with only a few wild goats as company. In the end he makes friends with a native-born refugee who managed to escape being eaten by the cannibals who captured him, and the pair are characterised by all the inherent features of colonialism.

But in fact Robinson is never alone. The reader is always with him, invisible but by his side. That is what makes the story so magical. If the reader keeps his distance and only peers into the text, the intimate relationship between the reader and the story that all novels aim to create never occurs. But in *Robinson Crusoe* the reader is invited to take part. He lies there in the sand, just as much a castaway as Robinson.

In my second-year class at primary school in Sveg, Miss Manda Olsson handed out small grey notebooks. We were to invent stories that we should then write down in the book. After a week, we were expected to hand in a written story – long or short, it didn't matter. I went home, locked myself in the lavatory and wrote a version of *Robinson Crusoe* on one page. I handed the book in proudly the very next day. By then I had filled it with stories and adventures to the very last page. Miss Olsson said afterwards that she couldn't make out anything of what I had written because it had all been done so quickly and carelessly. I had been in too much of a hurry. But I was given a new notebook, and urged in friendly terms to rewrite everything in a way that could be read and understood.

Now, in my study, I shifted to one side all the unread books and made a pile of the ones I wanted to reread. I would be threatened by no surprises. I would be wandering around in familiar territory.

Everything went well until I began my first cycle of chemotherapy. It transpired that one of the side effects was that the mucous membranes of my eyes became irritated, and produced constant tears. If I read too much there was a sort of mist between my eyes and the text. I couldn't see the words clearly. If I rested for an hour, it went away. But it soon came back again.

And so I began to alternate reading with looking at images of works of art. Again I chose ones that I was already familiar with. Never more than one picture a day. I began with the artists who have meant – and still mean – most to me: Caravaggio and Daumier. No matter how strange the world they create is, I always feel at home in it. I sometimes think about the fact that although Caravaggio painted such a variety of motifs, he never painted the sea. As for Daumier, a lot of people are familiar with his political caricatures, but not so many know that he was also a painter and sculptor of significance.

Every picture that means something special to me also has a story to tell, even if they open different doors from the ones opened by written texts.

I am constantly reminded that we human beings are basically storytellers. More *Homo narrans* than *Homo sapiens*. We see ourselves in others' stories. Every genuine work of art contains a small fragment of glass from a mirror.

My third way of thinking about something other than my illness was of course music. If you ask people suffering from severe pain or devastating sorrow what gives them the greatest relief, most of them say music. I started going through my record collection, switching between jazz, classical, and everything from African folk music to electronic music.

Most of all I listened to Miles Davies and Beethoven. Occasionally also Arvo Pärt and blues from the southern states delta.

I succeeded in diverting my attention from my illness by never breaking my routine. Books, pictures, music. With these it was possible to counter the almost intolerable pressure to devote all my attention to the disease, the treatment, and constantly looking for signs of new symptoms. That also gave me more strength to cope with the times when I had no alternative but to consider what I was stricken with. I was not simply a person who had been diagnosed with a serious illness: I was also the same person as I had been before, myself and no other. It was possible to live in two worlds at the same time.

But on certain days not even the stories, pictures and music helped. Days when I barely had the strength to get out of bed as a result of the exhaustion brought about by the effects of the chemotherapy as it attacked the tumours and metastases. Some days I hovered in a weightless state in an empty and cold universe, without meaning and without purpose. At such times I could understand that some seriously ill people can choose to put an end to their own lives.

I could understand it, but at the same time it was something I couldn't want for myself, and could never do. I wouldn't want to subject my nearest and dearest to the agony of always wondering if there was more they could have done, despite everything.

After about two months, when I had reached the middle of the first basic cycle of chemotherapy, I had the feeling one morning that a new sort of normality had entered my life. Nothing would ever be the same as it had been before I received the diagnosis, but nevertheless it was as if life was now taking on a form that in my darkest moments I would never have thought possible.

The days were getting lighter. Not a lot, but midwinter was past. One morning, all too early, a blackbird started singing from its perch on the television aerial. It occurred to me that this was something I could record on my gravestone.

I have heard the blackbird. I have lived.

But I thought less and less often about death. It was there all the time anyway, without my needing to lure it out from the shadows. Now I read my books, looked at pictures and listened to music – all things that had to do with life.

One day when I had finished a book I'd read before – Conrad's *Heart of Darkness* – I went to look at the pile of unread books I had put to one side almost two months earlier.

I was unable to pick any of them up. But only a few days later I started reading books from that pile as well.

Light had been travelling for a long way, but at last it had arrived. Just then, at least.

32

Paris in flames, 1348

ONE NIGHT I AM WOKEN BY DREAMS OF THE GIGANTIC RATS I SAW when I was living in Paris during the 1960s, especially when I was out late at night walking along the Rue de Vaugirard on the way to my flat in Rue Cadix.

The rats were as big as fat cats, and galloped into view before disappearing down drainpipes.

When I think of rats I also think of cats. And as I lie there in the darkness of night I recall how, according to legend, Paris went up in flames during the winter of 1348. Like all such unexpected events, this inferno was immediately interpreted as a sinister omen.

In the summer of 1348 the Black Death reached Paris. As always when epidemics threatened, Paris was badly placed: overcrowding in the city centre meant that anybody who didn't leave town would be unable to protect themselves from the plague. But where would the poverty-stricken – who made up the overwhelming majority in the city – be able to flee to? They remained, and they died.

Needless to say, nobody knew where the plague came from, or how it spread from house to house, from person to person. But as always, there was a search for an explanation and for a scapegoat.

In this case a rumour soon spread to the effect that the cause of so many human deaths was all the cats in the city.

It could equally well have been the Jews who were singled out as scapegoats, or Romany gypsies, or anybody else. But on this occasion it was the cats that were found guilty. It was a well-known historical assumption that cats and witches harboured dark secrets.

And so there was a furious attack on all the cats in the city. Hardly any escaped their fate of being killed and thrown into the Seine.

That meant that the real culprits, the rats, no longer had to fear their natural enemies. Their numbers exploded, and they and the flease they carried spread the infection far and wide. Before long eight hundred people were dying in Paris every day. The cemeteries were full. There were no people left to bury the dead. They remained in houses and in the streets, their bodies rotting away. Priests abandoned the dying when they realised that they themselves were infected and had to prepare for their own deaths.

Anybody who could fled Paris: rich businessmen, aristocrats and the top layer of clerics. Every day their carriages would hurry away from the stench and the misery. Many of them died even so, but just as many survived because they had the resources and the ability to flee.

Those who remained and had not yet been infected lived as one always does when death seems inevitable. They turned their last days into orgies. An unknown chronicler described Paris at this time as 'a city in a state of total collapse when it comes to morality and decency'.

The plague continued for eight months. When it finally came to an end half the population of Paris had died. The cemeteries were so full that arms and legs were sticking up out of graves. Every night the city's dogs would find their way there in order to feast on bodies lying under a thin layer of soil.

For a whole year there was a foul stench of dead bodies hanging over the streets. It was about 1350 before the nobility cautiously began to return to Paris.

But the dead cats! Perhaps they can be seen as an appropriate symbol for our history? That we killed the cats instead of allowing them to catch the rats?

Human beings are risk-takers. Risk coupled with our constant curiosity has taken us to where we find ourselves today. But if a third element is missing – caution – it can be dangerous. Perhaps the presence of caution would have meant it took longer for us to get to where we are, but it might also have meant that we would have avoided some of the devastating consequences and catastrophes that have hounded us in the footsteps of progress.

The question is: how much of this lack of caution and consideration is deeply embedded in the nature of mankind? Young men kill themselves the very same day they acquire a licence to ride a motorbike or drive a car. Deep down they are well aware that speed kills, but nevertheless they floor the accelerator, overtake impulsively and suddenly find that their radiator or bonnet has smashed into a tree or a cold, hard stone wall.

Girls of the same age are significantly more careful. They acquire their driving licences, but they don't kill themselves by driving like lunatics. The reason for this caution is of course the biological fact that they are here on earth in order to give birth to children. They normally give birth to more boys than girls, which is necessary in order to achieve a balanced society because so many more boys than girls die at a young age. On the Normandy beaches in the summer of 1944, for instance, or on the battlefields in France between 1914 and 1918, it was young men who ran headlong into the bullets and shrapnel. There were no women present. It had never occurred to anybody that women should be sent out to war, except in the roles of nurses, drivers or office workers. On the contrary, their role was to stay at home to make the shells that would later kill the young men belonging to what was called the enemy.

Let us move from the munitions factories to the town of Alberta in northern Canada. In an area as large as Florida are the world's richest deposits of oil-bearing sand. But there is no drilling for oil here; the method used is a kind of mining called fracking. In the last ten years the USA has imported more oil fracked in Alberta than has been acquired from Saudi Arabia.

With a short-sighted view of the world, this is of course a sensible political decision. But fracking has a devastating effect on the environment. The dangerous carbon dioxide emissions from the oil harvested in Alberta are almost twice as great as those from Saudi Arabia.

Some scientists believe that the expensive and environmentally damaging fracking exceeds the tipping point for whether or not we shall be able to control global warming.

James Hansen, who works on questions of climate control at NASA, says that 'the game is over when it comes to controlling global warming'.

Obviously the most important aim is to reduce all use of fossil fuels. This is something we all know, except perhaps for the most fanatical and corrupt climate experts who work for the industry and energy companies. But it could be that fracking in Alberta is one of the clearest examples of how we avoid taking into consideration the consequences of our actions before we embark upon projects we always maintain are for the good of mankind.

In 1977 *Voyager 1* and *Voyager 2* were launched from Cape Kennedy. Those space probes have made the longest journey in human history, a journey that is still continuing. Today those small rockets are at a distance of 19 billion kilometres from the sun, and even further from the earth. Radio signals sent from our planet to *Voyager* 1 and 2 and then returned need thirty-four hours in order to cover that distance.

Today those space probes (which I would like to call Travelling Men after the Swedish ship that sailed the seas 250 years ago) are at the outermost edge of our solar system. It is still the solar winds and magnetic fields that control everything in the closest universe that the spaceships can report to us about. But at any moment the Travelling Men could leave our solar system and disappear into another part of the universe where different magnetic fields will be dominant. Nobody can say when that will happen, except that it will be 'soon'. In a universal perspective that could be a matter of months, or years.

Our Travelling Men will continue their solitary journey following the same course until they fall to pieces. They will continue to send their signals and tell us about the unknown waters that comprise our universe.

When I think about all the scientific and engineering triumphs that lie behind this journey, I cannot but be astonished that we were able to achieve them with all the 'ifs' and 'buts' that had to be sorted out before the spaceship was launched. This means I must also believe that one of these days cancer will be defeated. And that we shall find a satisfactory way of taking care of the nuclear waste we are collecting.

Meanwhile the Travelling Men disappear deeper and deeper into a world we know nothing about.

Perhaps a world we could call 'Eternity'?

33

How long is eternity?

I AM REALISING MORE AND MORE HOW SIGNIFICANT FOR ME THE
period was that I spent in Paris when I was very young. It formed
me in so many ways.

Not all of them positive, perhaps.

For instance, for a long time there was a woman I wanted to see
dead.

As I have already said, after a month (by which time my money
had run out), I managed to find a job as an assistant repairer of
clarinets and saxophones. Monsieur Simon cleaned them and
renewed moving parts before it was time for me to reassemble the
instruments.

His little workshop was located in a backyard high up in the
working-class area of Belleville. He had another employee, an elderly
rotund man who was both unpleasant and cowardly. When Monsieur
Simon was around he said nothing; but when the owner left his
workshop in order to travel around various music stores to collect
or deliver instruments, the fat little man would start making rude
comments about my work. I arrived too late in the morning, I worked
too slowly, I wasn't skilful enough. Above all, I was illegally employed
and could be whisked away by the police any day.

I never responded because his obsequious cowardice reminded
me of one of Charles Dickens's fools. I relied more on Monsieur
Simon, who was a kind man.

As I lived at Porte de Versailles I had a very long journey to and from work. I had to change three times on the metro. Work started at seven, and I always fell asleep on the train in the mornings. I often didn't wake up until long after I ought to have changed trains. Monsieur Simon would glare at me when I turned up late, or rather gaze at me with a certain amount of melancholy, but he never said anything.

The station I had to get off at was called Jourdain, and from there I had a ten-minute walk. Every morning I would pass a toothless old woman who used to stare at me. I don't know where she was going to. As I frequently arrived at different times I hoped every morning that I might escape seeing her – but she was always there, as if she knew when I would be coming. She was dressed in black and chewed her lower lip with her toothless gums.

I didn't know her, never greeted her, had no idea who she was. Nor had she done anything to me. Nevertheless, I came to hate her. She was like a black cat, or a witch, who wanted to do me ill by always staring at me when I appeared every morning, tired and unsteady on my feet.

I don't think I can explain this emotion in any kind of rational way. Today it seems to me that unfortunately it is a very typical human trait. I was looking for a scapegoat onto whom I could unload my anger at having to strain myself so much in order to scrape together enough money to pay for rent and food. She just happened to get in my way.

Thirty years after leaving Paris I went back to Belleville. I got off the train in Jourdain once more and walked the usual route to Monsieur Simon's workshop. I gave a start when I saw the old woman coming towards me on the pavement, a little creature all in black. But it wasn't her. No doubt she was long dead.

Naturally, on other occasions I have also felt that I wanted to kill or at least injure people who have offended me or behaved badly in some other way. But they have been transient attacks of emotion that have passed quickly, and in most cases I have forgotten all about them. I have every reason to be grateful that I tend to forget things easily.

It was only that woman in the street who was not spared from my long-term anger before I returned thirty years later.

Nevertheless I refuse to allow the concept of 'evil' to pass my lips. I don't believe in it. The fact that people in all times, including those in which we live today, have done wicked things is just not the same. Those who suggest that some people are born evil are sending us back to times when original sin was still something we believed in. People were born evil just as they were born with freckles or red hair.

In my life I have met people who have committed horrendous and barbaric acts. I have met child soldiers who have murdered their parents or their siblings. But they were not born evil. They have carried out those brutal deeds when guns were aimed at their own heads. They have had to choose between their own lives and those they were forced to kill. What would I have done as a thirteen-year-old in that situation? The only honest answer I can give is that I don't know. I can hope that I would have acted differently, but I can't be sure.

Not even when neighbours in the Balkans begin to slaughter one another has an inherent force of evil come to the surface. Once again it is the horrendous circumstances that have taken the upper hand. There is always somebody who speculates and benefits from barbaric atrocities.

'Barbarism always has human traits. That is what makes barbarism so inhuman.'

I wrote that nearly forty years ago; I have no reason to change that view today.

I have been exposed to the hatred and violence of others. Not often, but often enough for me to have used up a number of the extra lives that all humans are born with.

I haven't been involved in all that many fights. Of course I squabbled with others in the schoolyard and I was usually the loser because although I was fast I wasn't all that strong. I also had the unfortunate tendency to take part in fights that I knew I was bound to lose. I always hoped I would manage to land a telling blow, and it did happen very occasionally.

When I was fifteen I worked for a while in the Swedish merchant navy. I was employed by a shipping company that exported Swedish iron ore all over the world and Middlesbrough was a frequent port of call. I went ashore one evening, got drunk and couldn't find my way back to the boat. I asked a young girl the way. Perhaps she didn't understand my English, who knows, but suddenly several young men came racing up and accused me of addressing her as if she were a prostitute. I was beaten up and somehow managed to lose my shoes. I found my way back to the ship in my stockinged feet. It was raining, and I had a lot of blood in my eyebrows and on my lips. But even that wasn't too awful. When I went on board I was met by the Norwegian third mate, who simply smiled somewhat ironically and suggested that the next time I went ashore when it was raining I should remember to wear my shoes.

But sometimes I have been seriously attacked. On one occasion I was convinced I was going to die.

It was in Zambia's capital Lusaka in the spring of 1986. After dinner one evening I was heading back to the Norwegian-run international aid building, where I was lodging. As usual, I kept a close eye on the rear-view mirror. It was not uncommon for four-wheel-drive vehicles to be hijacked and stolen by gunmen. I couldn't see any suspicious-looking vehicle behind me when I turned off the main road into the housing estate where my room was located.

But I was mistaken. One of the cars that had overtaken me earlier knew where I was going to stop – they must have had the house under observation since early in the evening.

As usual I drove up to the entrance gate in the stone wall and sounded the horn twice: that was the signal for the guards to open the gate so that I could drive in. It was not unusual for them to be asleep, or for it to take some time for them to open up. The guards had begun to open the gates at last – but when they saw what was happening they did the only sensible thing: they stopped, and said nothing. If they had started making a fuss it would have been impossible to stop guns being fired.

A car drove up behind me and blocked my line of retreat. Suddenly a revolver was pointed at my forehead through the open car window. I did what I knew was appropriate in the circumstances: I showed that my hands were empty and made no rapid movements.

But it was clear that there was a big risk I would get a bullet in my head. That was what usually happened when robbers struck. In Zambia in those days the death penalty was the standard punishment for wielding a gun, even if it was a dummy or unloaded: if caught they would die in any case.

I could feel that the gun pressed up against my temple was a real one. I was dragged out of the car and had time to notice that the black man holding the revolver had bloodshot eyes and smelt strongly of drugs. This was not unusual either. No more unusual than Swedish bank robbers often taking drugs before striking; those men are also filled with fear when they enter the bank.

When I was bundled down onto the ground I was sure I was going to die. I thought it was an unusually pointless way of dying. And too early. I wasn't even forty at the time.

But I don't recall any panic-stricken fear of death. All I felt was resignation. And the smell of soil pressing against my face.

Perhaps I thought that was the last sensation I was going to experience: the smell of wet African soil. But then the car took off with a screech of tyres and the robbers disappeared.

Then came a reaction, of course. I started shaking, my pulse rate rocketed and I didn't sleep for several nights. But I don't remember feeling any hatred towards the man who held the gun to my head. It was as if my relief that it wasn't fired was so much stronger.

There is an epilogue to this event. A month or so later I received a message from the police: they had managed to recover the car, which had been about to cross the border into Congo to be sold. One of the robbers had been shot dead. I was asked to identify the man from the photograph the police had taken.

Despite the fact that I had only seen his face for a few seconds, I knew immediately that it was him. I was told that he was nineteen years old and in all probability had already killed three or four people.

Life is short. But death is very, very long.

'How long is eternity?' asks the child.

Who can answer that question?

34

Room number 1

I ALWAYS HAD MY CHEMOTHERAPY TREATMENT IN THE SAME ROOM in the Oncology Department of the Sahlgrenska hospital in Gothenburg. It was a somewhat shabby room, but always immaculately clean. The visitor's chair was tucked away in a corner – the room was small and space was at a premium – and had a light blue cover; the wooden arms were scraped and worn. The only window in the room was high up. When I lay on the bed and looked through the window I could see a patch of sky, which was usually grey these winter months.

It started with one of the nurses sticking a needle into one of my arms or hands. As I have deep-lying veins that are reluctant to yield any blood, and are keen to prevent needles sticking into them, it could take half an hour to fix the cannula through which the infusions would pass. It sometimes happened that one of the nurses would give up and ask a colleague to try instead. The veins would occasionally become cramped or split, but in the end the nurses always managed to fit the cannula.

The cytotoxins came in transparent plastic bags, and most often there were five of them. One was red. When I asked why, I realised that I should have been able to work that out for myself: the contents were light-sensitive, and hence it was not possible to use a transparent bag.

I would get to room number 1 shortly before half past nine, and the process would be finished about five hours later, by which time the contents of the bags had been absorbed into my bloodstream. Most of the time I was alone in the room – nobody needed to check that the infusions were flowing as they should. Now and then some-body would come in to check that I had been to the toilet: it was necessary for my kidneys to be working normally.

They were. I drank water and tea. After an hour I got up and shuffled to the toilet in the same room, carrying with me the stand with all the tubes and bags attached. I sometimes saw a confused-looking bird fly past the window. Perhaps the birds have their own hospitals, I thought. But can an ordinary little Swedish bird develop cancer? I still don't know the answer to that, but I think they can.

During my third cycle of chemotherapy I had an unexpected visitor in room number 1. I was lying on top of the bed and had fallen asleep. One of the nurses had just connected up the third bag, the one with the light-sensitive contents. I heard the door opening.

But it wasn't one of the nurses. Standing in the doorway was a girl who couldn't be more than twenty years old. I hadn't seen her before and wondered if she was one of the health-care assistants I hadn't yet met. But she wasn't dressed as if she was working at the hospital.

I realised she was in fact a patient, just like myself. She stood there looking at me. Her eyes were glazed, her movements slow, as if every step, every gesture, required an almost impossible effort. She was very thin, her face pale, and around her eyes were deep hollows making it look as if her tiredness had been applied like mascara.

Then I noticed that she was wearing a black wig. It was not her own hair.

Chemotherapy and radiotherapy are always associated with hair loss. I had been spared this inconvenience, but I had noticed that people I met often glanced at my hair.

This led to me also glancing surreptitiously at fellow patients' heads when I attended the clinic. There were some who wore wigs, and others who didn't bother about their baldness. I imagined it must be worst for women. But that was my prejudice; in fact more men than women hid their baldness under wigs.

The girl stood there looking at me, like somebody who had just been woken up out of a dream.

She didn't look Swedish – whatever that means. There was something Semitic about her features. But of course she could have been born in Sweden even so; our country is based on immigration and emigration. My own ancestry can be traced back to France and Germany.

I nodded to her, smiled, and asked if she was looking for someone. She didn't seem to understand what I said. She swayed from side to side slightly, and sat down – or rather, collapsed onto the visitor's chair with its worn armrests. She leant back and closed her eyes.

It dawned on me that she was very ill. The earth was already pulling her down, despite the fact that she was so young. Her tiredness was pure exhaustion: she was already half gone, leaving life behind.

Then the door opened again. A woman in her fifties came in. She merely glanced at me before gently taking hold of the girl on the chair. She was speaking Arabic. I couldn't understand what she said, but she was obviously the girl's mother.

Then her father appeared – a short, timid-looking man with a furrowed face. He took no notice of me either as I lay there with the infusion dripping into my arm. All the pair of them cared about was their daughter. With extreme tenderness they helped her up and supported her as they left the room.

I didn't exist. All that mattered was their sick daughter.

The door closed. It echoed in a way reminiscent of a heavy church door. Death has paid a visit, I thought to myself, and didn't try to overlook the fact that the encounter with the girl and her parents had scared me. Why had the girl opened the door to room number 1 in the first place? What was the message she had brought with her? Was death in the habit of sending out couriers?

When one of the nurses came to connect the next bag of

cytotoxins, I couldn't resist telling her about the unexpected visit I had had. I said I had the impression that the girl was very ill. She nodded as she changed the bag and checked that the new infusion was flowing through the plastic tubing as it should.

Then the nurse confirmed that the girl was indeed very ill. She said it in such a way that I understood death was just around the corner. But I didn't ask exactly what cancer she was suffering from. Nobody speaks about other patients. Everybody has their integrity.

But I couldn't help asking one question that wasn't directly connected with her illness.

'Why did she come to room number 1?'

I assumed there would be no answer, but there was.

'She was moved here when there was a leak in the room she usually uses. There are no spare beds in the intensive care wards. She was in here for a week before she was able to move back to her usual place.'

And then came something I shouldn't really have been told.

'Her brain has been affected by her illness. She disappears sometimes. Her parents look for her until they find her. They are always here. She is their only child. Their other children have all died in some war they came here to get away from.'

I was told no more. I don't know if she had a brain tumour or if her mental confusion was due to something else. But in any case, it doesn't matter. When she came into my room she was on her way to somewhere but didn't know where.

As far as she was concerned, even though I was lying there on the bed, the room was completely empty.

I never saw her or her parents again. I don't even know her name. Nor do I know if she is still alive.

But every time I return to room number 1 for chemotherapy or a blood transfusion, when my blood counts have become so poor that I can't stand up without losing my balance, I think I can see her there, sitting in the visitor's chair with its worn-out armrests.

There was something she wanted to tell me, this courier sent to me by death. But I still don't know what that message was.

35

The road to Salamanca, Part 1

It was 1985. I was thirty-seven years old. I had set off two days earlier at four in the morning, from the Algarve in southern Portugal on my way back to Sweden. I spent the first night over the workshop of a petrol station north of Lisbon that rented out a room smelling of diesel and engine oil. The car I was driving was small and light; I didn't need to put it in a garage overnight as hardly anybody would have wanted to steal it, or even to break in as it was almost empty. All my belongings fitted into a suitcase that I took with me to my room.

The next day I continued my journey northwards. It was August, and very hot. Traffic was heavy because the European holiday period had just begun, and the big cities emptied out as lots of people travelled to the south – to the Riviera, the Spanish Costas and the Algarve. I was on my way home with a manuscript that was almost finished. I had rented a flat from a waiter at a cafe in Albufeira, where I had a view over the sea as I sat writing.

I had got quite a lot done. A circus was pitched nearby for a month: I got used to the music and the applause. I was present at their last performance. The following day, the circus and I both gathered together our belongings and left.

I listened to the news on the car radio, with reports coming and going from all over the world. Nothing important seemed to have happened. But on the other hand it was claimed that lots of important things had happened. As so often, the news broadcasts were more or less incomprehensible.

I had decided to turn off eastwards before reaching Porto, and drive over the mountains into Spain. I would have to wait and see where I spent the night, but I was counting on driving quite a long way.

At the time I was in charge of a theatre, and thought a lot about how I came to decisions. I could see in the rear-view mirror that I was suntanned, but my thoughts were white. Or at least, pale. I had spent the whole summer struggling with a nagging worry: how could I summon up the strength to be in charge of such a difficult and complicated operation as a theatre always is and probably has to be?

I drove along the winding mountain road that forms the border between Portugal and Spain, and by the afternoon I had got as far as the endless plains that lie in the west of Spain: mile after mile of dead-straight road through a scorched landscape. On one stretch I drove over thirty kilometres before coming to a slight, almost indiscernible bend in the road, which then continued in the same never-ending straight line again.

At one point I stopped and sat in the shade of a parched tree. I ate the food I had brought with me, and spent some time fighting off the flies before continuing.

In the evening, when darkness had already fallen, I arrived in Salamanca where I decided I would spend the night. I drove around the town centre and eventually found a hotel that didn't look too expensive, with a car park quite close by.

The room was very narrow and had probably once been a corridor in a rich family's home that had been converted into a hotel. But the bed was comfortable. I had a shower, changed my clothes and lay down on the bed. I heard the faint sound of two people quarrelling very quietly – I could only make out the occasional word. They seemed to be bickering over what everybody argues about: money.

I slept for a while and dreamt about the long way I had travelled that day. But there was something odd about the dream, it wasn't simply a straightforward reproduction of the journey I had made a few hours earlier. The car was the same, as was the landscape; even the news on the radio was a repetition of what I had heard already.

But I wasn't alone in the car. There was somebody in the seat beside me. There was probably somebody in the back seat, too, but I never dared to turn round and see who it was.

I was driving the car, but I was also sitting in the passenger seat. Myself as a teenager. Neither of us spoke.

I lay there on the bed and tried to work out what message the dream had been trying to convey. I believe that whatever one dreams about is always about oneself, even if there are different people in the dream. This was a message to the effect that myself as a young man was still important for me as an adult. I became increasingly convinced that it was also me sitting in the back seat – but perhaps I hadn't dared to check in case it was me as an old man? I couldn't know for sure.

It was high time for my dinner. I wondered if I ought to ask the receptionist, an elderly man with a club foot, if he could recommend a nearby restaurant, but when his telephone rang I desisted and went out. It was a warm evening. The darkness was as silkily smooth as it can be in southern Europe and Africa. I strolled around the streets, where the evening noises were just the same as everywhere else: laughing or simply loud young people, cars, dogs barking, blaring music from some bar or other. And church bells suddenly penetrating the blanket of sound.

There was something timeless about that evening in Salamanca. I felt relaxed as I usually do when absolutely nobody knows where I am, or who I am.

From Sveg to Salamanca, I remember thinking. A long way from a snowy and melancholy little town in central Norrland to the ancient Spanish town of Salamanca. The journey had taken many years. Nobody could have foreseen that eventually, one warm evening in August, I would be wandering around here looking for a restaurant.

I hesitated in the doorway of several establishments but kept going until I came to an eatery that looked as if it were a sort of local bar, patronised by people who lived in the area and not primarily a restaurant for tourists. I went in and was shown to a rickety little table and chair in the corner. The waiter, who was dressed in black and white, came up and suggested that I might like to eat veal. It was the evening's best dish, he assured me. He realised that I didn't speak Spanish but understood a fair amount, and was careful to speak slowly and clearly. He recommended a local wine. I said yes to all his proposals. He was in his sixties, roughly as old as I am now as I write this. His hair was thin, he had a grey moustache and a nose that was strikingly large and pointed. He moved from table to table seemingly unaffected by all the work he had to do.

I ate my veal steak, drank my wine, which was a bit on the sour side, and then had a cup of coffee. Customers started leaving; more and more tables became empty. The long journey and the concentration I had needed to cover the endless stretches of straight road safely had left me tired; I can't remember a single thought I had while at the table.

Suddenly a quarrel broke out at one of the tables. An elderly man and a younger woman began complaining to the waiter in loud voices. There was something wrong with the dessert that had just been served. The man pushed it away angrily and – I think – claimed it was inedible and the fact that it had been served at all was scandalous. The waiter stood there listening, without saying a word – not with his head bowed like a schoolboy ashamed of himself, but all the time eyeing the couple at the table. When the man seemed unable to think of anything else to say, the woman joined in. Her voice was shrill, and as far as I could tell she more or less repeated what the man had said.

All the time the waiter was holding his tray balanced on one hand; it contained used glasses and coffee cups destined for the dishwasher.

What came next happened very quickly. The woman was still complaining in her shrill voice when the waiter suddenly lifted the tray up over his head then flung it down onto the floor, smashing all the glasses and cups. Then he calmly took off his white apron, threw it onto the floor and walked away. He left the restaurant in his shirtsleeves, didn't turn round, and disappeared.

The silence in the restaurant became even heavier. The chef had come out from the kitchen, but the man at the cash desk hadn't moved. He shouted to a black man, who emerged from the kitchen wearing rubber gloves and began picking up the bits of broken glass and china. Then the man at the cash desk stood up and apologised to the few remaining customers for what had happened. They all hurried to finish their meals and pay. In the end I was the only one left. The kitchen hand swept up the remaining fragments. I paid the man at the cash desk; he flung out his hands in a gesture of resignation, but still didn't say anything.

I went out into the Castilian night. On my way back to the hotel I passed through the Plaza Mayor, one of the biggest town squares I have ever seen. There were still a lot of young people around – after all, Salamanca is a city where one-fifth of the residents are students.

Just as I turned off into one of the streets that led to my hotel I saw the waiter who had thrown down his tray and discarded his apron. He was standing in front of one of the travel agencies, studying their illuminated window. He was smoking a cigarette, and seemed to be deep in thought. I stopped and observed him. The window contained posters advertising journeys all over the world.

When he had finished his cigarette and stamped on the glowing butt with his heel, he walked off. I watched as he disappeared into the shadows between two street lamps. I never saw him again.

That night I lay in bed awake for a long time. It was as if the waiter's sudden violent outburst, his indication that he had endured all he could take, and his determined exit from the restaurant amounted to a challenge for me as well. I was in the middle of my life, at the point one usually reckons is the time when both risks and opportunities are greater than at any other period.

I could see more clearly than ever before that I really must make up my mind how I was going to spend the rest of my life. My allotted time was not as long as it had been ten years previously.

As I lay awake until dawn broke, I flung my symbolic tray onto the floor, took off my apron and went out into the warm night.

It seemed to me that the only really important stories were about breaking free. The breaking free of individuals, or the liberation of whole societies via revolutions or natural catastrophes. I decided that writing was shining my torch into dark corners and doing my best to reveal what others tried to hide.

There are always two types of storyteller who find themselves in constant conflict. One type buries things and hides them, the other digs things up and exposes them.

I eventually fell asleep as dawn broke, and dozed for a few hours. When I woke up I had a sore throat and a temperature. The thought of driving a couple of hundred miles to Milan and then to the coast, northwards towards France, was not attractive. I decided to stay for another night at the reasonably priced hotel.

That evening I went back to the same restaurant. But I didn't go inside. I could see through the window that an entirely different waiter was working there that evening.

I continued my journey the following day. The road from Sveg to Salamanca had been very long, but now there was also a journey from Salamanca and I didn't yet know how it would end.

A tray is thrown onto the floor. China and glass are smashed to smithereens.

There is a breaking free. A question is asked.

36

The man who dismounted from his horse

MY ILLNESS HAS MADE ME MORE FORGETFUL THAN EVER. I DON'T know how much time I spend every day looking for spectacles, papers, my mobile, packets of tablets, books and half-eaten apples.

But I spent many years looking for a tree without being the slightest bit forgetful.

It was supposed to be somewhere along the old main road between Cambridge and London. There was even supposed to be a plaque marking the spot where a young man dismounted from his horse and sat in the shade of a tree in order to make a life-changing decision.

I never found that tree. Mainly because I never gave myself enough time to search in earnest. I regret that. But I know that it is there, preserved as a memory of somebody about whom history has more or less forgotten.

The man's name was Thomas Clarkson. Thomas was six years old when his father died. From then on he lived in poverty-stricken circumstances, but received help so that he could study in the Theology faculty of Cambridge University. Nobody doubted that he was very talented and had a deep-seated faith. His future as a clergyman in the Church of England seemed assured.

The modest scholarship Thomas Clarkson had been given was only sufficient to cover the basic necessities. He was always forced to raise money in other ways in order to get by.

One day he saw an announcement about a competition for

clergymen requiring entrants to write an essay on slavery. This was in 1785. The French Revolution would soon take place and proclaim the inhumanity of slavery. In England it was particularly the Quakers who protested more and more vociferously about the assumption that anybody could own other human beings and exploit them accordingly.

Thomas Clarkson decided to take part in the competition. What attracted him most was not the theme, but the possibility of winning a sum of money that would help him to pay his way through university.

Clarkson travelled to Liverpool and interviewed managers of slave-ship companies, and their skippers. He also met in secret slaves who had escaped and now lived extremely difficult lives in the city's slums.

Not everybody was keen to talk to him. The slave trade had a huge financial turnover, and those who made money out if it were not prepared to risk their lucrative incomes. On one occasion some unidentified people tried to throw Clarkson off a jetty into the sea.

But Thomas Clarkson could no longer fight shy of the facts he had in front of him. His thoughts about the attractive sum of money he might win began to fade, and instead he became obsessed by the sordid lives African slaves were forced to lead on the sugar plantations in the Caribbean or in the cotton fields of the southern USA.

Clarkson wrote in the evenings with a paraffin lamp as his only source of light. In the shadows he could hear the voices of the people he had spoken to and picture the faces he had seen. Among them was the arrogant ship owner who regarded the Africans as just one more form of cargo. Perhaps they were living creatures – but so were goats and exotic animals. He remembered the words of slave-ship captains to the effect that brutality and strict discipline were necessary to ensure that the cargo of black people didn't cause chaos and unrest, didn't take part in mutiny or commit suicide by jumping overboard.

But he thought most of all about the slaves who managed to

escape and now lived their lives in terror, fearful of being traced and captured and returned to their 'owners'. How they would be flogged before being placed on a new ship and transported to a destination where they would be auctioned off.

Thomas Clarkson wrote his essay and sent it in to the prize committee. When he heard some time later that he had won and was called to the formal ceremony at which his winning entry would be presented, he wasn't at all sure whether or not he ought to go. Perhaps he should, and in his acceptance speech refer to the shadow that lay over the British nation like an evocation of unjust human suffering?

He did in fact attend and received his prize with due ceremony, but he said nothing about his real thoughts.

Thomas Clarkson's first incumbency as a clergyman was in London. Early one spring morning he mounted his horse and set off for the capital. It was a very pleasant day, but the closer he came to London the more he worried about all the implications. Around midday he stopped and dismounted from his horse. He was in the vicinity of Wadesmill in Hertfordshire, where there is nowadays a motorway that became the first one in England to apply toll charges. He sat in the shade of the tree that I searched for in vain some two hundred years later. His horse grazed nearby. It was a peaceful spring day, but a storm was raging inside Thomas Clarkson. He knew that he had to make up his mind.

Clarkson left no written or oral account of how long he sat there in the shade of the tree before making his life-changing decision. The distance between Cambridge and London is about sixty-two miles, so he had time to sit there for quite a few hours.

When he finally stood up, re-saddled his horse and continued his journey he had made up his mind. In fact, he had done so a long time previously, but it was only now that he spelt it out for himself and for the God he would always remain faithful to.

He was not going to become a clergyman. He was going to spend his life devoting his strength to the abolition of slavery and the setting free of all slaves. The literary competition he had entered by chance had turned his life upside down.

Thomas Clarkson lived long enough to see the passing of the Abolition Act, which made slavery and the owning of slaves illegal throughout the British Empire.

His life was never straightforward, often dangerous. The powerful enemies he had made when he first visited the centre of the slave trade in Liverpool continued to harass him. He survived several assaults and attempts to murder him, but he lived for another sixty-one years after making his fateful decision, and eventually died a natural death. He knew that his life had been worth all the pressure he had placed himself under.

Today Thomas Clarkson is more or less forgotten. Apart from the plaque on the tree that I never managed to find, there are no significant memorials to him – just a few busts, the odd painting and of course the memories in his book about the people who eventually brought about the abolition of the slave trade.

Thomas Clarkson is one of those shadowy heroes – men, women and surprisingly often children and young people – who belong to the highest ranks of humanity. They have been active in a vast range of subject areas: they have taken enormous risks and overcome the fear they must all have felt many times over.

But what I have written isn't quite true. The slave trade does still exist in the modern world. Even if Thomas Clarkson and others cut through the roots of the slave trade that existed within the laws of many countries, the brutal attraction of earning money by selling people never went away. Nowadays slave trading is widespread throughout the world. It is no longer sugar cane that is harvested in the Caribbean islands or cotton in the scorching hot fields of the southern USA. Now the slave trade often involves prostitution, child labour in horrendous conditions and people being forced to pick tomatoes, berries and nuts in slave-like circumstances. Those involved have no rights, are often swindled out of their wages and forced to live alone, separated from their families.

Prostitution in the world may currently be worse than it has ever been before in the history of mankind. Those who are exploited are often very young. They are forced into submission by violence.

As in the past, individuals protest. Opposing violence and oppression is not only something we have a right to do, but something we actually can do. We must never accept it.

Even today we need people who dismount from their horses and sit in the shade of a tree while they make crucial decisions.

They are always there somewhere. Despite everything.

37

While the child plays

I AM NOT RELIGIOUS, AND NEVER HAVE BEEN. AS A CHILD I TRIED to say my prayers in the evenings, but it didn't feel right.

Now that I have cancer I often think about people who derive consolation from their faith. I respect them but I don't envy them.

But I am certain about one thing when it comes to the people who might be living on our planet many thousands of years after long and difficult ice ages. It is that they will possess a fundamental joy of life, a feeling of happiness at being alive.

People cannot survive without that. It would be like amputating a person's soul.

We may have developed no end of survival strategies, but the basic source of energy behind our successes is our zest for life. If that is coupled with constant curiosity and thirst for knowledge, we have an image of the completely unique ability of mankind.

Animals do not commit suicide. Human beings do so when they have lost their zest for life, often due to severe physical or psychological pain. Who was the first person to take his own life is a meaningless question, because it is not possible to answer it. But we have copious documentary evidence for the fact that suicide has haunted humans like a shadow throughout the ups and downs of civilisation. Even if Cleopatra didn't actually use a snake to bite her, we can be sure that she committed suicide. Throughout history vast numbers of people have hanged themselves, drowned themselves, shot themselves or poisoned themselves. In many cases we can understand why somebody finds life impossible to endure; in other situations we are worried and astonished, filled with fear to discover how little we knew about the person who has just died.

Albert Camus wrote some famous lines: 'There is only one really serious philosophical problem, and that is suicide. Deciding whether or not life is worth living is to answer the fundamental question of philosophy.'

The answer to that question is: the zest for life.

Just what comprises zest for life is something we know much more about now than we did only thirty or forty years ago. It is ultimately to do with chemical processes. Whether we like it or not, our spiritual experiences are a matter of various measurable physiological happenings.

When I wrote before about the young man who has decided to become a neurologist, it is these processes that he will try to investigate and understand. The efforts to do so are strenuous and the results are difficult to analyse. But our understanding of the innermost processes that make us human beings is growing by the day.

There are those who react negatively when they hear that even the most passionate feelings of love are basically a matter of chemistry. We think that love and erotic passion must be something different. And indeed they are something different. These chemical processes that blossom forth thanks to the magic of love lead to actions – everything from the giving of gifts to the writing of poetry, endless sleeplessness, jealousy or all-consuming happiness. But to start with it is cells and chemical processes that decide how we feel and how we think, how we love and how we suffer from the humiliation of jealousy.

I find it difficult to understand how these chemical processes should be thought to involve a degradation of human passions. On the contrary, I am bound to say. Michelangelo would not have painted any less brilliantly if he had known what we know today about the wonderful, invisible processes that drive the most important events and decisions in our lives.

But zest for life? It seems to me this could be illustrated as follows: a young child is sitting alone, playing. Totally absorbed in its own games and its own thoughts. And the child is singing – a wordless, humming song.

The child is like an island in an ocean, with waves flowing gently towards the beach. There are no dark banks of cloud, no threats, no fear, no pain. Life is quite simply a pleasant experience when one is able to play and hum to oneself.

Time has stood still. It doesn't exist. The walls of the room are soft and billowy. Looking out or looking into oneself is the same thing.

The child hums and plays. Life is perfect.

Perhaps the fact is that there are emotions so strong that they can't be expressed in words, but have to be sung? The child's humming expresses the same thing as a Portuguese fado singer, or a soprano singing the Queen of the Night aria from *The Magic Flute*.

Without a zest for life, human beings cannot exist. Anyone who has been robbed of his dignity and is fighting to recover it is fighting just as hard to recover his purpose. The people who try to escape from attacking armies or poverty-stricken agricultural communities to the richer parts of Europe and are washed up dead on the beaches of Lampedusa and Sicily were also on a journey to recover their desire for life.

Many of the emigrants who enter Europe illegally are often dismissed scornfully as 'fortune-hunters' or 'gold-diggers'. Which of course they are. We all are. Why did millions of Europeans emigrate to North and South America 150 years ago? For exactly the same reason.

The humming child is always sitting there on the beach or in the garden or on the pavement. *inside us.*

There is no humanity, no civilisation, without the humming child. In the spartan world of biology the only imperative is that we should keep reproducing. But a more penetrating definition of the meaning of life would say that every generation has an obligation to pass on unanswered questions to the next, which must attempt to find the answers we have failed to discover.

One day, of course, this long-dance we embarked upon deep down in the mists of time when we bade farewell to the chimpanzees and went our own way, will come to an end. One thing we do know about our history is that sooner or later all creatures and species die out, or are transformed into something quite different. There is no reason to believe that this will not happen to the species we belong to. The fact that we are the most successful creatures we know of is unlikely to prevent us from dying out one of these days.

Nobody knows when or how. We might well suspect that we have such inbuilt destructive forces that we shall exterminate ourselves. But we can't know for sure. Even today a madman with access to large nuclear weapons arsenals can put an end to everything simply by pressing a button.

Against what I have written here one could set up something I would call 'The History of Barricades.' All revolts or revolutions are ultimately about people at the bottom of the heap in a society demanding their right to a zest for life. Just as often as they occur, these revolts are suppressed brutally by people who claim to have the right to decide the living conditions of others.

After the student revolt of 1968 in Paris, the French authorities asphalted over the streets around the Sorbonne. Nowadays it is impossible to break up the paving stones that lie underneath. But of course nothing can prevent revolutionaries from finding other ways of building up their barricades.

Meanwhile the little child continues to play, humming its wordless melody. — *The Little Green Fairy*

Elena

BUT NOT ALL CHILDREN PLAY.

Here is a story about two children who devoted all their time to surviving.

About fifteen years ago two brothers lived in the street just outside the theatre where I work in Maputo. One of them was about five years old. He wasn't sure, but between us we were able to work out that his brother, whom he took care of, was three.

Yes, a five-year-old looked after a three-year-old.

For a while they slept in an oblong-shaped cardboard box that had been used to deliver a refrigerator in the days before new refrigerators were wrapped up in plastic. When the big cardboard boxes were no longer used, many street children lost their homes.

The two brothers slept huddled up closely together in the cardboard box. In the mornings the elder boy used to wash the younger one. But of course, they were unable to change their clothes. I have never met anybody, before or since, who was so utterly devoid of personal possessions. They lived in the spirit of St Francis of Assisi, even though they had no idea who he was.

During the day they wandered around the town, begging. Naturally enough many people were emotionally touched by the two brothers – but as Maputo was full of orphaned street children who lived like rats or stray dogs, they were not especially successful in their begging. As dusk fell they would creep back into their cardboard box.

They lived there in the street for several years. We allowed them to sleep inside the theatre when the weather was too awful. We also gave them clothes, which they immediately changed into something to eat by selling them to other street children for crusts of bread. Despite the fact that they were totally dependent on what others gave them, the elder brother had a strange but completely natural dignity. It was as if he knew that he was carrying out an impossible task brilliantly well – being the parent of his brother.

But I never saw them playing. Their life consisted of surviving, and not much else. There was a grim, or perhaps rather a dogged, seriousness about the elder child's desire to keep his brother reasonably clean, and to make sure he got something to eat every day. There was no time or space for play.

They were usually silent. When the elder brother spoke to the younger one, he always did so in a soft voice, speaking close to his ear, as if he had important secrets or pieces of confidential information for him alone.

One day some people from a Roman Catholic mission came to collect the boys. A week or so later they were back in the street again – but by then their cardboard box had disappeared. The house had been taken over by other street children. They spent some time sleeping on a staircase before they managed to find another cardboard box – a smaller one this time as it had been the container of a freezer rather than a refrigerator.

One afternoon they appeared, dragging with them a scruffy-looking puppy. God only knows where they had found it. It had to squeeze into the cardboard box together with the two brothers. One day it had gone again, just as suddenly as it had appeared. Somebody had seen the boys selling it to another street child for half a chicken.

I tried to talk to the two boys, but the elder one kept watch like a hawk over his brother. He wouldn't allow anybody he didn't trust to come anywhere near – and he didn't trust anybody. Street children seldom have any reason to trust adults.

Street children have existed ever since early civilisations began to break up the system of tribes. And street children are not only a problem in the poorest countries and cities in the world: even in the richest metropolises there are children who live out their lives on the streets.

During all the years I have spent in Maputo I have stubbornly tried to make friends with various street children. It could sometimes take several years before I could establish contact that wasn't restricted to untruthful responses to my questions. Often these children died because their lives were so brutal. Some overdosed, others died of malaria or diarrhoea. A few were murdered.

But in the end I was able to converse with the two brothers. I gathered that they belonged to the large group of children who voluntarily run away from impossible family circumstances. The behaviour of male lions who take over a herd and kill off the offspring of previous dominant males is replicated in human life. If a man marries a woman who already has children, he sometimes throws them out into the streets. Or he makes their lives so intolerable that they run away of their own free will. And the mothers affected cannot protest: if they do they can be starved or even killed. Or prostitution becomes their only way out.

Never did I see anybody walking past them in the street who might have been a relative. The boys lived in a vacuum, without a past and without a future. Literally all they had was each other. An empty and barren universe began for them at the very end of their street.

But at the same time it was a deeply moving love story. When the younger boy had stomach ache, his elder brother would tenderly stroke his dirty hair. Expressions of love and care seem to be inherited, not learnt.

I was never sure about their names. The elder boy said he was called Joao, but then he suddenly changed it to Armando, as if that was the most natural thing in the world. The younger brother might have been called George, or perhaps Vitor. I never knew for certain. And they didn't have a surname at all. Naturally, neither of them had any identity papers.

One day the two brothers vanished. They must have been nine and seven when they disappeared. I never saw them again, although I often looked for them when I was out walking or driving through the city. Nobody I asked knew where they had gone to. They were simply no longer there.

However, something tells me they are alive. And that they are now grown up. Despite the fact that street children often have short lives, I believe that these brothers have survived. Because they had one another.

Other street children also survive sometimes. Some years ago I met a girl called Elena. As a newborn baby she had been found in a gutter by some Roman Catholic nuns. If she had been there for one more hour, she would have died. Her mother had left her there shortly before dawn, and then disappeared: she was never tracked down. Perhaps the search for her wasn't all that persistent because everybody knew it would be impossible to find her.

Elena was placed in a children's home where she grew up, went to school, and had a decent life. When I met her she was eighteen and was just about to start at university. I asked her what she would be studying.

'I want to become a lawyer,' she said. 'And I'm going to specialise in children's rights. I know quite a lot about that, of course. I was born in a gutter, after all.'

I always think about Elena whenever the two brothers crop up in my thoughts.

Of course.

39

The awakening according to Plato

THERE ARE PEOPLE WHO THINK THAT GOD IS A CLOCK.

But a clock that has stopped. A clock that used to work, but now stands still, perhaps because it hasn't been wound up, or the pendulum never started swinging. Or possibly simply because God has never needed a clock himself because he is synonymous with time.

For these people God is the clockmaker. His heaven is a miniature Switzerland, in which he wanders around watching his angels creating clocks which they then place in human souls by magical means.

God is time, and human beings have been given the means to measure it, to be frightened by it or to sanctify it.

Measuring time, calculating time, setting precise points in time – these are all things human beings have occupied themselves with for thousands of years. But those early attempts are only something we can nowadays deduce and measure from archaeological finds. Most probably people with developed brains have always been fascinated by 'time'. To begin with the instrument was in fact nature itself: the sun rose in the east and set in the west – but not always quite in the same place or at quite the same time as in the previous month. In those early days time was measured in terms of similarities and differences that were repeated from year to year. Nobody knew or imagined that behind these variations that kept repeating themselves was anything but the breathing of their gods.

The first measurers of time created and constructed by humans were sundials. Nature and the movement of shadows indicated the regularity displayed by the sun and the earth. If one scratched furrows in a circle on a rock, one could see how things repeated themselves. Then these markings were combined with changes in the weather, with heat and cold. It became possible to see when one should sow seeds, when one should go out hunting certain animals.

It also became clear that animals didn't have any sundials of their own. They didn't care about the breathing of the gods. That in turn must mean that they simply didn't possess a soul.

We are the only creatures who are aware that it is not possible to separate time and space. Time *is* in fact space. We cannot see time, but it exists and drives our existence.

Swedes sometimes say that the dead have 'passed away out of time' – which is basically nonsense, of course. Unless it is perhaps a poetic way of saying that our hearts have stopped beating like the biological clock we all have inside us.

I shan't have to experience it, but it would feel very embarrassing if when I die, one of my relatives were to say that I had 'passed away out of time'. I have never lived in time. I have always tried to live in the middle of my own and others' lives.

I discovered in Africa that many beautiful women wore watches that didn't work. They wore them on their wrists solely as pieces of jewellery, not as time measurers. That taught me something about time. That it was not always necessary to be ruled by it.

Some 2,000 years ago the great philosopher Plato is said to have constructed an ingenious alarm clock in order to wake up his pupils each morning at the Academy in Athens. He used one of the earliest methods of measuring time, namely water. Using two bowls, some scrap iron and regularly dripping water he created a highly effective alarm clock. When the water had filled one of the bowls, it tipped over into the other bowl containing the scrap-iron. That bowl also tipped over, the scrap iron fell out and hit the solid base of the contraption with a deafening crash. Nobody could avoid being woken up.

The day had begun.

Plato constructed alarm clocks; but he also thought a lot about what time actually was. If you study the history of philosophy you will be unable to find any significant thinker who didn't devote a lot of effort to this phenomenon. What is time? What exactly is meant by the passing of time? What is the meaning of time? They have all commented in very different ways on time, from Aristotle to Wittgenstein. But none of them has been able to explain precisely what time means for an individual person.

You could say that time is what you make it. It's your own and nobody else's. What you do with it is up to you. You can shrug off time, or take it with you as a travelling companion on your journey through life, which ends with a return to the same darkness from which it originated.

But time has not only been measured by hands on a clock face. A picture still hanging on the wall in many a Swedish home is the famous staircase of age. The earliest examples were created in Sweden in the seventeenth century, but the most common versions are based on the highly decorated Dalecarlian floral staircases from the late eighteenth century onwards. Furthest to the left is a cradle, furthest to the right are two hundred-year-olds stepping off the staircase and into death. At the very top of the stairs is a man at the height of his maturity as a fifty-year-old.

Needless to say, this picture is influenced by the fact that it originated at a period when society was very different. It would be possible to make a better version describing today's society while remaining true to the basic concept of life and time holding each other by the hand.

Heartbeats are of course the most common symbol for how time ticks away inside us all. With slightly more beats per minute than a minute has seconds, the heart beats millions of times between birth and death.

Whatever time is, we always live with time in the past. At the very same moment that I think about a word and then write it down, time has changed it to something in the past. Whatever we do or remember or dream, there is no now, only a past. We always live with one foot in a time that has already passed and will never return.

Time and our ability to measure it can also disclose secrets to us. Time can be a scale in which we weigh our actions.

Right now as I write these words, an article in the newspapers tells us that a piece of Greenland ice that took over 1,500 years to form has melted in less than twenty-five years. The increasing amount of carbon dioxide in the atmosphere has disturbed the balance of our climate. Nobody can any longer deny that it has become warmer. The old ice is melting. Nor can anybody deny that this has been caused by the actions of humans.

Time has thus become a way of exposing the consequences of our actions.

And what does the future hold? Will there be anybody able to measure the passage of time?

Or has the clock stopped for good?

40

Winter night

I DISTRUST PEOPLE WHO CLAIM THEY ARE NEVER FRIGHTENED. I think they are lying. Not so much to me as to themselves.

What most people are most afraid of is dying. Looking back, I have quite frequently found myself in situations when I thought my life was in danger, but occasions when that was really true are less than the number of fingers I possess.

I once fell asleep at the wheel of my car and only just managed to avoid being hit by a lorry whose driver was sounding his horn frantically. I drove into a lay-by and got out of the car. It was in the winter, and nearly three o'clock in the morning. I stood there as one or two cars flashed by on the road. Fear came creeping up on me gradually. It had been so close. Out into the darkness, at the age of thirty-six and a few months.

But I have experienced worse than that. And I wasn't the one involved. I recall a night in Kitwe in Zambia when a heart-rending cry for help came from the radio: an Indian woman had been attacked in her own home, and she was convinced she was going to be killed by the robbers. Neither she nor I managed to contact the police. Listening to her terrified voice was among the worst things I have ever experienced.

I remember being convinced that the Indian woman must have been thinking the same as I was when I was attacked at gunpoint in Zambia. It was a horrible way to die. So young, so unnecessary, such a wasted life. All for a few Zambian banknotes, a wristwatch and a Toyota Land Cruiser that had seen better days.

Fear protects us, warns us, perhaps it even helps us to endure what is unendurable.

Fear and oblivion go hand in hand, of course. But no more so than fear and remembering.

If we hadn't needed fear in order to survive as a species, we wouldn't have been able to feel it.

The same applies to fantasy and imagination, which are also wonderfully precise instruments of survival.

41

Relief

DURING THE EARLY STAGES OF MY CANCER TREATMENT, I ENDURED many investigations. My head was X-rayed, for instance. The day Eva and I went to the clinic to hear the result of the scan was one of the worst. Had the cancer spread into my brain? If so, it seemed inevitable that my life would soon be over.

But Mona, who was my consultant on that occasion, said they had not found anything. Eva squeezed my hand tightly and said to Mona: 'Thank you! Thank you!'

I felt enormous relief. I remembered that boat journey down the river and the hippos that could have killed me. But I also recalled a football match in Fredrikstad in Norway.

I was sitting right at the top in one of the stands when I suddenly noticed a little boy down at the bottom looking up at all the rows of seats. His face contorted and he started crying: I understood why straight away. He had been to buy an ice cream or a hot dog, and now when he returned he couldn't locate his father or whoever it was he had come with. He felt totally alone and lost in this crowd of people. I was just about to go down to him when his father noticed him, stood up and waved.

I shall never forget witnessing the boy's relief.

In 1972 I finished writing the first book I had decided to send to a publishing house. I had written three manuscripts before that, but didn't think they were good enough. I had made up my mind not to submit anything until I was quite sure it would be accepted and published. That was of course a presumptuous decision. Nobody can be certain about such a thing in advance.

I took the manuscript to a postbox, but hesitated for quite a while before actually inserting it. It was a spring evening. I can still recall the whole scene – the feeling of loneliness as I stood by the postbox, the manuscript inside a brown envelope, before I dropped my future into a dark chasm. Would it lead to the abyss?

I waited for several long months. The silence seemed to go on for ever. But one day a postcard featuring a picture of the poet Dan Andersson fluttered down onto my doormat. The publisher to whom I had sent the manuscript wrote that he and his colleagues had now read it, and decided to publish it.

How did I feel? I remember standing naked by the front door, feeling the cold under my bare feet. Was I filled with joy? Jubilation? What I remember was enormous relief like a hot flush through my body. I had not been mistaken. The manuscript was good enough to be published.

I sat down on the floor, and took a deep breath. Then I exhaled.

Relief has been a constant presence throughout my life, at least as significant as feelings of happiness. Every time a theatre production for which I was responsible was reasonably well received, my first reaction has always been relief. Happiness, and perhaps a dash of pride, has been less important and above all short-lived.

Review days for new books can be painful. If the reviews turn out to be reasonably good, I feel relief again. If they are not so good, I can feel ill for a day or two. But then the unpleasantness fades away. Even in those circumstances a sort of relief ultimately takes over.

One man who must have felt boundless relief was an English country doctor in Gloucestershire called Edward Jenner. There is a portrait of him in which you can observe his large mouth with full lips, his clear and wide-open eyes, his rather big nose. There is something convincing about his face, and he seems full of self-confidence.

The portrait dates from after 1797, when he had already felt his great and crucial relief at the age of forty-seven.

Jenner was born in Berkeley, the place where he ended up working for the whole of his life. He had assisted a local doctor before undergoing medical training in London. At the age of twenty-three, having passed all his examinations, he returned to his birthplace where his father was vicar.

Berkeley was a rural town. In his practice Jenner met all kinds of people; most of them were farmers who grew crops and raised livestock. He became familiar with their illnesses, but he also listened to what they had to say about them, and why they thought some people were affected and others weren't.

One such story in particular was constantly repeated, and stuck fast in his memory. It was the assertion that many milkmaids, often young women, who had become infected with cowpox appeared to be immune from the fatal epidemic of smallpox. Jenner thought deeply about this, and began to suspect why this was the case. But could he dare to test this suspicion? What would happen if he was wrong? He would be risking a person's life, as he would need to test his theories on a human being – and a child at that, since they were the ones worst affected by the recurrent smallpox epidemics.

In 1796 he experimented on an eight-year-old boy called James Phipps. He infected one of the boy's arms with pus from a cowpox pustule. When the boy was later exposed to infection during a smallpox epidemic, he proved to be immune.

What Edward Jenner experienced when the boy didn't fall ill and die must have been the greatest possible form of relief. He had been right. And he had dared to vaccinate the boy – the first time this had ever been done.

Jenner was subjected to what Schopenhauer would later call the three stages of truth. At first he was universally scorned, then scientists tried to prove him wrong, and finally the truth became regarded as self-evident.

In a satirical drawing from the beginning of the nineteenth century we can see people whose heads have been replaced by cows' heads after being vaccinated by Jenner. (*Vacca* means cow in Latin.)

As early as 1797 Jenner sent an account of the James Phipps case to the Royal Society: but they rejected it, claiming that his proof was insufficient. Jenner continued with his vaccinations, and even vaccinated his own son who was just over one year old when he was infected with cowpox. In 1798 Jenner presented his results to the Royal Society once more, but it was some time before his revolutionary research and experiments broke through the wall of doubt and prejudice. In the end it became impossible to deny that vaccinations had saved the lives of many people, and Jenner became famous. Truth was victorious in the end. Once again he must have felt enormous relief. He devoted the rest of his life to studying the possibilities of vaccinations and the risks that were also involved.

He lived until 1823. I imagine that occasionally he must have met, or at the very least thought about, James Phipps who, thanks to him, had been given the possibility of living rather than dying of smallpox.

Relief is one of the strongest emotions of which humans are capable.

42

Getting lost

I ONCE GOT LOST IN A DENSE AND OVERGROWN FOREST IN THE province of Västergötland. I danced a sort of ghostly ballet with myself among those trees in the gathering dusk. I was thirteen at the time, and had moved to Borås from the province of Härjedalen a few months earlier.

For me, Borås was a big city. The first Sunday morning I lived there I went out early for a walk around town with two aims in mind: one was to discover how many cinemas there were, and the other to find my way back to my place in Södra Kyrkogatan. I found six cinemas that morning. I can still remember the names of five of them, but the last one escapes me – perhaps it was the Palladium?

Later that spring we went off on a school trip. It was the end of April or the beginning of May. It was still chilly in the evenings, but light. I can't quite remember the reason for the outing, but I do recall that we travelled by bus, and I can conjure up blurred images of the faces of some of my schoolmates. We eventually stopped at a yellow conference centre in the middle of the forest. A very short and chubby man with round spectacles addressed us in a shrill voice about the history of Västergötland. The point of an ancient arrow-head was passed around.

Then we went for a walk through the trees to what might well have been a ruin – my memory of it is very uncertain. The man with the round glasses wasn't with us: instead it was a grey-haired woman who spoke to us about Varnhem. Her talk concluded, one of the teachers who had accompanied us said we should assemble at the conference centre in half an hour's time. He recommended that we should follow the same path as we had used on the way out – but we could take a short cut if we dared.

His last comment was sarcastic, of course: there are no predators in the Västergötland forests, and bears and wolves died out there over a hundred years ago.

I decided to take a short cut. It was about two kilometres to the yellow conference centre, and I was clear about the general direction. I rather fancied the idea of getting there first and waiting for my classmates to appear. I set off at full speed and was swallowed up by the trees after only a few metres. The forest was more dense and undulating than I had anticipated, but I didn't have far to go after all. I ran around a few little hills, found a passage between various blocks of stone that had been placed among the trees, and expected to see the yellow building at any moment.

But no building appeared. I was soon forced to accept that I was lost with no idea where I was. The forest was silent; there was only a faint sighing sound in the gathering dusk. No voices of my school-mates in the distance, no cars, nothing. As it was cloudy and there was rain in the air, I was unable to see where the sun was. I started by retracing my footsteps in order to find the main path, but there were hardly any marks on the ground and I couldn't establish where I had come from. Gaps in the trees and the blocks of stone seemed to be haphazard, with no obvious pattern. I could be right next to the ruin, or a long way away. The devil had followed me without making a sound, and removed all traces.

I tried walking in various directions, noting distinguishing features on the blocks of stone or large tree roots, but it didn't help. I suspected I was committing the usual error made by those who are lost, thinking I was walking in a straight line but in fact moving in circles.

I don't know how long I spent wandering around. I wondered if they had started searching for me. Or if they hadn't called the register and noticed that I was absent. I didn't have a best friend who would miss me. I hadn't lived in the town with six cinemas for long enough to have made a best friend.

I don't think I became really frightened that evening. Perhaps the gathering dusk was scary because it made it all the more necessary to find my way as soon as possible. But I'm not sure. Anyway, I continued searching because there wasn't really anything else I could do.

I suddenly heard voices. I stopped and listened. It was a man and a woman speaking Finnish to each other. The voices drew nearer. Then I noticed a path going right past where I was standing. I ducked down behind a fallen, half-rotten tree and saw a couple in their forties carrying two paper carrier bags. I remembered now that on the way to the yellow conference centre we had passed a few newly built houses that seemed to have been scattered at random in the forest, and I had wondered if all the dressmakers from Finland who worked at Algots clothing factory in Borås might live there.

When the Finns had passed by I followed the path and duly found the conference centre. The bus we had come in had left now, and the yellow building seemed deserted. But then a man emerged onto the stairs, smoking a pipe. He must have heard me walking over the crunching gravel.

'The Prodigal Son!' he said. 'Did you get lost?'

'I must have done.'

'Because you took a short cut?'

'Yes, I couldn't find my way.'

'Short cuts can be dangerous,' he said. 'You can get there quicker, but you can also get lost and never get to where you want to go.'

'Have they been looking for me?'

'They waited for a while, then I said I'd find you.'

He drew on his pipe and whistled softly. A dog came trotting out of the building.

'Stella can find anything or anybody,' he said. 'She has a fantastic sense of smell. I thought I'd wait for half an hour before letting her out, but you've managed to find your way back yourself. I'll ring your teacher and then call a taxi – the school has paid for it.'

I soon forgot about the goings-on in the forest. A bit of teasing from my classmates and a stern look from my teacher was all that happened. I suppose I thought the incident wasn't that significant.

But many years later I suddenly started dreaming about that yellow conference centre and my wanderings through the forest. In the dreams it was all very scary. The Finnish-speaking man and woman became a threat who would attack me if they saw me. The trees and the soft ground underfoot concealed old mantraps that could open up at any moment. When I came to the conference centre it was deserted. Everything was locked, and I couldn't get in. Then it suddenly became very cold, as if spring had faded away and it was midwinter again with severe frosts.

The dream kept coming back over and over again. I tried to interpret its message as if it had been a traumatic experience, but deep down I didn't believe it.

Now that I have cancer I understand that feeling of being lost. I am in a labyrinth where there are no ways in or out. Being stricken with a severe illness is to be lost inside one's own body. Something is happening over which you have no control.

Some years ago I went back to look for that yellow conference centre. It took me a few hours to find it, but it was still there – just as yellow, even if the paint was flaking off a bit. Now it belonged to an evangelical church. I strolled around for a while. The forest path had been replaced by quite a large road following a slightly different route, but the trees and blocks of stone were still where they had been. And the houses scattered around were still there as before.

I wondered what had happened to the Finnish dressmaker and her husband. Were they still alive?

I don't know, of course.

So many questions. So few answers.

43

The road to Salamanca, Part 2

IN MY DREAMS I CAN STILL DRIVE ALONG THOSE LONG, STRAIGHT stretches of road from the mountain border between Portugal and Spain.

In the dreams the road is just as long as it was in reality: the dream hasn't shortened the distance.

My memory of that day and night in Salamanca is not restricted to the incident of the waiter who suddenly decided he'd had enough and took off his apron. I have another recollection, just as remarkable in its way.

It happened the following day. It also took place at a cafe, one that served a few dishes in a room whose walls were covered in colourful photographs of handsome-looking racehorses.

I sat down at a pavement table. It was shortly after breakfast had finished, and a lot of chairs were unoccupied. I ordered a cup of coffee and began thinking about my onward journey. I thought if I had the strength I would drive as far as Lyon that day – but I realised that in that case I ought to have set off several hours ago. I told myself that passing over the French border would be far enough. I wasn't in that much of a hurry.

Haste is nearly always an outcome of imagined human necessity.

I noticed a lady in her sixties sitting alone at a table. She had a large glass of milk in front of her. Next to it was a glass of sherry. I watched her pour the sherry into the milk, then stir it with a long spoon.

She was elegantly dressed, with a sparkling bracelet and necklace – I couldn't tell if they were genuinely expensive jewellery, of course.

Then I noticed that she was frightened – so much so that her hands were shaking. I could see that from as far away as my own table. Or if she wasn't afraid, she must be in considerable pain, I decided. In any case, it was disturbing.

She was completely absorbed in her own emotions. She seemed not to be aware of passing traffic or people walking along the pavement. Her shaking hands marked the border of a world that was not hers at all.

She didn't touch her glass of milk. I'm still not sure why she fascinated me – perhaps her unapproachability and my curiosity as to why she so obviously wanted to shut out the rest of the world?

A police car with screaming sirens raced past, but she didn't react at all.

I must have been sitting there watching her for ten minutes when a waiter went up to her table and said something to her. She jumped to her feet and almost knocked over the glass of milk, but the waiter managed to catch it. She was inside the cafe in a flash, and when I turned to look I could see through the window that she had hastened up to the bar and taken a telephone receiver from the barman. She listened intently without saying anything herself.

It was a short call. She put down the receiver and flopped down onto a chair. I now had an explanation: she had been waiting for a message and was afraid of what it might say, but now she had received it and it was as bad as she had feared.

But I was wrong. I learnt there in that cafe in Salamanca that expressions of happiness and sorrow can be identical. Joy can appear to be relief, sorrow to be resignation – the person's reaction is the same.

She returned to the table with the glass of milk she had laced with sherry, sat down and drank half of it in one gulp. Her hands were no longer shaking. The whole of her face radiated relief – I have seldom seen anybody exuding such calm and yet jubilant happiness.

She was suddenly in a hurry. She placed some money on the table, left the remaining half of the milk and sherry, stood up and walked quickly off along the pavement.

Then I did something that still surprises me although I freely admit that I can be very curious about things that are none of my business – curiosity is an important source of inspiration for me. I beckoned to the waiter and asked him in my poor Spanish if he knew who the woman was that had been sitting there with the glass of milk. He nodded.

'Señora Carmen,' he said. 'She usually comes with her husband, but he is very ill. She just heard on the telephone that he's not going to die. Now she's gone off to her hat shop in order to open it up for customers. I'm so pleased for her. They have no children, only each other.'

I paid and left. An hour later I managed to worm my way out of town via the complicated web of roads and set off northwards.

That happened almost thirty years ago. I have never returned to Salamanca – but I sometimes think I ought to. As a sort of pilgrimage. We all have our Meccas, which don't necessarily have anything to do with religious thoughts and emotions.

In Salamanca I saw somebody cause an incident and make a break with his life so far. But I also saw that calm, almost invisible happiness on the face of a woman who learnt that she wasn't going to be left on her own.

I was about thirty-five at the time. Now I am almost twice that. Much in my life is still uncertain. There is of course no doubt that I have lived over half my life, nor that the most important decisions have already been made. I am not going to change my profession. There might be various hiccups, of course, but I can quite confidently tell myself that this is what my life will have been like.

I shall never visit Salamanca again. Other people will sit at a cafe table and watch somebody drink a glass of milk laced with sherry. Or visit a local bar where a waiter suddenly decides he's had enough and takes off his apron.

Growing older involves looking back. The memory of events and people can be experienced in different ways – like when you reread a book that you have read several times before. You always discover something new.

Since I was diagnosed with cancer I find myself more and more frequently noticing something unexpected in the memories that come to mind. It is only now that I see the waiter and Señora Carmen with the glass of milk with such clarity. Earlier their contours were blurred, but no longer. They have become images frozen in great detail. The waiter's apron has stood still in the air, like a broken-off wing. Señora Carmen's shaking hands stick out like claws.

Life is a tumult constantly changing between what frightens me and what brings me joy. If we are lucky we are able to create good memories during our lives – even if there are far too many people in the world who are forced to forget in order to live.

I shall never return to Salamanca. Nevertheless it feels as if I am always on my way there. In secret.

PART III

THE PUPPET ON A STRING

44

The earth floor

I ONCE SAT BY A BED IN WHICH A SEVENTEEN-YEAR-OLD GIRL WAS fading away.

The bed was a mattress covered by a tattered sheet. As it was very hot in the room she had only a thin piece of cloth over her. The mattress was lying on the earth floor.

There was no electricity. When I entered the room I was carrying a flickering candle.

Her mother and her siblings were sitting outside the little house in front of a fire on which they were preparing their food: a rice and vegetable stew.

None of them seemed to realise that their eldest sister was dying. They hoped I would take a look at the girl and assure them that she would soon be fit and well again.

She had been infected with HIV, and now it had developed into Aids. In the poverty-stricken African country where she and I lived at the time there was no chance of helping her. It was before the antiretroviral medication had been created.

She had a boyfriend who worked in South Africa, and had caught the disease from him. Now she was going to die.

I squatted down beside her in the darkness. She was lying with her eyes open, as if staring at some distant goal. Or perhaps she couldn't see anything at all? She was so exhausted that her mother and siblings had to carry her whenever she needed to go to the latrine.

I remember the first time I ever saw her: that was three years earlier, and she was fourteen. She was already very beautiful.

But she was not beautiful any more. She was emaciated, and her face was covered in sores from countless attack of herpes. Her hair had started to fall out.

It's now twenty years since she lay there, staring at some mysterious unknown goal. In my memory it is a faded black-and-white photograph. The image of her face is slowly fading away.

I have occasionally thought about her over the years. About how old she would have been if she had lived, what she would have done with her life, what she would have looked like.

I've thought about her as I have done about others who have died. I've never understood why you should have to stop mixing with dead people or having them as friends simply because they no longer exist as living beings. As long as I remember them they are alive.

Carlos Cardoso, the brilliant African journalist, was murdered in the street in broad daylight in Maputo fifteen years ago. He had exposed and challenged the widespread corruption among politicians who mixed with criminals. They condemned him to death and executed him.

I speak to Carlos almost every day. The conversations take place inside my head, but he is there and still of great significance as one of my best friends.

But this spring, when I received the first cycle of chemotherapy in what is called my 'basic treatment', I often thought about that girl who died. More often than ever. I started to wonder if I saw my own death in hers, even if it was hardly likely that I would conclude my days on an earth floor in a dark room with only a candle as a source of light.

In my memory I return over and over again to that evening when I saw her for the last time. Perhaps there was something there which I found meaningful for myself?

Nobody had invited me to the little village outside Maputo where she lived. I had got to know her and her family by chance after meeting one of her younger sisters who had lost both legs in a horrendous accident when she stepped on a landmine. I wrote about that girl, whose name was Sofia, in several books. Whenever I visited Sofia and her family, the older sister, Rosa, would be out in the distant field tending the vegetable patch the family lived off.

On this occasion, I had been sitting in my damp-ridden flat in Maputo, preparing for rehearsals we were going to have at the theatre the following day. The urge came from nowhere. Suddenly, I simply knew that I had to drive out to the village that same night. So I did.

In the end it dawned on me why I so often think about Rosa now. I remember sitting down on the floor next to her mattress and pressing the candle down into the earth floor to keep it steady. We said nothing. The only sound to be heard was the murmuring of her family as they sat round the fire outside their hovel. And her own panting breath, as if each one caused her almost intolerable strain. I tried to imagine what she was thinking, and what she might be seeing in the darkness.

When she eventually turned her face towards me and I could look her in the eye, I heard myself asking her a question.

'Are you afraid of what's in store for you?'

I could have bitten my tongue off. You don't ask a dying person, especially a seventeen-year-old who has not yet even had the chance to start living seriously, if they are afraid.

I think she smiled when she replied.

'No,' she said. 'I'm not afraid. What should I be afraid of? I'll soon be up and about again. I'll soon be well.'

A week later she was dead. One of her younger sisters had hitched a lift into town in a lorry and was waiting outside the theatre when I concluded the rehearsals. She mumbled in her low, shy voice that Rosa was dead.

I wasn't surprised, of course. Nevertheless, I burst into tears. Some of the actors who came out through the stage door were scared; they had never seen me cry before. Perhaps they thought that white men never cry?

I understand now, as I fight my battle with cancer, that I keep asking myself the same question that I put to Rosa. How afraid am I? Do I also reject the fact that death is always standing in the wings, as a possibility, once a cancer diagnosis has been made?

I don't know. But I think I try to be true to myself. No doubt I am afraid. High storm waves could come from nowhere at any moment and crash against my inner and outer coastlines.

I have tried to build up defences to ward off what scares me. If the worst should happen, if the cancerous tumours multiply and can't be stopped, I shall die. There is nothing I can do apart from summoning up the same courage that is necessary to lead a decent life. One of the most important arguments for maintaining this dignity and trying to stay calm is that I'm not seventeen years old and doomed to die before I've even started living seriously. At sixty-six I have lived longer than most people in the world can even dream of doing. I have lived a long life, even if sixty-six is not as old as it once was.

When I leaf through an old copy of the magazine *När Var Hur* ('When Where How') from 1964 and read about 'those we have lost this year' I find that the majority of them were aged between sixty and seventy. There are a few eighty-year-olds, but not nearly so many as there would be today.

One thing that can be frightening of course is that death can be painful. But there are fewer reasons to fear that than there were ten years ago. There are not many pains that can't be kept in check nowadays.

There is also a final way out that makes me feel secure when I think about it. If an intolerable pain cannot be prevented, I can ask to be put to sleep. Then I would fall asleep and bid farewell to life and the world. Rather that than feel myself compelled to commit suicide. I don't want to do that for the sake of my nearest and dearest. If I were alone, that could perhaps have been a possibility: but not as things are now.

My deepest fear is something quite different. Silly, childish. I'm afraid of being dead for such a long time. It is a pointless fear, almost embarrassing. In death there is no time, no space, no anything. My role in the long-dance of death will be over. I shall have fallen off the staircase of life on the final step.

But perhaps that is the most confidence-inspiring aspect of death? That my fear is based on a meaningless presumption that death will be reminiscent of life? That the same laws and same concepts would apply? Which they won't.

I shall never know if Rosa gave me an honest reply when I asked my disgraceful and insensitive question. I shall never know if she was deceiving herself, or telling me the truth.

It is as if the seventeen-year-old African girl is helping me to answer questions and steer the right course through the difficult channels between life and death.

As I write this I have just completed the fourth cycle of chemotherapy in my basic treatment. In a few days from now I shall know whether or not the cytotoxins have worked.

Of course I am worried and tense. Sometimes, especially during the night, I wake up in a state of almost panic-stricken worry. Then I get up and go out into the chilly spring darkness of the terrace. An oystercatcher impatiently waiting for the dawn cries out from the beach below.

It usually doesn't take long for me to become calm again – a fragile calm, but calm even so. And then I sometimes get the feeling that Rosa is close by. Not as a ghost or some kind of evil or benevolent spirit, but just as a memory and an unresolved sorrow on my part.

And most important of all: a reminder of what happened that evening on the earth floor.

45

Moving silently from darkness to darkness

WE CAN ONLY REMEMBER THE PAST. THE FUTURE CAN GIVE US NO memories. Time is an arrow flying in only one direction: forwards. We can't change time and ask the arrow to fly backwards. Time machines don't exist. Mathematical theories, sometimes in model form, can investigate the possibility of reverting to the past – and play with the idea of preventing Grandma and Granddad from meeting so that you yourself are never born. But all such theorems are no more than thought games: in practice I can't possibly make myself unborn. The thoughts I think would never have been thought if such a journey through time were possible. My memories would never have existed, and hence could never be obliterated.

Questions about time and the universe are the biggest and most difficult. The sharpest minds work away at them. The chemical processes in their brains operate at the highest possible rate and occasionally amazing new breakthroughs take place.

I can remember what nobody knew when I was young and what we know today. From a universal perspective the black hole question is completely new. Analysis of human DNA is another scientific breakthrough that nobody could have foreseen seventy-five years ago.

All theories about thought are ultimately about trying to discover a meaning beyond the basic biological requirement of reproducing ourselves. They are just as much about survival of the human race as about ensuring that our questions, as yet unanswered and possibly not even formulated, shall be set before the enquiring minds of future generations.

We all wonder. It is something we have in common. I don't know anybody who hasn't gazed up at the stars and wondered about the meaning of life.

Many people give up, stop asking such questions, shrug their shoulders and continue their daily lives as if there were no unsolved mysteries. Some give up when they are still young, others continue wondering until later in life. But in the end they give a philosophical shrug of the shoulders. I can understand them. For millions of people it is an unattainable luxury to be in a position to set aside time for thought.

This is one of the most disturbing injustices in the world we live in: the fact that some people have time to think while others never have that opportunity. Searching for the meaning of life ought to be written into the global declarations of human rights as a matter of course.

Some people find the truth in religion. Others gaze up at the stars. Once, when I was a young child and unable to sleep on a cold winter's night, I saw a solitary dog appear in the flickering light of an overhead street lamp and then slink silently off again into the darkness, as if on tiptoe. I sometimes think that all my questions about life and death and the past and the future are linked to that dog, moving silently from darkness to darkness.

Our ability to wonder and ask questions is what makes us human beings. In a way that starry night sky is a mirror in which we see our own faces. It seems to me that my face is most accurately reflected when it is filled with wonder.

In my world truths are always provisional. Nothing I have ever thought in my life has remained the same. Truths are ships sailing across the sea; you have to steer them in the right direction, avoiding reefs and rocky shallows. The speed has to be varied, or the number of sails increased or reduced.

A ship returning from a voyage is not the same vessel as it was on setting sail. The same applies to truths cruising around inside my head and in my life. In order for those truths to survive, I sometimes need to question them and find a suitable way of adjusting them.

When I was in my twenties the USA's aggressive war against Vietnam was in many ways a significant watershed. At the time I thought it was right to campaign against the American invasion, and still do. But when the war was over and the American troops had been driven out of the country, Vietnam then attacked its neighbour, Cambodia; it became every bit as justified to condemn Vietnam as it had been to condemn the American invaders.

To my surprise, at that moment rationality was replaced by sentimentality as far as many people were concerned: how could I criticise the brave Vietnamese? People flopped down on their sofas weeping profusely and insisting that the Vietnamese had every right to attack Cambodia.

For me that was a significant insight. Sometimes the truth has to be stood on its head in order to appreciate its true stature.

Bertolt Brecht wrote that thinking is one of the most enjoyable activities there is. I agree with him. Trying to solve a problem by means of concentrated thought, sitting at a desk or out walking, is both liberating and invigorating. And also fun.

It is possible to think about anything. There are no protective fences or trenches or minefields in the world of thought. Everywhere is open country.

The people who run dictatorships or tyrannical governments know this so they use various methods of forcing their subjects to conduct more or less voluntary self-censorship. To dig trenches inside their brains where there were no such barriers before.

I know what self-censorship involves. On several occasions twenty-five years ago we chose not to stage some productions in the theatre in Maputo. Our arguments were rational: audiences wouldn't turn up, we didn't have actors suitable for the roles, the play or the theme was perhaps not quite as important as we had originally thought. We created no end of arguments to demonstrate that we had made a sensible decision, but deep down we all knew that in fact we were practising self-censorship. There was a risk that the powers that be in Mozambique at the time would not react positively to our production, and we would have problems. In the worst-case scenario the theatre might be closed down. I myself might be given what was known as '24/20', which meant that I would have twenty-four hours in which to leave the country, and my luggage must not weigh more than twenty kilos!

Whether or not we did the right thing is open to argument. I am still not sure. But the theatre is still there – it was never threatened or closed down. Now we can state openly that our decisions were dictated by self-censorship, rather than by our free and unbiased creative aspirations.

The biggest challenge of all is to have the will to explore new thoughts, not to hesitate to question what others regard as truths, and to go in other directions.

Let me give an example. If I were ever asked to write a play about a strike, I would probably choose to write about a strike-breaker. That would mean I would approach the topic from an unexpected angle. Querying the justification for the strike might lead with luck to unexpected and different reflections. New thoughts, new conclusions.

Vital discoveries in various branches of industry often come from the factory floor, not from the offices in which engineers are paid to find solutions to problems. Developing our ability to think has to do with our survival, of course. We want to live, not to die. Every time I see someone rooting in a rubbish bin, I see this simple axiom before me: we want to live. At any price.

Perhaps we can turn this argument around? Everything we do is because we want to avoid death. At any price. Despite everything, life is something we know about. Death is foreign to us, even if we know that dead bodies rot away and eventually all that is left is merely bones.

But we also think about what death implies. Are there other worlds? Or is it simply darkness? or just "nothing."

People die, They rejoin the earth, the earth moves on, Their life spark

This also means that sooner or later we find ourselves standing in front of the wall I have spoken about earlier. What came before time and space? What existed before anything existed?

Are 'nothing' and 'eternity' the same thing?

My paternal grandmother lived to be almost one hundred. During her final years she suffered periodically from an acute fear of death. She would lie down on her bed and close her eyes – tightly, like a child who thinks it can make itself invisible.

I sometimes sat on the edge of her bed. Then she would slowly open her eyes. I would ask what was troubling her, despite the fact that I knew already.

'Death,' she would say. 'I can see it in front of me. Then I need to stop thinking. To banish all thoughts, just try to survive that moment. That's all I can do. Until the next attack comes.'

Perhaps that is the most difficult thought of all – to stop thinking and banish all thoughts?

46

Mantova and Buenos Aires

MANY YEARS AGO I VISITED THE TOWN OF MANTOVA IN ITALY. I was taking part in a literary festival. It was a warm spring day, and somewhat absent-mindedly I wandered around looking for a restaurant where I could have lunch.

I found myself in Mantova's biggest square, where people were gathering in a circle around a spot where a street theatre performance would shortly begin. I thought I might as well see how it started and joined them.

In fact I watched the whole show, which lasted for fifty minutes. When it finished I looked around and could see that nearly all those who had been there at the start were still present. Many of them seemed to be as impressed by the performance as I was. The hat lying on the stone paving of the square was soon filled with coins and notes.

The show had been performed by just two actors, a young man and woman. They were dressed in what seemed to be the costumes of medieval fools. That had worried me at first – I had seen all too many performances in which the illusion of medieval jugglers had been forced and embarrassing rather than convincing. But these two young actors soon demonstrated that they were more than capable of doing justice to these costumes. In a sort of timeless no man's land they recreated a love story with aspects of both tragedy and comedy. They didn't say much as the square was filled with the noise of busy traffic, and on all sides were cafes with music blaring. But they overcame the bedlam and established a remarkable intimacy with their audience. The performance was subtle and constantly exciting. I didn't simply stand there waiting for the end, but kept asking myself: What will happen next?

The young actors portrayed love and all its difficulties amazingly effectively. There was never any trace of pretentiousness, everything was consistently credible.

When they had finished it dawned on me that I had just seen one of the finest theatrical performances it had ever been my privilege to witness. As the crowd melted away I remained standing there, watching the duo packing up their few props. Then they squatted down in the shade and counted their earnings in the hat. It became clear that they were a couple in real life, not just on the stage. Their joy over the contents of the hat was such that they hugged each other passionately.

I wondered if I ought to go up to them and say how much I had enjoyed their show, but by the time I started moving towards them it was too late. They had already stood up and scampered over to a battered old banger of a car. I watched them disappear into a side street.

I have always been irritated by the fact that I failed to thank them. I have so often hidden my lack of genuine enthusiasm and thanked actors for their performance, but on this occasion I had really loved what I had seen.

I have no idea who they were, what the play was called or who wrote it. All I know is that the actors were very young and very gifted. It is still one of the most outstanding artistic experiences I have ever enjoyed.

There is another performance that has been haunting me for over fifteen years. Seeing it was just as much of a coincidence as the one in Mantova.

I was in Buenos Aires to talk about my books. I had visited the city once before, but all too briefly. On that occasion I was searching for material in connection with the book I was writing, but now I had more time and had taken a whole evening off.

It was a South American autumn when I left my hotel in the centre of town to look for a restaurant where I could have a late dinner. I hadn't gone more than a few metres before I noticed homeless people curled up all over the place in entrance porches or underneath illuminated shop windows. Not just individuals, but in many cases whole families. I was walking through people's bedrooms and living rooms. I knew about the crisis in Argentina, of course, but I wasn't prepared for the fact that it had such a devastating effect on those who had already been living in poverty.

It was a heartbreaking experience. I turned off into a side street that was so narrow there was no room for people to sleep there. I continued walking around and eventually found a little restaurant full of Argentinians.

I can't remember what I ate, but I do recall that the waitress had a limp; despite this, she worked more efficiently than any other I had ever come across.

At about eleven o'clock I paid and left, heading for my hotel. After a while I came to a junction where a crowd of people had gathered, making it difficult to walk through them. They were standing in a circle, watching some kind of performance. I could hear music – an Argentine tango – coming from a loudspeaker. In the end I elbowed my way through to the front and saw the reason why the crowd had gathered there.

Four couples were very skilfully dancing the tango on the street corner. They weren't simply dancing, but also performing a play in which jealousy and other emotions were interwoven and constantly changing. Two of the dancers were at least seventy years old, and another couple could hardly be much more than twenty. They kept swapping partners and adopting different styles of dancing. The only light came from swaying overhead street lamps. They had chosen exactly the right place to perform. The audience was outside the range of the lighting, but the dancers were illuminated dramatically as they moved from the bright light to the shadowy dimness.

Nobody said a word. Sometimes they stopped dead, as if suddenly frozen, then they would continue, changing partners and telling a story about the joys and curses of passion.

It was absolutely brilliant. Technically superb dancers with a theatrical ability to express something more as they flitted through the shifting landscape of the tango.

One of the dancers, the youngest of all, had something extra special about her. I couldn't quite pin it down at first, but then I realised that she was blind. Even so she closed her eyes when the man she was dancing with closed his.

After the performance I managed to make my way closer to where she was standing, wiping the sweat from her face. She was just as exhausted as all the others, and was clearly thrilled by the sound of the coins and notes clinking and rustling into the hat that the others took it in turns to carry round.

Just as had been the case in Mantova, the performers obviously lived off what the audience put into the hat. That evening I thought about all the thousands of hats that were being passed around or placed on the ground every day by street artists, some of them miraculously skilled. Really great artists, like the actors in the square in Mantova and the dancers in the street in Buenos Aires.

It had turned midnight by the time the performance ended. One of the male dancers was talking to his wife, who was holding a little child in her arms. Those who had been performing were tired – dancing the tango non-stop for over an hour takes a high level of fitness and well-trained muscles. I don't know how many performances they had given that evening. Two? Or perhaps the one I had seen was number three?

I walked back to the hotel through the night, past the families curled up asleep on the pavements. It was distinctly chilly. I thought I would remember my visit to Buenos Aires thanks to those tango dancers. Just as much as to those families sleeping out in the streets.

The corner where the tango dancers had performed was like a cave, with house walls looming up and disappearing into the darkness, the faint light from the overhead street lamps, and the sound of the music bouncing off the house walls.

Sometimes you just know that something you have experienced will always remain in your memory. Something that can never be replaced.

47

The stupid bird

ON ONE OCCASION IN THE MID-1980S I WAS LOOKING FOR A TYPE-
writer. I was living in Zambia, on the border with Angola, and I had
to travel as far as Mauritius in my hunt for the machine.

A Norwegian author had left it there. My own typewriter had
broken, and I couldn't find anybody who could mend it. I knew the
one I was looking for was in a hotel with the peculiar name of 'The
Colonial Coconut'. It was owned by a Frenchman who had once
studied philosophy under Michel Foucault in Paris. Planted on the
slope down to the sea outside the hotel was a specimen of every
coconut tree known to man – hence the name.

The owner of the hotel, who came to visit me the very evening I
arrived, seemed to be an enthusiast for every aspect of old-fashioned
colonialism; I never managed to work out whether he really felt that
way, or was just being ironic. He lived alone in a house beside the
hotel, and occasionally invited me there. Always after midnight. His
big passion was discussing philosophy. We used to sit talking until
dawn, and as far as I can remember we never agreed about anything
at all. But we didn't quarrel. There was something soothing and
unreal about those nocturnal discussions.

Anyway, the green typewriter was there all right. My intention
had been to take it back with me to Zambia, but it was too heavy
and so I only used it for the ten days I stayed on the island.

I hired a car and used it to pay visits to Pamplemousses and the
big botanical gardens there. The island is covered in damp, heavy

greenery, and in many places there are large sugar-cane plantations. The population is a mixture of Africans and Indians, and of course there have also been a group of whites, mainly Frenchmen, since colonial times. It's only twenty years since Mauritius became independent of France and formed a republic.

The last thing I did on Mauritius was to visit the capital city, Port Louis. Apart from wandering around the city streets and watching the local population carrying out their everyday business, I had a specific aim: I wanted to go to the museum with a skeleton of the extinct bird Swedes call the *dront*, and the English, the *dodo*. If I remember rightly there was also a model replicating what the bird looked like, with flesh on its bones and a coat of feathers.

It is a remarkable experience, standing in front of a species that is now extinct. But the dodo didn't die out like the dinosaurs millions of years ago; there were living dodos as recently as four hundred years ago.

The name 'dront' comes from 'dodo', which derives in turn from the Portuguese 'doudo', which simply means 'dumb' or 'stupid'. Portuguese sailors who landed on Mauritius noticed that this wingless bird was totally unafraid of people, since it had never before seen creatures walking upright as human beings do. And so it was very easy to kill dodos. You didn't need to hunt them, or trap them, or shoot them. All you had to do was to walk calmly up to them and hit them on the head with a stick, or wring their necks. The birds had no idea how to preserve themselves.

Dodos were large. A fully grown bird could weigh as much as twenty kilos. If they were short of food, sailors simply needed to go ashore and collect as many birds as they required for the cooking pots. The meat wasn't regarded as a delicacy, but of course it was better than nothing. Moreover, they could eat the eggs and pluck the feathers.

The dodo lived only on Mauritius. Individual species of animals living on remote islands is something that happens all over the world. As the dodo had no natural enemies until sailors came to the island, it had lost its ability to fly.

...e dodo became extinct very quickly. Reports suggest that there
...e still large numbers of the birds on Mauritius in the late sixteenth
century, but two hundred years later it was more or less extinct. A
few living birds were taken to England, and others were painted by
sailors who were also artists.

Human beings had nothing to do with the dying out of the dinosaurs – there were no humans at that time. But as far as the dodo is
concerned, there is no doubt about it: it was human beings who
exterminated 'the stupid bird'.

Today several thousand species of animals are threatened with
extinction. People no longer go hunting in order to exterminate
frogs, deer or tigers. But rhinos are being hunted to extinction
because some Asians imagine that their horns contain aphrodisiacs;
they grind the horns to powder and inhale it. It would be a clever
move to saw off all rhino horns to make poaching the beasts a pointless exercise; the animals would not suffer much. But if nothing
dramatic is done, our grandchildren will only be able to see rhinos
in zoos.

The extermination of animals is the price we have to pay for the
way we live. Even if we are much more aware now than we were ten
or twenty years ago of the consequences of our stripping the earth
of its riches, we continue to plunder all we can.

Needless to say, there is opposition. Individuals join together to
protest, and argue that by ruthlessly exploiting natural resources to
improve our living standards and acting in ways that lead to the
extinction of other creatures, we are belittling ourselves and endan-
gering the future of the human race.

Can an individual species of bird be all that important? Yes. There
can be no concessions when it comes to protecting our environment.

Of course, not everything that is done in the name of protecting
wildlife is good. A lot of actions are not properly thought through
and result in the opposite of what was intended. Releasing mink from
mink farms in Sweden has resulted in the extermination of large
numbers of seabirds in the Baltic Sea area, notably velvet scoter and

eider ducks, thanks to the mink taking the birds' eggs. Mink are not natural members of the fauna among the islands of Östergötland and Småland. No matter how much sympathy one had for the caged mink there could be no justification for the subsequent annihilation of so many seabirds whose numbers were previously regulated by organised hunting in the spring and autumn. There is no point in liberating one species and in so doing annihilating another. Who could possibly entertain such an idea? Only a human being, of course!

I have always spent a lot of time in the Swedish archipelagos. Every summer while I was growing up, and for many years after, I spent several weeks on an island in the Östergötland archipelago. Fishing was one of my favourite pastimes. The idea of perch one day disappearing altogether from the central islands was totally alien. It would be the equivalent of the moon ceasing to shine at night.

In the summer of 2013 I saw only one single perch, not much more than five centimetres long. The previous year I saw none at all.

The same applies to Sweden's largest beetle, the stag beetle. They live in and around oak trees, and on the island I am talking about oaks are almost the only trees growing there. Stag beetles have never been numerous but they certainly existed and if you wanted to see one you didn't need to search all that long. Now there aren't any.

This unobtrusive extermination of animals and plants is taking place all over the world. Tigers and rhinos attract the greatest attention, while nobody thinks much about stag beetles. But it is the same thing that is threatening so many animals, irrespective of their size, wildness and beauty: our boundless urge to consume what the earth can give us only in limited and quite specific doses.

There is a battle taking place between those who in various ways are trying to protect animals and plants and put a stop to the current senseless plundering, and those who look the other way and think that everybody in the world who wants a car and has enough money to buy one should be able to do so.

How many new cars appear on the roads of China every day? Forty thousand? More? And what will the purchasers of these cars

...ven the multi-lane motorways are so clogged up with ... that it is almost impossible to go anywhere?

... images and comparisons that describe most clearly the overcrowded world we live in, there is one I think about more than any other. It is a photograph taken from an aeroplane or a helicopter over the network of motorways around Los Angeles. No doubt a similar photograph could be taken of roads around any large city in the world – Shanghai, São Paulo or Mexico City. The winding and clogged-up lanes are reminiscent of the conveyor belt sequence in Charlie Chaplin's *Modern Times*. The ant-like motor vehicles are jammed together in endless queues, and hovering above them is the foul-smelling air characteristic of modern cities.

These motorways, exhaust fumes and the extinct dodo are all linked together.

Our rate of progress is dizzying, but the constructive and destructive outcomes of that progress are increasingly out of balance.

Nowadays there is talk of being able to recreate extinct animals as a result of modern DNA techniques. But surely that is no more than wishful thinking, glossing over everything that has happened and is still happening?

Death exists. As does extermination. In the rational world nothing returns from the dead.

The skeleton of the dodo will be all we have left of that bird that had no chance of surviving once the first sailor had set foot on the beach in Mauritius.

The dodo didn't know what an enemy was. And hence, of course, it was considered to be stupid.

48

Who will be there in the end to listen?

ENTERING A CAVE IS LIKE GOING INTO A DENSE FOREST. LIGHT changes. It gets darker until eventually it becomes pitch black. The sound that surrounded you on all sides becomes fainter, and in the end all is silent.

But deep inside the cave another phenomenon occurs, which has captured our imagination down the ages. There is an echo. You can whisper something, and the echo comes back to you much louder. If you move just a few paces in any other direction, the echo changes. It can come from many directions at the same time, or it can flit around you in circles. The echo is alive.

It is hardly surprising that people living some 40,000 years ago were convinced that echoes were the voices of supernatural beings. In the pitch darkness inside a cave, the walls began speaking. You couldn't see any faces or bodies, but the voices were there. And they spoke the same language as human beings.

But echoes are even more surprising than that. A marvellous discovery was made by archaeologists about thirty years ago.

In the mid-1980s the music researcher Iégor Reznikoff went wandering alone through the French caves at Arcy-sur-Cure in Burgundy. It is a cave system with a large number of wall paintings that are at least 20,000 years old. Reznikoff noticed that most of the paintings were where it was darkest and most inaccessible, more or less as far into the caves as it was possible to go. He also noticed that the same thing applied in many other caves. Why had the people who made the paintings not chosen locations where the light was better and the working conditions easier?

He wandered around in the darkness, speaking loudly and softly, sometimes whispering, sometimes singing. All the time he listened carefully to the echoes and how they changed. In places where the echo had very special characteristics he would stop. It transpired that in such places, without exception, the number of wall paintings increased. It couldn't possibly be just a coincidence. He researched one cave system after another, searching for spots where the echo had special characteristics in the darkness, then switching on one of his torches. According to the results he presented later the outcome was always the same. The echo and the wall paintings were interrelated.

He could also see that the motifs of the paintings could be linked with the special acoustic form of the echoes. If the echo was especially loud, or a conglomeration of many echoes coming from different directions, he could be certain of seeing a herd of large buffaloes or mammoths looking as if they were running away.

When the echo had different variations there could be individual splashes of colour on the cliff wall, or a line of dots – sometimes even the impression of a hand.

This is not just a phenomenon that has been discovered in Europe. Exactly the same patterns occur in various ravines in Utah and Arizona. The paintings on the cliff walls correspond to the shifting character of the echoes.

We cannot be certain why these wall paintings were made, nor why the echoes played such an important role. Cave paintings from those times depicted images from real life – animals, hands, ships. But it was a long time before the Lion Man was created. The cave painters were not yet artists in the sense we give to that term nowadays – i.e. that they use their creativity to produce images of things that don't exist in the real world. Abstractions which assume that people observing the work of art have the ability to create associations implying its significance.

The cave painters were influenced by echoes. Their decisions about *where* they would paint and *what* they would depict were in direct relation to how the echoes changed. But does that mean the cave painters experienced echoes as a kind of 'music'? We cannot know the answer to that. What we do know, however, is that at the same time as cave painters were listening to echoes, other people were making flutes that they could play music on.

The people living 40,000 years ago couldn't explain those echoes. There were no echoes on open plains. Cliff walls or caves were needed to produce them. They presumably thought that echoes were magical beings or spirits living inside the rocks and talking to human beings by means of returning the sounds people made in a somewhat distorted form that might be so deformed as to be almost unrecognisable.

Echoes were both magical and divine. We can't prove it, but we can well imagine that human beings could pray to sounds in the same way as they prayed to the spirits within rocks or trees. Very early in the history of mankind there may have been some sort of priest whose calling was to speak to echoes.

It is possible to take a step further along these lines. The caves in which echoes were particularly outstanding could have functioned as cathedrals, or even as a kind of theatre. Illuminated by flaming torches at spots where shadows and light brought the depicted animals to life, almost as if they had broken free from the cliff walls, people might have gathered to pray to them, and their many voices could have transformed the echoes into a remarkable choir. Perhaps the people also performed rhythmical dances – either all of them together or just those leading the rituals.

The ceremonies need by no means have been characterised by solemn seriousness. Perhaps their prayer sessions were full of joy and lust for life? It is easy to imagine our forefathers being gloomy and melancholy as their lives were so hard, food so difficult to obtain and survival anything but a foregone conclusion.

The echoes are still there in the caves, just like the wall paintings.

Maybe the very sound of praying gave people the strength to go on?

The feeling of magic is never far away. Although we can now explain echoes as an acoustic phenomenon, that does not undermine the fact that the experience was uplifting at that time. Perhaps the reverse is true. Maybe the magic moment when the echo flitted around the cliff walls gave those present the strength to survive in a way that is beyond our present-day comprehension?

What happened inside those caves is a mixture of the credible and some kind of reality that we can only guess at. Were the magical and religious rituals something of what we would nowadays call 'ceremonial occasions'?

The people of those days were probably not so very different from us. One might even be justified in expressing it thus: We are like they were. We are and will always be members of the same family.

How did those early forefathers of ours regard the opposite of those sounds and echoes – silence? Was it important to them in a comforting sort of way, or was it frightening? Since they lived in a world that was so very much quieter than ours, perhaps they regarded silence as normal. There were no machines, no cities, no mechanical vehicles or loudspeakers. The world was silent, apart from the sounds created by nature – the sighing of the wind, the roaring of storms, the twittering of birds.

Nowadays silence is increasingly rare. I sometimes wonder if silence is on the way to becoming extinct.

But echoes will outlive human beings. Even when our voices no longer exist, stones will become loose and fall with a crash that is multiplied and amplified by echoes.

But who will be there to listen to them?

49

Salt water

I ONCE HAD A WELL DRILLED DOWN INTO THE ROCK OF AN ISLAND. The well that had been dug a hundred years earlier was no longer producing sufficient drinking water. As the island was not in an inland lake with fresh water but out in the sea, I decided to employ some experienced well-drillers. They turned out to have a surprising ability to deduce the geology of the archipelago's rocks and to find the exact spot for reaching fresh water and thus avoid having brackish or salty water coming up through the bore hole. They didn't have special technical equipment, but relied on experience.

They loaded their drilling machine onto an old adapted cattle ferry and came to the island one day in early September. There was a clear sky, no wind at all, frost was coming closer by the day and the last of the migratory birds had left for southern climes, usually at night. All one could hear was a swishing sound from their wings; they left Sweden without being seen, but their wings sang to us.

It took just over half an hour to walk round the island, which was divided by a ravine between two high, rounded hills. When I played there as a child I thought of it as a vast wilderness in which cliffs, precipices, caves, anthills, stag beetles and the occasional adder provided plenty of opportunities to inspire my imagination. It was Moomin Valley and Winnie-the-Pooh country at one and the same time. But it was also the barren deserts of unknown continents – Australia and the parched African plains.

The two well-drillers had selected the spot where they were going to start drilling. They were going to dig down into the rock beyond sea level, and after that they were not sure how deep they would need to go before reaching water. They were aware that things could go wrong, that the rock could be damaged and split, and that the nearest they had to a guarantee for finding drinking water was their combined experience, which told them this was the best place to drill.

The hours passed as they drilled down through the rock – ten metres, twenty metres . . . Around noon they came to water – but it was not just brackish, it was very salty seawater. But that didn't seem to worry the pair.

'It's a pocket of salt water,' they said. 'When it's emptied it will fill up again with fresh drinking water. All we need to do is to pump out the salt water.'

One of them took a glass out of a rucksack and polished it with a handkerchief. He held it up against the autumn sun to check that it was clean. Then he filled it with salt water from the bore hole and handed it to me.

'Taste that,' he said.

'What?' I said in surprise. 'Salt water?'

'Dip your tongue into it. Swallow a few drops. It won't kill you. Afterwards I'll tell you exactly what it is that you've been drinking.'

I thought at first he was having me on – a bit like tricking passengers unused to boats into drinking the delicious liqueur created by the wake. But something told me that wasn't the case. I took the glass and swallowed a few drops. It was distinctly salty. I handed back the glass.

'What you have just drunk,' he said, 'comes from a pocket of salt water forty metres down in the rocky ground. That water has been lying there ever since the last ice age 10,000 years ago. When the ice melted away some of the salty seawater collected in pockets like that. It's been lying there now for 10,000 years – or about three hundred generations, if you like to put it that way. Only now has it come up to the surface again.'

I have often thought about that moment when I swallowed a few drops of ice-age water. But never so often as now, when I've been stricken with cancer. In dark moments I have tried to work out how long I've lived and how long I can reasonably expect to go on living, given all the varying circumstances. Will I be a long-term survivor, or do I have only a few years left? How long in terms of days, hours and perhaps minutes? How many more seconds do I have to live? The calculations are pointless. Neither life nor death can be redefined like fractions or second-grade equations. You can count the number of heartbeats and the number or red and white blood cells, but life can never be an expression of geometrical measurement.

Nevertheless, there is a sort of consolation in the memory of that glass of ice-age water I was given by the well-drillers. It puts into perspective how a human life can be stretched or shrunk in so many different ways. Since the last ice age about three hundred generations of human beings have wandered around the Scandinavian peninsula. Ahead of me, way beyond my lifetime, another three hundred generations will wander around there before glaciers once again cover our country and compress the earth's surface. New pockets of salt water will be formed, and perhaps one day new well-drillers will bore down through the rocky ground.

My desk is by a window as I write this text, and outside is an ash tree. It doesn't come into leaf until after the tardy oak has attained its full springtime glory. I sometimes imagine that the ash is the shepherd keeping watch until all the other trees' leaves have turned green before it comes into leaf itself.

That ash tree was outside the window the day I was born, and it will also be there when I die. Nearly all the trees in my garden, apart from a few slender birches, were here when I was born, and will still be here when I have passed away.

Today I can think that there was a sort of eternity in those small drops of salt water. A lifetime varies. It is misleading to consider measurements of time in connection with one's own life or that of others. Some people live longer than others. One can regret the death of young people who die before they have even had the chance to start living seriously. But there is no such thing as time when it comes to death. When you are dead you are dead, if you are not religious and don't believe in resurrection or reincarnation.

Death is life's great mystery. Today I can think about those well-drillers and wonder how their salt-water pockets deep down in the rocks affected their own view of life. I don't believe those who maintain that most people brush aside all thought of their inevitable death. I wasn't the only one who, when I was eight or nine years old, had periods when I thought almost every day about death waiting for me somewhere over the horizon. All children had such thoughts, and still do.

Something that does worry me is the fact that in Sweden today one can spend one's whole life without ever seeing a dead person apart from on a flickering television screen or in a cinema. If we hide death away, life becomes incomprehensible. I'm not suggesting that pre-school children should be dragged off to mortuaries on study visits, but how can we get young people to respect life if death has been relegated to hospitals and funeral parlours? The fact that death has disappeared in a country like Sweden is a gross cultural lapse that doesn't bode well for the future.

The well-diggers left the island with their machine. The converted cattle ferry disappeared from view, towed away by a fishing boat with an old, thumping Säffle engine. I had been given instructions about how to drain away the salt water and then allow the water to keep flowing 24/7 until the reservoir had lost all trace of salt.

'How long will that take?' I wondered.

The elder of the two men had evidently been asked that question many times before.

'It's impossible to say,' he said. 'It varies. But taste your way forward. Once the water is completely drinkable without a trace of salt, you don't need to carry on running it.'

It took about a week before the salt fully disappeared. Since then the water has always tasted as it should – even when the washing machine has been going full steam for days on end, the water has never run out.

I don't really understand how it all works, but when I am feeling very worried about my cancer I can think about the well-drillers, their machine and the glass of water from an ice age ago, and I feel calmer again. There are no logical reasons for that, no emotional ones either. But that's the way it is. The water had been lying down there in the rocky ground ever since the covering of ice melted away and the land arose once more from under the sea. Many of those salt-water pockets will remain in the ground and be dispersed only when a new ice age affects our part of Europe.

I am living between two ice ages. The trees that were standing in my garden before I was born will still be there when I have passed away – but they won't live for ever. They will also disappear one of these days, just like all islands, all reefs, all sandy beaches, all of everything I have experienced during my life.

That's the way life is: a few drops of salt water in a glass.

Taste your way forward.

50

The buffalo with eight legs

WHAT WERE THE PAINTERS THINKING WHEN THEY CREATED THEIR pictures, mainly of animals, on the rocky walls of those caverns that were so difficult to penetrate? The caverns where they sought sanctuary from the worst of the weather and from predators that threatened their very existence – and yet they were also places that they decorated.

Did they have any idea that their pictures would survive and be judged by future generations? Or were the pictures intended to be enjoyed just during their own lives, in their own time? As the brains of human beings developed an ability to think ahead, to make plans, that might have played a role for the cliff-wall painters. But what role exactly? Were the pictures meant to be messages and greetings from one era to another? Or did they imagine that the animals they depicted on the cave walls might eventually come to life and leap out into the real world where they could become food for human beings, not merely mysterious images to which shamans in a trance could appeal in the hope of keeping starvation and illness and predators at bay?

Perhaps the cave paintings were intended to be sacrifices to gods? Instead of slaughtering a bull or a reindeer for that purpose, could the pictures be offered up and the real animals be used as food for humans?

In a cave in the Swabian Alps, at Chauvet, there is a picture of an animal that is dramatically different from those in any other caves known to man.

It is a buffalo with eight legs. It is as detailed and accurate as any of the other paintings around it, apart from the astonishing fact that it has eight legs.

It doesn't take long to understand why. The artist's intentions are clear and obvious: he wanted to portray an animal that was moving. In his own way, at least 30,000 years before moving films were invented, he has tried to capture the leg movements of the running animal; the distance between each leg and its changed angle depicts the fraction of a second in which the movement would have taken place in reality.

We know of only one picture of a buffalo with eight legs – it is possible of course that there are other as yet undiscovered caves containing paintings of animals whose legs are moving, but so far we have only this one example. The unknown artist was inspired to attempt something totally new, something he might never have tried before: to depict movement at the moment when it was taking place – something that in the real world happens so quickly that a human eye is unable to detect it.

What happened when the artist completed his painting? What did his companions say when they came and saw the eight legs? What did they think? Were they curious or angry that the artist had broken a taboo? All we can be sure about is that the picture still exists – it wasn't scratched out, or painted over.

But the picture tells us something more than that. If you study it carefully, you realise that the moving legs and the buffalo's eyes imply that it is running away from something. Beyond the painting, on the cave wall, another animal or perhaps a group of human hunters might be chasing the buffalo. It is fleeing for its life. The picture is attempting to depict the animal's instinctive urge to escape from danger and death.

Whoever it was that painted this fleeing, terrified buffalo has created a great and inspired work of art. The whole picture is on the point of exploding, thanks to the animal's fear of death. It is as if the buffalo is tearing itself away from the cave wall in order to increase its speed and leave the predator or the human hunters behind.

Not a single line seems to have been changed. There have been no attempts to paint over any part of it. The artist knew what he wanted, and had no second thoughts.

This is not the work of a beginner. People in those days seldom lived to be older than about thirty, but this man has obviously been painting for a long time.

Every picture needed time and effort. Just like the creator of the Lion Man, this cave painter must have been fed by others who were happy to let him spend all his time painting.

In the same cave there is another collection of animals, notably horses and rhinos. When I scrutinise the paintings I get the distinct impression that it was the same artist who produced all of them. In other caves one can see that various artists have produced the pictures, but just one man seems to have created all those we can study today in the Chauvet Cave.

The first individuals suddenly begin to emerge from the darkness of history. They are not people, but animals. Before long the first sculptures of individual human faces –discovered by us over a thousand generations later – will begin to be made.

In what is now Slovakia, a five-centimetre-high ivory sculpture was discovered a few years ago. It depicts the face of a woman, and is sometimes called 'The Original Mona Lisa'. The face is about 35,000 years old. It is a statuette that reproduces all the woman's features, but especially remarkable is her left eye. Her eyelid is drooping, her eye is injured.

Her mouth suggests the beginnings of a smile.

There was presumably a living model, most probably in the same family or clan as the artist. Perhaps she was the artist's mother, or his sister, or a woman he lived with? But in any case, from the darkness of history emerges an individual – one of the first human individuals we can really see.

What did she think when she saw this little sculpture depicting her face? She must have been surprised that somebody was able to make a copy of her that was so small. She must have wondered if there was a spirit inside this little piece of ivory that was similar to her own soul.

Her smile has followed me throughout my life since I first saw that little statuette. There is something introspective about her face, as if she knows that she is being looked at.

She also awakens another thought inside my mind. When I first travelled to Africa some forty years ago, I was quite sure I would discover many differences between Africans and myself – an assumption that turned out to be completely wrong. All I found was similarities. I realised that we all belong to the same family. As human beings as a species originated on the African continent, it follows that we all have an ancient matriarch who had black skin.

Whenever I look at that sculpture, created over 30,000 years ago, it occurs to me that the model for it also belongs to my family. She is not a stranger. In that hint of a smile on her lips I can see something I understand and recognise.

It is a fact that we laugh and cry for the same reasons.

I am at home with the cave painters, and they are at home with me.

51

The secret of cave painters revealed

LAST SPRING, WHEN I STARTED ON NEW CYCLES OF CHEMO-
therapy treatment, the day before the first infusions I went to a
bookshop and bought some books. Doing so gave me a feeling of
consolation – or perhaps it was an advance reward for what I was
about to go through.

When I lay down on the bed in room number 1, ready to receive
the last infusions of the first round of the new cycles, I had in my
hand a little book with what would turn out to be the misleading
title of *The Oldest Enigma of Humanity.*

I read through the opening pages somewhat suspiciously, but
when I had finished reading it I realised that it was just the title
that was idiotic and aimed at selling as many copies as possible.
The book itself was fascinating. It threw a radical new light on many
questions regarding the origins of art – the paintings in inaccessible
caves.

In it a French graphic designer, Bertrand David, poses a series of
crucial questions about the techniques used by the cave painters,
not least about the way in which they seemed to make things as
difficult as possible for themselves. Why did they choose places that
meant they had to worm their way along dark, narrow passages in
order to get there?

Another thing that baffled him was why the eyes of the animals
were often in the wrong place when the rest of their anatomy was
accurately reproduced. Then one day David thought he had stumbled

upon the cave painters' secret. He arranged a series of experiments in his cellar and invited others, including children, to take part. The outcome was both surprising and convincing.

He concluded that way back in the depths of time the cave painters chose the darkest space for a very special reason. It was precisely that darkness that they wanted. They placed small carved statuettes of the animals they wished to depict in front of primitive sources of light, and with the help of the shadows cast on the cave walls they were able to trace the outlines in a realistic way. But the eyes of a lion or an ox or a horse did not cast a shadow, and the artist had to place them as best he could.

This is a technique anybody can use. You only need to stand outside your door on a dark winter's night and allow the light from inside the house behind you to cast a large shadow on the ground; you will be big or even giant-like according to how far away you are from the source of light.

David and Jean-Jacques Lefrère, a literary historian, combined to write the book I was reading as the cytotoxins were infused into my arm. I hardly noticed when Marie or one of the other nurses came to replace an empty bag with a new one.

As soon as I got back home I went down into the basement with the little statuette of an elephant I had brought back from Africa many years ago. I pinned a large sheet of white paper onto the wall, lit a paraffin lamp and placed the elephant in front of it. It immediately turned into a giant with the shadow of its body filling and overflowing outside the paper on the wall. By moving the statuette and adjusting the distance between it and the lamp I was able to use a felt pen and trace the outline of the elephant.

I then drew in the animal's eye – and might not have placed it in exactly the right position.

Therefore we can assume that the cave painters traced their subjects on the walls. They didn't even need to have any artistic ability. Although it is unlikely, it would have been possible for children to trace the contours of shadows projected onto the wall.

For me it was a giant step forward into the world we know so little about – those paintings of animals in the darkest corners of underground caverns.

The French graphic designer and his professorial colleague also presented a bold thought about what those animal pictures were intended to be. Rather than creating a world of spiritual or religious symbols, perhaps the painters were creating memories of dead relatives. If people had names in those days – which is probable, although we can't be sure – the likelihood is that many of them would be named after animals. Could these animal pictures be a sort of gravestone of dead people that the family, the group or the clan wished to remember? That might also explain why over many thousands of years those animal pictures have been painted over with different images. It would be no more remarkable than the fact that in our modern cemeteries the earth is dug over at regular intervals, resulting in the disappearance of old gravestones and crosses.

This possible explanation of cave paintings is of course no more than speculation. But more certain is the shadow-projection technique, which in all probability explains the secret behind the cave painters' method.

The only artistic assessment observers can make regarding the unknown, unnamed cave painters is how successful they were in placing such details as an animal's eye on the shadow projections. Some were more accurate than others, and sometimes not only was the position more anatomically correct, but the expression in the eye was also more alive.

No one eye is exactly like another. The artist who placed it where he did had to make an artistic choice.

This discovery in no way reduces the value of all those animal images that capture our attention nowadays after so many thousands of years, no matter whether we see them in pictures or on film or in the caves themselves.

In other words, art has always been on a journey throughout the history of mankind until it developed into what it is today.

And tomorrow it will develop even further, becoming something new and unexpected.

imagination casts shadows
What this "explanation" doesn't
explain is how/who did
the small statue used to cast
the shadow on the cave
wall — if that's how it
was done

52

The happiness brought by a rickety lorry in the spring

WHEN I WAS A CHILD, EARLY SPRING WAS THE TIME I USED TO dream about the imminent arrival of the travelling circus.

Most people of my generation who grew up in small places where nothing unexpected ever happened remember when the snow melted away at last and the travelling circus finally arrived. During the long winters I would occasionally picture in my mind's eye the painted wagons, the strong men with sledgehammers preparing the ground for the ring and the tents, the strange foreign-sounding languages echoing between the caravans in which the artists lived their mysterious and incomprehensible everyday lives.

Of course it was naive and romantic, and of course it still is. But it was also very real. The outside world had come to visit us. It was a sort of greeting from a country and people beyond the endless forests that radiated out from the little valley with the freezing-cold river where I lived.

It started with the arrival of a battered and rickety lorry, often with a broken exhaust pipe, carrying men with long brushes and buckets of thick white paste who proceeded to display colourful posters. They were always in a hurry, and were gone as quickly as they had arrived, leaving the sticky white paste splattered around.

A few days later the cavalcade of wagons would come rolling in. Only the biggest circuses arrived by train and the place where I grew up was too small. We had to make do with the more modest ones that comprised caravans, lorries and other wagons pulled by tractors emitting clouds of smoke.

One of those circuses was called Scala; there were others whose names I have forgotten. Their performances were often very similar, apparently produced from the same mould.

If one was lucky and able to attend a performance, it was a very special occasion. All normality disappeared. High up under the roof of the tent acrobats would hover in an apparently weightless state; I can still recall their shouts as they jumped into the waiting hands of their colleagues.

Down below in the ring other artists would juggle with a seemingly endless series of balls or clubs, or with each other. The clowns were the closest to normal human beings in the programme: they would stumble and trip, squirt water all over each other – but all their awkwardness and stupidity made them similar to us sitting all around the ring in the stands. Although none of those people could ever be as funny as Charlie Chaplin.

Dogs would perch on horses' backs, sea lions would shuffle around, and the ringmaster would invite first silence, then applause. He was in complete control of his little band of performers, and prompted the audience to follow the slightest gesture of his raised whip and white-gloved hand. He was a frightening person, the only one I was put off by in the whole ensemble. While all the others transformed dull reality into an exciting paradise, he was the link with reality. He was the strict teacher, or the local drunk who would sometimes stagger along the street and frighten children who came too close to him.

I don't know if there are still circuses travelling round to small remote places every spring or summer and arousing the locals from their everyday mood of unexciting normality. If not, it is proof that there is still a trace of poverty despite all the modern welfare and buzzing, constantly surprising technological developments. Even if we can see the best of the best of circus arts on the television or via the Internet, that cannot be more than a pale imitation of the reality. A circus demands that spectators are present. We need to be in the same location as the acrobats and the jugglers. We must be a part of the same community, call a halt to time and be united in what I call, for want of anything better, a state of elevated happiness.

The great adventure is actually seeing that what these artists do is possible. The rubber man really does have a skeleton despite the fact that he can tie his body into knots. The woman really can keep all those plates spinning round on those slender sticks without any of them falling down into the sawdust.

A circus is simply a demonstration of human capability that has been achieved and maintained thanks to strict discipline and training.

Every day during the summer half of the Swedish year, thousands of tonnes of sawdust were tipped into the circus ring. The Big Top was erected, poles fixed and secured, and canvas put in place.

And that still happens in some places.

The art of the circus is constantly developing. Something new came along unexpectedly twenty or thirty years ago. It was even called 'The New Circus'. The company responsible was called – and still is – Cirque du Soleil, and constantly tours the world with different troupes. The basic features are the same as they always were: acrobats, jugglers, clowns. But what was 'new' was that they told a story. They didn't just present a series of individual acts after which the artists would all come into the ring together and share the applause. In the New Circus there is a continuous love story or something similar – it can be interpreted as a saga presented not in words, but in actions.

But circus artists are actors. They entrance us by means of the same ability as actors on a theatre stage; I sometimes think the only thing that distinguishes them is the sawdust.

Whenever I see a really good circus I immediately want to take part. Needless to say, I couldn't start flying around beneath the Big Top, or do dramatic things with a dozen clubs; simply walking in and out of the ring carrying the props the artists need would be good enough for me.

The same applies to theatre performances. When I sit in a theatre watching a play that doesn't inspire me, I want to leave as quickly as possible. But if the performance is good I am overcome by the same irresistible lust that grips me at the circus: I want to get up on stage and sit at the same table as the actors are seated around as they eat a scrumptious dinner.

In a very short time the New Circus performances have developed the art in astonishing ways. They usually avoid sentimentality and create emotionally effective stories that take place before our very eyes. The creativity that these circus artists – who are often very young – display arouses my admiration, but it also makes me even more convinced than before that there is no limit to the human ability to *create*. The step from the artist who once sat down and created the Lion Man out of a piece of ivory tusk to the flying acrobats under the roof of the circus tent is perhaps not all that great after all.

Dolphins fly over the waves in the palace at Knossos. Acrobats hang weightless under the roof of a Scala circus tent visiting a little village in the north of Sweden.

Those of us sitting in the audience see what is happening. But we also take part. At the same time.

those of us reading a book
learn / imagine whats presented
in words + thereby take
part in seeing/feeling new worlds "new
emotions new ways of
looking at ourselves + other
cultures, + God forbid any
idea of intersectionality
or "Woke" "ness".

53

The war invalid in Budapest

ONE DAY IN THE EARLY SPRING OF 1972 EYVIND AND I MET AT THE
Hovedbangården railway station in Copenhagen. We were colleagues
– theatre directors who also wrote plays. We were going to take the
train to Milan where we had been promised we could attend the theatre
La Comune, run by Dario Fo and his wife Franca Rame, and watch
them in action. We slept our way through West Germany and left the
train in the evening at Milan's large central station. That first night we
shared a cheap hotel room, and then began looking for a suitable flat.
We didn't have much money. We were offered a garage in a building
due for demolition: no beds but the guaranteed presence of rats. We
declined, and carried on looking.

That same day we met Dario Fo, who had completely forgotten
that we were coming. The theatre seemed to be just as disorganised
as his memory. Before entering one needed to endure an elaborate
security check. Dario Fo and Franca Rame were under constant
threat of being murdered, and they were busy rehearsing a play that
was later entitled *Accidental Death of an Anarchist*.

In the evening Eyvind and I drank coffee at an outdoor cafe. We
agreed that we really did need to find a cheap place to stay, otherwise
our intention of spending some time in Milan would not be finan-
cially feasible. Someone came to our table and tried to sell us a watch,
but we said no thank you. It's possible that one of us might have
smiled, I don't remember; but in any case some of the watch sales-
man's friends appeared out of the shadows – young men in their

twenties who accused us of not taking their friend seriously. Eyvind had his nose knocked askew, and I was kicked in the genitals, but the only consequence was a few days of pain.

After a sleepless night Eyvind flew home, and had his nose adjusted at the hospital in Malmö. I stayed in Milan and wondered what to do next. Perhaps Dario Fo wondered what on earth had happened to those two eager young Swedes who had said they were going to stay around for a month.

In fact, I left Milan and took the train to Vienna, and then to Budapest. I had never been to Hungary before, and was also a bit embarrassed at the thought of returning to Sweden so soon. Would it be fun to stay in Budapest for a while?

In the station I saw a man who must have been a war invalid. He was drunk, and was begging. A Hungarian Railways employee appeared and kicked the beggar to the ground. His crutches were sent flying and the coins in his cap were scattered all over the dirty stone floor. While the invalid crawled around on the floor the railway employee simply adjusted his cap and walked away.

It had all happened so quickly that it seemed unreal. People were rushing back and forth, and the echoing station hall was filled with deafening announcements from a loudspeaker, which to my ears sounded like an outburst of furious anger. But nobody helped the invalid crawling around and scrabbling for his crutches as he collected the scattered coins he had begged.

It was a devastating experience. The brutality seemed to be self-evident, and was accepted by all those who happened to witness it. Not even the man who had lost his crutches protested. He acted as if what had happened to him was perfectly normal.

Nobody helped him. Not even me. It was a horrifying incident. When the official who had kicked him returned I was afraid that it would all happen again, but the invalid hopped out of the station building on his crutches. So his crime had been begging inside the station. The official couldn't care less about whatever happened outside the premises.

I spent my days in Budapest in exactly the same way as I did in my youth in other places I visited without having planned anything in advance. I wandered around, ate and drank in cheap cafes, went for boat rides along the river, called in at bookshops, and tried to read the posters outside any theatres I passed. But most of my time was probably spent thinking about the journey home that lay ahead of me.

One evening I splashed out on a phone call to my father in Stockholm, to tell him where I was. I gave him the hotel's telephone number in case anybody asked for me. It was a very short conversation – and the last time we ever spoke to each other, although of course neither of us knew that at the time.

He died that same night. When people started looking for me they didn't know that my telephone number was scribbled down on a scrap of paper in his trouser pocket.

But I have never forgotten that invalid, and how nobody – including me – reacted. It was as if it was some kind of act in which everybody knew their role, even the man with the crutches, and kept it up until he had left the station building.

Until then I had never seen such crude and undisguised brutality in the real world. Experiencing it in the cinema or on the television is quite different; there role-playing is shifted into another dimension in which you kill people for large payments.

Many years later I experienced a different sort of brutality, which was nevertheless a sort of link with the treatment of the invalid in Budapest central station. It happened in Maputo, at the end of the 1990s. I still find it hard to recount the story.

I was living in a three-storey house in the centre of town. It had been badly built in the early 1970s, when the national liberation movement Frelimo was approaching from the north. A few months later the military leaders in Portugal would revolt and the fascist dictatorship crumble, which in turn accelerated the defeat of Portugal in its African colonies. Building continued, but there wasn't even enough time to allow the cement to set properly. Shortly after I moved in all the walls were dripping with water.

In the same street lived a Portuguese couple who had been in Mozambique for many years. They had servants, including a black girl aged about twenty. She started work every morning at about six o'clock by serving breakfast – having left home in a distant slum at about half past three to walk to her workplace. She had a long working day ahead of her before returning home for a few hours' sleep. There were minibuses covering part of the distance, but she was so badly paid that she couldn't afford the fare.

One day she announced that she was pregnant. The lady of the house wanted to sack her on the spot, but her husband pointed out that she was clean and made decent coffee. She was allowed to stay on.

The child was duly born. The girl stayed at home for about a week after the birth, but then her long working day began once more. And she carried the baby with her on her back. But the lady of the house forbade her to take the baby inside; it had to lie in the outside porch. When it needed breastfeeding, the girl had to go outside to do it.

I heard about it from furious neighbours who insisted that this racist behaviour, this disgraceful treatment of the young mother, must be stopped. Hadn't Mozambique been an independent country now for nearly twenty-five years? How could this ancient colonial brutality be allowed to continue?

We joined together to make a formal protest, wrote a letter and threatened to involve the police if the young woman wasn't allowed to take her child into the house. The result was that she was sacked without further ado. As we knew that was a risk we were taking, we had already arranged another job for her.

Admittedly I have experienced even worse things since then, not least child soldiers killing their parents. Nevertheless, it is the memory of the incident in Budapest and the servant girl in Maputo that is written over the gate leading into my private archive of experiences from hell.

54

A visit when something both begins and ends

LÖKSKÄR IS AN ISLAND AT THE OUTERMOST EDGE OF THE GRYT archipelago in Östergötland in eastern Sweden, just south of Stockholm. I generally try to visit there once a year, most often in the autumn. It is nearly always impossible to moor there; I have to jump ashore from Tommy Ljung's boat and try hard not to slip and injure myself. He picks me up again a few hours later.

It is a remote island exactly where Sweden begins or ends, depending on which direction you are coming from. It is silent, dumb. The rocks cannot speak. The island broods over its history.

It is forbidden to land on Lökskär during the bird-nesting season. It is also so far away from the mainland that the birds are not disturbed by the mink that cause havoc on neighbouring islands.

Once upon a time people used to live in the silence and loneliness of Lökskär. How they could bear to live in those conditions is beyond me. If a storm blew up they would have to row out in their primitive boats to retrieve their nets and cages, and they often drowned. Sometimes their bodies would be found entangled in a net, as if death wished to exhibit its booty. Sometimes they simply vanished and were never seen again.

They arrived there during the eighteenth century – or at least that is when we first find their details recorded in the church registers: 'Inhabitants of Lökskär'. As late as the 1850s the occasional inhabitant is listed, but after that the island was deserted again. The temporary visitors vanished just as quietly as they had arrived. Perhaps the island raised a stony hand and waved them goodbye?

For me, visiting Lökskär is an annual pilgrimage. I walk over the island as freezing-cold stormy winds blow, and think about the years that have passed and those that are yet to come. Among those bare rocks are no escape routes, no excuses. It is not possible to lie to yourself there. The rocks polish all truths and turn them into knife edges that cannot be obscured.

I sometimes think I can discern the shadows of the people who once lived there. They are still there, keeping watch as I pass by. Their faces are ingrained in the grey cliff walls, which sometimes have patches of rusty brown here and there.

One occasionally finds remains of the huts in which the poverty-stricken fishermen used to live. All the wood has rotted away, of course, but it is still possible to come across corner stones of the huts in slight hollows on the north-west side of the island, protected on all sides from the wind. The huts are hardly any bigger than a boathouse or even a playhouse. But that is where they lived, totally dependent on what the sea had to offer. They can't have kept more than a single cow, for there was hardly any grass and the heather was red and impossible to eat.

I often stand and observe the stones that were once laid there by immigrants who had been forced out onto this outermost island as those islands closer to the mainland became overcrowded. If I stand there for long I sometimes get the feeling that the stones are slowly moving back to the place from which they were first taken.

Dense thickets of thorn bushes grow all the way down to the narrow inlet where they kept their boats, protected from the wind.

There are no other traces of their life there. Nothing is scratched into the rock walls, there are no iron hooks or mooring rings in the cliff walls facing the deepest part of the inlet. Local history enthusiasts with metal detectors might have been here, but as far as I know they have found nothing at all.

There are not even any graves of the one-time inhabitants. When the ice was thick enough to walk on or the water calm enough for rowing or sailing, dead bodies were taken to the church in Gryt and buried there. But there are no gravestones for Lökskär inhabitants in the churchyard there.

You can sometimes find records of these people in the church registers, however. On day in 1837 a little boy scalded himself by knocking over a cauldron of boiling water. 'He died very quickly,' wrote the priest in sprawling handwriting. A few lines further down it states that Emma Johannesdotter has drowned. Life out on the remote island was always difficult.

Nevertheless, even on this isolated and inhospitable island there must at times have been feelings of great joy. Nights when one could make love and sleep soundly. I sometimes imagine I can see a woman lying in a rocky hollow allowing the sun to shine on her bare arms.

Brief moments of peace. Hopes that perhaps one day life will get better. But that can only happen if they can leave Lökskär and move to a more hospitable island. Or to another country. To another world. But which world would that be?

Seldom if ever did the coastal population of Sweden leave home and head for America during the big surge of emigration during the nineteenth century. Compared with the people of Småland, they always had their fish even during the worst years of starvation.

Once when I was rowing around the island on a fine, clear day in early autumn I noticed a drift net that had somehow come loose and was now slowly floating out to sea. The sunlight penetrated deep down into the water, and I could see several dead fish and a sea duck trapped inside the net.

It struck me that this was what I imagined freedom was like. Freedom. Always fleeing from something. From whatever or whoever tries to restrict it.

I can't say for sure who was the last person to leave Lökskär, but those who know these things say it was an old woman who gave the island back to itself. She was the last of several generations who had experienced and survived endless hard work in order to make a living.

But there is nothing left of all their heroic efforts. As I walk around the island on this freezing-cold autumn day it seems to me that everything must look exactly as it did 150 years ago. The stones, the low trees, the heather and the constant sighing of the sea. Seabirds hover motionless in the upwinds, hoping that I might throw them some food.

When I reach the highest point of the island I imagine that I have come to the top of a church tower. If I look westwards I can see small islands and rocks that gradually seem to form an unbroken line of land. In all other directions there is nothing to be seen but the sea.

It is difficult to imagine that everything I can see will eventually disappear when the next ice age arrives. What is bluish-grey today will become white, or beige, depending on whether or not the ice is dirty. The sighing of the sea will be replaced by the rumbling of the ice as it twists and turns before settling down. Where I am now standing, on the highest point of the island, the ice will be several kilometres thick. Lökskär will never reappear after the ice melts.

Sea or no sea? Land or islands? Deep ocean or shallow fresh-water lagoon? It's not possible to say. The exact movement of the ice cannot be foreseen.

But if there are people there, the maps will have to be redrawn.

At the very edge of a precipice on the eastern side of the island is a rock formation that has taken on the shape of a chair with a high back. I usually sit there for a while and curl up to protect myself from the wind that is always so cold.

On this occasion I suddenly notice in the distance a sailing boat heading for some unknown harbour – one of the last autumn sailors escaping from the approaching winter.

Even this island will soon be closed down – a museum of the past settling down to rest for the winter.

55

The woman with the sack of cement

I DON'T KNOW HOW MUCH OF MY LIFE I HAVE DEVOTED TO RELA-
tionships with women. In my particular case the beginning of such
relationships was not especially uplifting. I didn't get to know my
mother until I was about fifteen years old. She had done what men
often do, and deserted her family. That was most unusual in the
1950s. Fathers running off and staying away was old hat – we still
live in a world where lots of fathers are non-existent, never-present
in the families they helped to create. But not having a mother was
something very suspicious in the little town where I grew up.
Needless to say, I was aware of the oddity of my situation. My elderly
paternal grandmother, who rarely spoke and spent most of her time
darning socks, created some sort of balance in the household, but
my missing mother was a constant presence in the back of my mind.

There is a photograph of me and my mother that I think was taken
by the photographer Fåhraeus. I think the picture tells me that my
beautiful mother, holding me on her knee as a small child, would
have preferred to put me down, stand up and leave the room. Which
is what she soon did. I don't remember her at all from my early
childhood.

Being rejected by one's mother is no doubt the worst thing that
can affect a small child. Anyone less thick-skinned than I would
probably have blamed himself and thought he wasn't good enough.
But I don't remember thinking like that. I was surprised more than
anything. For some odd reason I always think of my reaction as being

like that of a child whose brightly coloured balloon suddenly bursts and turns into a useless bit of rubber. A sort of astonishment at having a mother who can't be bothered to be there when you wake up in the morning or go to sleep at night. I met her for the first time at a restaurant in Stockholm. It was in Stureplan, but has closed down now. Every time I walk along that street, I recall our meeting. She was sitting alone at a window table. I had seen photographs of her and knew that physically – face, hair, eyes – I was very like her. I approached her in a state of curious expectation. When she saw me walking towards her table, she raised her hands like a sort of shield and said: 'Don't come too close! I have a cold.'

I shall never forget that. Every time I write a play or a film script I try to create something more dramatic than that situation and comment, but I wonder if I shall ever manage to do so.

We remained somewhat hesitant and reserved during the ten years or so she remained alive. I think we both tried to hide the distrust we had of each other. On a few occasions I attempted to talk to her about what had happened when I was a small child, but she would always go out into the kitchen and there was a strong whiff of whisky in the air when she returned. I would let the subject drop, we never completed the conversation. She was no doubt ashamed, and didn't have the strength to face up to the fact that she had abandoned her children.

Today, when her failings have long since faded away, I can understand how she felt. She had four children, but was not cut out for motherhood. She was too restless, lacked patience, always wanted to be somewhere else. I recognise aspects of myself in her. In many ways her life was a great and certainly unnecessary tragedy; but in those days a woman who was married and had children didn't have much choice. I can now feel a degree of respect for her abandoning us, which must have been difficult and troubled her in so many different ways.

Whenever I think of her I also recall the memory of a woman and a sack of cement. The images of my mother and that African woman are totally different, in both time and space; nevertheless they are each standing on opposite sides of the river of life and death waving to one other.

I saw the incident from the window of a car just outside Lusaka in Zambia. An African woman was kneeling by the side of the road and next to her were two men heaving with considerable difficulty a sack of cement onto her head. The sack weighed fifty kilos. They then helped her to stand up. I saw her staggering away with that immense burden on her head, apparently walking straight into the sun with the dirt and dust from the road whirling around her.

Only then did I react. I went over to the two men, who were sitting in the shelter of a tin hut, and asked if they realised that carrying heavy burdens like that on her head would destroy the woman's back very soon. To them, I must have seemed an extremely aggressive white man.

Without the slightest trace of irony in his voice, one of the men said: 'Our women are strong. They'll manage it.'

He seemed proud as he said that.

That woman personified a truth about the world we live in. Her burden wasn't just on her head, it was just as much *inside* her head.

As a teenager I can't claim to have had an especially respectful attitude towards women. All my early erotic experiences were characterised by the fact that it was the woman who was at risk of becoming pregnant; it was nothing to do with me.

Today, of course, I can see very clearly that one of the most important movements after the Second World War, at least in the Western world, was the liberation of women. Even if it is still one of the major political challenges in the developing world, one cannot ignore the fact that major changes have taken place. The big challenge is exposing the views of those who base them on a false reading of religious teachings, especially Islam and Judaism. Women must still sit right at the back of buses as far as the Orthodox Jews in Israel are concerned. Women in Islamic countries are still fighting to obtain basic human rights, not least the ownership of their own bodies.

I once met a very old woman in a small village in the north of Sweden. She told me about a life-changing incident. She had grown up poverty-stricken, married a lumberjack and given birth to seven children before she reached the age of twenty-six. She felt that she simply didn't have the strength for any more children, but the thought of denying her husband his only pleasure was impossible for her to entertain.

Then she heard about a remarkable woman who was travelling around the country talking about love. It wasn't a word she ever used, except perhaps when talking to or about her children; it was too alien, too fancy for her and her husband. Saying such a word would have been embarrassing, as if she were trying to make herself seem a cut above other people.

But eventually she went to a talk at the community centre in the nearest sizeable town, ten kilometres there and ten back home again, in order to listen to that woman talking about love. Her name was Ottar, and she spoke a remarkable mixture of Swedish and Norwegian; even so, every word she said was understandable. The most important message was that it was not necessary to become pregnant with unwanted children when the winter nights were long and cold. Afterwards, in a freezing-cold outside toilet, Ottar gave the woman a pessary, which meant that she would no longer need to be afraid of conceiving. Her husband wouldn't need to give up his pleasure and she too would be able to share it.

'Ottar changed my life,' said the old woman. 'What had been painful torture became something I could appreciate as a pleasurable part of a dignified life. Before that making love with my husband had been tinged with despair.'

One of the greatest challenges facing the world is giving women more influence. For most women the responsibility for producing children and preparing food is great, but their political and economic influence is non-existent.

I don't believe that men and women think all that differently. Too much credence is given to what is called 'male and female ways of thinking'. What the world is really suffering from is a one-sided male way of thinking in which the voices of women are not heard at all.

It results in a preposterous way of life. It is a reflection of the old classic bourgeois custom of men gathering together after dinner while the women left the room to socialise somewhere else. If a woman tried to behave otherwise, she was immediately disciplined.

But if a new way of behaving is to take over, the men must take a step back and make room for women. Refusing to believe that this will happen is to have very little understanding of what change really involves.

Today there is still a battle going on between those who carry sacks of cement, and those who place them on their women's heads.

56

A winter in Heraklion

IN THE WINTER OF 1978 I SPENT A FEW MONTHS IN A HOTEL IN
Heraklion, the biggest town on Crete. It was the last time I made a
really long railway journey. I started one cold morning in the
Östbanestation in wintry Oslo, and arrived in Athens several days
later. Our train was pulled through Yugoslavia, which was a unified
state in those days, by a steam engine. In the morning, as we
approached the Greek border, I put my head out of the window in
order to breathe in some fresh air that was at last no longer wintry
– and was hit in the eye by a fragment of coal from the engine. As
a result I had difficulty in seeing anything during my first week in
Crete.

My hotel was simple, charmless and cheap, and I was more or
less the only guest. Breakfast was usually watery coffee, dry bread
and a smear of marmalade. A man sat in reception apparently perma-
nently occupied by attempts to solve strange mathematical problems
he had scribbled down on hotel notepaper.

I had gone to Crete because I wanted to see Knossos, and the
house where the great Greek author Kazantzakis had lived. But most
of all I wanted some peace and quiet.

I had with me a rucksack and a suitcase: both were crammed full
of books. In order to get them all in I had needed to remove some
of the hard covers. Most were books about cultural history, both
general and specialised, from the dawn of classical European civilisation to the present day. During the autumn that had passed I had

realised there were big gaps in my knowledge of how European civilisation had developed. Everything earlier than Voltaire, Diderot and Rousseau seemed blurred and not really connected. But now I was going to read up on all that with the intention of gaining a thorough grasp of the most important events that had created the world I live in, and hope to be able to help to change.

The fact that Crete had been a centre of this historical development had not been all that relevant to my decision to travel there; the most important thing was that a good friend had informed me that during the winter, hotels in Crete cost next to nothing.

Every morning I got up early and went for a walk that usually ended up at the end of the long pier at the entrance to the harbour. After a meal at some cafe or other that made up for the awful breakfast I had been served at the hotel I would sit down in my room, hang a shirt over the mirror by the desk and open my books. I still remember looking forward to learning something new that I hadn't known the day before. I didn't go out again until the chamber maid knocked on my door at about eleven o'clock. It was often raining, and I bought an umbrella and wandered around for several hours.

I would have lunch at the cheapest local restaurant I could find. It was almost always freshly caught fish. Then I would carry on reading, with a pause for dinner, and continue reading into the night.

I learnt something new every day. I don't think I've ever slept as well as I did in that room with its uncomfortable bed. Knowledge is a good sleeping pill.

On New Year's Eve I sat in a bar so long and drank so much wine that I got lost on the way back to the hotel. The receptionist was asleep when I eventually came staggering in. With considerable difficulty I collected my room key from the rack.

The following day I woke up very early, with a bad hangover. My head ached and the nausea kept rising in my throat – anybody who has drunk too much inferior Retsina knows the feeling. I read nothing at all that day. Instead I did what was usually no more than a vague intention and wrote what I now thought about the concept of civilisation in my diary. Despite my headache, or perhaps because of it, I managed to express my thoughts quite well.

There was something unsatisfactory about the way the concept of civilisation was used. The word was often coupled together with the concepts of culture and tradition without it being clear why. I had begun to wonder if there was something wrong about the concept of civilisation itself. The most common aspect in the analyses and definitions I had read was its use as the antithesis of barbarity. A civilised person had left primitive human life behind.

But was this really the case? Ancient Greece was a slave state. Freedom of thought and action was restricted to a number of selected men who satisfied the criteria of being citizens, whether the city involved was Sparta or Athens. Great thoughts were thought and great deeds performed in societies that can by no means be called civilised. There was always somebody else who prepared the food, looked after the children and cleaned the floors. And those who did that were often badly treated – not simply regarded as inferior individuals, but terrorised physically and psychologically.

And that is by no means the end of the story. Even today there is a mass of faceless and nameless individuals who are forced to live in a state of deepest humiliation and fear. And they exist in all the continents.

When you travel through Arab countries, for instance, you are constantly aware of these shadows behind the white facades. They appear briefly and then disappear again. Nearly all these people come from poor countries in Asia or Africa and work non-stop. They are often very young, and their opportunities for keeping in touch with their families are limited. And they have no rights whatsoever. The slightest protest or unwillingness to carry out their daily tasks can result in immediate dismissal. Back to poverty and a life on a rubbish dump.

But how then should the concept of civilisation be defined? What is a civilised person? There have been many answers to those questions throughout the course of history, and they have all been based on the assumption that civilisation is something you learn, whereas the uncivilised are stupid or lacking in means and hence have not been lucky enough to become 'civilised'.

The concept of 'civilisation' has often been used as an excuse for aggression. During the nineteenth century, when efforts to acquire the riches of Africa began in earnest, it was often used as the motivation. The European countries taking part in the rush to take over Africa had three weapons, all of them beginning with the letter 'C'.

The first was cannons, in other words: firepower. It was always in the background as a threat, and was used whenever necessary, often totally without discrimination. Civilised people had a right to exterminate the people who opposed the imposition of what was seen as being good for them. The only midway position between civilisation and barbarism was death. Nothing else.

The second was the cross. During the colonisation of Africa a helmet was placed on the head of Jesus and a sword in his hand. The only way of elevating all black people, the wild and barbaric beings, was for them to acquire the one true belief. The gods and animistic teachings that had sustained most Africans for centuries should be banished. The missionaries sent to Africa regarded themselves as soldiers of God. They were warriors with white safari helmets and Bibles instead of cannons, prepared to use them indiscriminately.

The third was cashbooks. Anybody who failed to respect the Western world's financial laws and the inherent brutality of the capitalist markets could not achieve the desired level of civilisation.

The secret weapon of colonialism was lying. I wonder if there has ever been so much and such systematic lying as during the nineteenth century's wave of humiliating attacks on the African continent. No doubt there were many Europeans who believed every word of what they preached about civilisation, but the driving force behind the brutal attacks was to simplify the colonialisation processes. They wanted to create peace and quiet while they stole Africa's natural resources, just as they had previously robbed Africa of its population.

I spent a lot of time thinking about these questions during the period I spent in Crete over the winter of 1978. It made me doubt whether it is at all possible to create anything worthy of the name civilisation as long as the world is being dominated by tyranny and a lack of freedom. Can true civilisation, without slavery and other more or less hidden processes of subordination, ever be achieved if it only applies to a limited part of the world?

Perhaps it is an impossible dream to create worldwide civilisation that isn't based on the suppression of some minorities?

Impossible or not, it is essential to have such a dream. It is highly unlikely that the next generation will be much cleverer than our own. But it is possible that later generations will be less stupid than we have been and still are.

I keep on remembering that winter in Crete, when I spent such a lot of time reading. And enjoying a solitary existence that was undisturbed.

57

Catastrophe on a German motorway

ONE SUMMER IN THE MIDDLE OF THE 1980S I DROVE TO WHAT WAS then called Yugoslavia. It was not the best of times in my life. I was a theatre director, and had realised too late that it was both naive and foolhardy to combine those duties with continuing to write books and plays. To make things worse, my year at the theatre had resulted in a lot of personal conflicts, which meant that I had to make several unpleasant but necessary decisions.

Now, having taken the ferry from Limhamn to Dragör early that morning, I was more or less fleeing southwards in my car, driving non-stop. Late in the evening I found myself not far from Hanover; I decided to carry on for as long as I could, and then sleep in the back of the car. I had removed the back seat and replaced it with a mattress.

The feeling of running away lessened the further I drove. As my car, a very old Citroën, didn't have much in the way of horsepower I was constantly being overtaken, but I was no longer in a hurry. I would reach the Yugoslav border sooner or later. I didn't know what would happen after that. Perhaps I would travel to the island of Krk and stay there until I had to go back north again. By then I would have made up my mind how to handle the coming year in the theatre. I didn't want a repeat of the past year, during which I had made every possible mistake.

South of Hanover, I began to feel very relieved. I had at least thirty days ahead of me during which nobody would knock on my door and present me with new problems – no furious actor who had argued with a producer, no trade union leader complaining about new regulations regarding lunch coupons. It became easier to think. I was reminded of an aphorism I had read somewhere: 'Don't take life so seriously – you won't come out of it alive anyway.'

A bus overtook me on the autobahn. I glanced at it and saw it was full of young people – a school trip, perhaps, or a sports team. The bus pulled in in front of me. It had an open sunroof, and a teenage boy stuck his head and upper body out through it. He waved to me, but I don't remember whether or not I waved back. He stuck his upper body even further out – there was no risk of him falling out as his lower body from the thighs down was tightly jammed inside the bus.

He continued looking backwards towards me, and nobody inside the bus, including the driver, realised what was about to happen.

Ahead was a low viaduct. The bus would pass under it without any problems – but nobody had thought about the boy sticking out of the sunroof. When the concrete edge of the viaduct struck him at about neck level, it crushed his head. Bits of bone, skin and battered brain flew through the air and onto my windscreen. I wasn't going very fast and was able to pull over onto the grass verge despite the mess all over the window. The bus had skidded to a halt at the side of the road, brakes screaming. Cars were stopping on all sides. Most people didn't know what had happened, and it was only later that I realised I was the only one who had seen how he had died.

The boy's severed body was still hanging out of the sunroof. I remember I had my hand on the windscreen wiper control when I stopped myself. I just sat there. I was in deep shock, my heart was pounding and I burst into tears. What I had just experienced was incomprehensible. What affected me most at the time was that the boy had had no idea of what was about to happen – not just that he had no chance of slipping back inside the bus, but that he didn't realise his life was about to end. He died without knowing it.

Ambulances and police cars came racing up together with fire engines. I got out of the car and beckoned to a police officer. He gave a start when he saw my windscreen. In halting but fairly comprehensible German I explained what I had seen. He made notes and then gestured to a forensic officer who had just arrived. The latter scraped bits of the mess into a small plastic tube, then signalled that I could wipe the windscreen clean.

I set off again and didn't stop until four in the morning. I had travelled quite a long way south by then and stopped at one of the petrol stations that are characteristic of German motorways. I parked between two long-distance lorries; their cabin curtains were drawn and I could hear snoring. I lay down on the mattress in the back of my car, with the noise from the autobahn in the background. Two people walked past, and one of them laughed for some unknown reason.

I eventually fell asleep. Only then did I no longer see the image of the boy waving at me from the roof of the bus.

After waking I continued to Krk and found a cheap hotel where masses of cockroaches scattered every time I switched on the lavatory light. I stayed there all summer, lacking the strength to go on looking for goodness only knows what. It was a restless summer and I spent much of it soul-searching. I eventually decided how I would try to improve my performance as theatre director during the coming year. As I only had one year left after that, the whole thing would soon be over. When I left Krk at the end of July and drove back north, I adopted what I convinced myself was a fighting spirit.

And that second year did pass much better. In fact, I stayed on for just over another twelve months, and to my surprise was offered the chance of working there even longer, as well as being offered other jobs as theatre director. I turned them all down, of course. All that mattered now was getting down to my writing again after an involuntary gap of over three years.

My contract eventually ran out, but I didn't travel abroad that summer. And I sold my car. On the evening my contract formally came to an end, I hired a car and drove from my home in Skåne to the theatre in Växjö, although the theatre had already closed down for the summer. I spent the evening in my empty office, which I had cleared of everything I no longer needed. The black desk was completely empty, apart from a letter I had written to my successor. I wished her good luck and reminded her of the unwritten rule that says the best day of a theatre director's work is the first one. After that, somebody is always dissatisfied. If you bear that in mind you are better prepared for all the problems in store.

I placed a mini-bottle of champagne beside the letter. Then I put my wristwatch on the desk in front of me, switched off the light and sat there in the late-summer darkness. My job would be over at exactly midnight. I didn't think of it as being released from prison – it hadn't been quite that bad, especially during the second half of the contract. The theatre had even won a prize for one of its productions. I regarded my visit to the empty office as rather embarrassing, but I still sat there waiting for the clock to strike midnight.

Then I suddenly saw again in my mind's eye that boy who had been decapitated. I had hardly thought about it since I returned from Krk, but now I could see him again, waving merrily at me during the last few seconds of his life.

Why did I think about him at that moment? I didn't know, but as the clock struck midnight he was the only other thing in the room, like a sort of shadow.

I felt nothing. No relief, no sense of freedom, no optimism for the future. It was as if I now had to start all over again from the beginning. Would I still be able to write? Had my ability to do so withered away during my years as a theatre director?

Then I stood up, switched off the light, locked the door and slid the key in through the letter box. It was as if I were locking up inside the office the memory of the boy in the bus.

I got into my hired car and drove off. Without a backward glance, as they say after something final.

Many years later, about a month after I had been diagnosed with cancer, I received a thick letter through the post. I couldn't read who the sender was, just some initials I didn't recognise and Stockholm as the place of origin; but no postbox number, no street name, no postcode.

Inside the thick envelope were several letters addressed to Henning Mankell – but they were not written to me. Eleven in all, dated 1899, 1900 and 1901. They had been sent to my paternal grandfather, also called Henning Mankell, who, in 1899, was thirty years old and lived in Cardellgatan in Stockholm. In 1905 he married Agnes Lindblom and they moved to Floragatan where he lived until his death in 1930.

I read the letters. They were all written by somebody called Harald, but no surname was ever given. He was about twenty and living and studying in Uppsala. In other words, there was a ten-year age difference between the pair of them – but there was no indication of their relationship.

The letters were unusual. There was no chit-chat, no questions about one's state of health, no greetings to mutual friends. Harald wrote to Henning about his dissatisfaction with life, his difficulties when it came to finding a meaning to his existence, and constant musing about various moral questions. He often referred to the erotic passion he felt for certain women, but his total lack of love for them. Some letters broke off in the middle of such thoughts, and the next one would start by asking the same questions once again.

It was impossible to read from the letters what Henning's response had been. They could only be read as a sort of monologue written by a young man studying unknown subjects at Uppsala University who quite often spent evenings with friends drinking punch in pubs. But he grew tired of the vulgar chatter of his friends and went home to write letters to Henning.

I read the letters and put them to one side. My grandfather died eighteen years before I was born. There is nobody around today who can tell me who this Harald was. There was no information about his surname, no photographs, only these letters sent to me by some unknown person.

I hadn't thought at all about my cancer while I was reading the letters sent to me. But I recognised quite a lot of myself in Harald, things I had thought when I was his age.

The next moment I also thought about the boy on the bus who died over and over again in my memory as his last wave was cut short by terrible tragedy. He must have sneaked out of that theatre office where I thought I had locked him up for good. I now realised that I could see aspects of myself in him as well. Harald's unrest and the smiling young boy are both a part of me. Or perhaps, rather, I am a part of them. You don't see yourself in others; you see yourself in *all* others.

It is the end of May as I write this. Those awful mornings in January and February when I had to keep attending the Sahlgrenska hospital for new examinations and tests before the chemotherapy could begin are now in the past. The first series of cycles is over, and I have survived without too many serious side effects. I feel very tired, yes, but the treatment has not been too devastating. I have only lost a couple of kilos in weight, on two occasions my blood count has fallen so much that I have needed a transfusion, but my immune defences have been up to the challenge.

I am currently receiving a lower dose of chemotherapy infusions every third week. I need to spend about an hour at the hospital. How long the treatment will last depends on how my tumours respond. If they continue to shrink, or at least stop growing, the treatment can continue for months or even years.

As I write this I suddenly remember a photograph. I have to search through albums and boxes before I find what I am looking for. It is a black-and-white photograph from 1957 of Class 4 from Sveg primary school. I am standing in the middle of the back row, looking very serious.

In the bottom right-hand corner of the photograph are three boys. The fact that they are standing together is pure coincidence: they were not close friends and didn't mix at break or after school – they simply happened to be standing next to each other.

All three are now dead. One drank himself to death – latterly on methylated spirits, I have been told. One shot himself in the face with a shotgun. The third died of some illness or other.

But as they sit there in the photograph they have no idea they are going to be the first pupils in the class to die. The picture gives no indication.

However, I can also recognise aspects of myself in them. I carry images of the living and the dead inside me, and I assume that I exist similarly in the minds of others who recognise themselves in me.

Or at least I did, for as long as they were alive.

58

Jealousy and shame

ONE SPRING NIGHT MANY YEARS AGO I WAS WANDERING AROUND a small town in northern Sweden, riven by jealousy.

It was as if the town around me had lost all its colours, and the environment had suddenly become a glassy black and white. The pavements swayed under my feet. There seemed to be hollows everywhere that might suddenly open up into abysses.

I had recently met a woman in another country and fallen passionately in love with her. We spoke every evening on the telephone.

But that evening she had not answered when I rang. My worries drove me out into the streets, from telephone kiosk to telephone kiosk. I rang every ten minutes, but there was still no answer.

It was like living under a curse; I had never experienced such a feeling before. Being let down by friends when I was a child or broken promises by adults were nothing compared with what I was going through that night.

It was over forty years ago, but I think it is one of the moments in life I can still recreate with absolute clarity. A moment when life was centred upon just one thing: the hope that a woman would answer the telephone and confirm that our love was still alive.

The spring night was quite light, even though it was raining on and off. By about three in the morning I was soaked through, but I continued my humiliating walk from telephone kiosk to telephone kiosk. A police car drove past me occasionally and the officers inside it regarded me with suspicion. But I wasn't staggering as I walked, nor was I carrying stolen goods, so they let me be.

Now, long afterwards and with hindsight, I can recall it as a black shadow extracted from one of Dostoevsky's novels. It wasn't a Swedish town I was prowling through at night, it was Moscow or St Petersburg.

I also had physical pains. My stomach was tied in a tight knot, and every breath was torture. I tried to think of a reason why she wasn't answering, but could only envisage in my mind's eye an unknown man at that very moment holding her against his naked and aroused body.

At one point I walked across a long bridge over a river, suddenly stopped and cried out loudly. Edvard Munch's *The Scream* embodies a deep human truth.

It was dawn before she answered the phone. I burst into tears when she eventually picked up. The explanation was simple: she hadn't replaced the receiver properly the previous evening, and had slept soundly all night.

Relief was all-consuming. My jealousy no longer existed. The knots untied themselves and loose strands whirled away into the distance.

Later in life I have sometimes felt jealous, but never as badly as on that occasion. And I have learnt to notice when other people are suffering from jealousy. It is usually linked with love, infidelity, fear of being abandoned. But jealousy can occur in the most unexpected circumstances. In a theatre the distribution of roles can lead to a sort of hatred that is basically jealousy. In literature there is a supreme description of jealousy in Shakespeare's *Othello*.

A long list of examples could be compiled. Among writers it can concern anything from reviews to sales figures. And I have seen farmers fuming over the excellent harvest reaped by a neighbour when their own fields have not been nearly so productive.

I once saw two taxi drivers fighting at a rank. I heard later that it was because one of them thought the other had a better car than his own.

But where does this jealousy come from? And why?

I remember a time in the 1980s when Aids was a new and frightening phenomenon. I asked a few friends how they would react if they heard they had been infected. In those days such a diagnosis was in effect a death sentence; antiretrovirals had not yet been found and medics were unsure about how the virus functioned once it had found a home in a new host.

I received all kinds of different answers, as can well be imagined, but one came over and over again and was horrifying. It was a response the person concerned would not have made public, of course, if they had been asked by a journalist or a doctor. But they had no inhibitions in telling me.

'I would infect somebody else. I don't want to die alone.'

My reaction was obvious: 'Why would you want somebody else to die? You always die alone.'

'I couldn't bear the thought of somebody living longer than I did.'

That reply is born of extreme jealousy. Other people will continue living after I am dead. Indeed, quite a lot of people will be cheeky enough not to have been born when I breathe my last.

This is both grotesque and inhuman. But I have met people who find it hard to conceal their jealousy of their own children – the ones who will live on after they have gone. I see people in their fifties wearing tight jeans that are far too youthful for them in an attempt to deny the fact that death is shadowing them.

The dream of the elixir of life will never desert some people. It's not good enough for them that nowadays we usually live longer than our parents. We can't do anything about our genetic inheritance. Not yet, at least. But perhaps the time will come sooner than we expect when people start to clone their children into exact copies of themselves, minus any possible snags in their DNA profiles.

There is a difference between the jealousy of men and women. If you have seen a male lion taking over a herd of lionesses, you have seen man.

Jealousy is about survival, about the biological imperative for reproduction. In a biological sense, the person with whom we conceive children can be irrelevant. But complicated social and financial circumstances play a role.

Love is a modern invention. Earlier generations were exclusively concerned with placing children in advantageous social and financial environments.

In many ways that is still the case, of course. In many cultures children are married off soon after they are born. In those circumstances what we call love is something that might come about after marriage, not before.

It is hardly surprising that female and male jealousy is different in a world where it is the men who have power and the women who have responsibility. Men are jealous if they suspect their chosen woman might have children with another man, but they themselves feel free to kick over the traces all their life.

Women on the other hand are jealous if they suspect another woman might be taking their man away from them, since if that happens she will be left alone with the children.

These are generalisations, but the only jealousy I feel in relation to women was on that spring night long ago in a northern Swedish town.

Jealousy is hard to cope with. It is appropriate that the French have a special code for 'crimes of passion' in their legal system. That is in accordance with human nature. Even if other countries don't have the same clear attitudes as in the French system, law courts nearly always take into account jealousy if it is hovering in the background of a crime.

They say people are ashamed of being jealous, that it is regrettable to have such weakness of character. That is something I find hard to understand. Why should I feel ashamed because I am acting in a way that comes naturally to humans?

Deep down, being jealous means that I am able to express my highly human feelings.

I once knew a man called Olof. At the age of eighty-seven he suspected that his eighty-six-year-old wife Irma was being unfaithful to him with another man in the old people's home where they lived. His jealousy was as rabid and humiliating as mine had ever been.

They were reconciled later when it was established that she had not been unfaithful.

Irma lived to be a hundred and one and Olof ninety-nine. When Olof died Irma did something she had been wanting to do for a very long time: she searched through his papers for the answer to something that had bothered her for sixty years. Had he been unfaithful to her when she was expecting their second child? She found among the documents the proof she had been looking for.

She said it hit her like a tidal wave. A wave of black, murky, oil-like water. Jealousy.

But it passed. Olof had not abandoned her. She could forgive him. And she lived for two more years, and died having fallen asleep with an unfinished crossword puzzle on her chest.

59

The twenty-eighth day

ONE UNUSUALLY COOL DAY IN 2013 IN MAPUTO I HAVE LUNCH with a doctor from Switzerland. He is just over fifty, is called Renée and during his years in practice has carried out heart operations on some 4,000 children. He is a quiet, undemonstrative person and earlier in the day had spent three hours operating on a 'blue baby' that would otherwise have certainly died, if not immediately then definitely before it reached the age of five.

I ask him what it feels like when his daily work is saving the lives of children who would never otherwise have had the chance to grow up and wonder about the meaning of life. Somewhat hesitantly, he says it is of course a constant pleasure – but that he is only doing his job, like everybody else.

Then he starts talking about three cases when he thinks he failed. The children died, and although he had made no mistakes, he was responsible for their deaths.

I can't see that he should bear any personal responsibility whatsoever. His description of the three cases seems to me to be a combination of unfortunate circumstances and unexpected complications.

Then he tells me about the meetings he had with the children's parents. They were shocked at their loss, and furious with the doctor. Naturally he could understand that they were looking for a scapegoat to blame, but his pain is still difficult to live with.

Our discussion has continued for some considerable time, despite the fact that he is tired out. Together with his team of specially trained nurses who flew out to help him, he has performed fourteen operations in one week. Later this evening he will fly home to Lausanne, and after a couple of days will be operating again in his own hospital.

4,000 operations – often on tiny hearts, which he will enable to pump blood for the next eighty or so years.

He starts talking about how he loves the organ known as the heart. What he says sounds almost lyrical, but essentially he is very objective.

The heart is a muscle. Nothing more. Just like a thigh muscle or a spinal muscle it has a special function. It pumps blood.

Then Renée begins a fascinating account of the heart's secrets, which are totally unknown to me.

'When a child is born, its heart has already been beating for a long time,' he says. 'It has been working for ages before the child comes into the world. After conception, the heart's muscles start moving slowly on the twenty-eighth day, and after a warming-up process lasting three days it begins to beat properly on the thirty-first day.'

'As precisely as that?' I wonder.

'Yes, as precisely as that. There have been a few cases of it happening after thirty-two or thirty-three days, but if the heart isn't beating before the thirty-fifth day the child won't live.'

My thought process is inevitable. When a child is born its heart has already been beating for eight months. All the crucial physiological processes are established from the very beginning by this obstinate muscle pumping blood around the body.

Renée relaxes after his intensive week's work by sipping a glass of red wine. His smile is friendly all the time. The heart interests him. His heart, my heart, your heart. I suspect that at some time he has amused himself by calculating how many heartbeats there are throughout the world during one minute or one hour. A quick calculation suggests that the number of heartbeats for a human being who lives for eighty years is a twelve-digit figure.

The heart is a muscle that occupies him every single day.

I ask him about tortoises that can live to be 150, and am informed that their hearts are simpler than ours in their make-up. As they move so slowly, their hearts can carry on working for a very long time – whereas animals with a faster heartbeat might only live for one or two years.

Then he starts talking about another remarkable fact relevant to the heart muscle. It is actually programmed to live for about thirty-five to forty years – which was quite a high age only a few generations ago, even in Europe, and it is still the average lifespan in a lot of poor countries. But the heart muscle proved to have an unsuspected ability to live for longer than was thought; it carries on working, even when it has to pump twice as many times as it was created to do.

Renée maintains that the heart is perfect because there has never been any doubt about what it is supposed to do. Other muscles in our bodies can make a variety of different movements, such as when we are doing strenuous physical work or indulging in sport. But the heart has only one job to do: to pump our blood around hour after hour without a break.

I ask Renée why nature chose this particular system for pumping blood around our bodies; there must have been alternatives in the early stages of life on earth.

His response is that the enormous advantage of the heart's way of working is its simplicity, which enables it to work for so long. Also, it means we know all there is to know about the heart, its formations and its function – unlike the brain, for instance, which is still largely unexplored territory.

Renée is not surprised that the heart has become a symbol for everything from patriotism to the most passionate love that nature is capable of arousing. He talks of 'the wonderful heart'; its clockwork mechanism as 'a measurer of life' just keeps on going, and it can endure the most painful human experiences such as privation and starvation before finally being forced to submit.

The heart is the most loyal of servants. It is the yardstick for love

– at the height of passion our heartbeat increases and our cheeks turn red. And it is the heart that execution squads aim at. A white rag attached over the heart is the target the gunmen aim at.

In former times – and perhaps even today in some places – men used to eat the defeated enemy's heart in order to take over his strength.

When a person becomes overweight or stops exercising, the heart continues pumping blood round the maltreated body for as long as possible. The heart is our ultimate hero. Yet at the same time it is a perfectly normal muscle, albeit one with remarkable resources.

Renée gets ready to leave for the hospital in order to pack up his instruments and say goodbye to his African colleagues. He will soon be back, once he has collected enough money to cover his expenses in performing new lifesaving operations.

Before he leaves I ask him what the human heart will be like a million years from now. Will it have developed? He doesn't think so. The muscle is the perfect pump to keep us alive. Every person's heart pumps as much blood during their lifetime as the Victoria Falls pours water down that gigantic African ravine over several hours. Other body muscles will no doubt change – in a world where more and more people lead sedentary lives, changes to our muscles will occur, even if it takes a very long time.

'How long?' I ask before he leaves. 'A hundred thousand years?'

'If this restaurant is still here, the people serving and eating here will be very similar to us inside their skins,' he says. 'A hundred thousand years is a very short time.'

After he has gone, I think about what he said.

'A hundred thousand years is a very short time.'

Hard to grasp, but of course perfectly true.

60

Meeting in an amphitheatre

ONE DAY IN AUGUST 1983 I BOARDED A BULGARIAN AIRWAYS PLANE to Athens, full of great expectations. We landed in Berlin, Prague and Sofia, if I remember rightly. There were delays at every stage. The food on board was dry sandwiches, but none of this mattered. I wasn't in a hurry. I was going to spend a few weeks in the Swedish guest house in Kavala in northern Greece. My aim was to write a play I had been commissioned to produce.

One day that autumn I understood what the feeling of entering a both timeless and historic situation involves. It happened quite unexpectedly, like nearly all major and life-changing events.

It was still very hot, but everybody I spoke to said there would soon be a change to more autumnal weather. I had completed the first act of the play, and so I took a day off.

There was another reason why I allowed myself a free day. The previous day had been a Sunday, and in the morning I went out onto the balcony of my room and looked down at the church below it: I found myself staring into an open coffin. A young man of about my age, wearing a dark suit, was lying in it, surrounded by hysterical, weeping mourners.

I left the balcony and closed the door. I had seen dead bodies before, but my unease grew and grew.

At the time I hadn't quite resolved my relationship with death. I was perhaps on the way, but it wasn't until later, during my early years in Africa, that I could seriously recognise death as a part of life rather than something extraneous to it.

I slept badly that night. The next evening I went down to the harbour and checked the times of ferries to Thasos. I got up at dawn, and the ferry left on time.

When I got to Thasos I didn't realise that there was a classical amphitheatre there. I had previously seen the one under the Acropolis cliff, and the mother of all amphitheatres in Epidaurus, but when I walked along the stone-paved path to the theatre on Thasos, past the ruins of the Dionysus Temple, and saw the old theatre spread before me, it was one of the most moving experiences of my life so far. It was reminiscent of the time I stood outside the community centre in Sveg and discovered that I was myself and nobody else.

On that occasion I discovered myself. Now, on Thasos, it became quite clear to me that my identity was linked with that of others who had gone before me and those who would come later.

It was not a new thought, of course, but it was precisely then that I realised its momentous significance. I saw what I had seen before without properly comprehending it.

It was the first time I registered seriously what the long-dance of the generations implied.

The theatre was surrounded by tall, sparse trees. Beyond them was the sea. One could see the setting sun from the tiered seating as well as watching the play reaching its climax.

It was morning when I came to the theatre. I stayed there almost the entire day, apart from a brief visit to a little restaurant for lunch. I spent most of the time walking around the stage, or sitting in various seats provided for the audience.

A little boy who happened to be visiting at the same time helped me to test the acoustics. He whispered or shouted loudly or spoke normally when I asked him to. In the end, despite the fact that I don't speak Greek, I got him to understand that I would like him to sing a children's song. I sat right at the back, looking down onto the stage, where he seemed little more than a dot way down below. But his voice reached me loud and clear, despite the fact that he wasn't singing especially loudly.

He was interrupted by his mother, who was either anxious or angry and had come up the hill to the theatre looking for him. The last I heard from him was some sobbing, drowned out by his mother's telling-off as she dragged him away by his ear.

For a brief moment I took part in the play myself when the mother noticed me and shouted several angry questions that I didn't understand. I simply shook my head and thrust my arms out wide.

Afterwards, I have since read that there is documentary evidence to show that both Aristophanes and Euripides were performed in this theatre over 2,000 years ago. There are also indications that Aristophanes visited the theatre in person.

But that day, when I discovered the theatre quite unexpectedly, I was able to imagine what had taken place there. The appearance and voices of the actors, their temperament, masks and movements. I sat there playing with the thought of all the rest of the audience sitting around me, whether I was at the very top at the back or in the VIP seats just in front of the stage itself.

The human connection, I thought. This is how it was. We all do the same things in order to find food and survive. We do the same jobs, and we share the same secrets hidden in the art form that is the theatre.

The thought was very simple. Once upon a time actors stood on this stage performing plays that are still performed today. Some of which I myself have directed in theatres. There is an invisible link between them and me that is so strong, it can't be broken. If I stretch out my left arm I can grasp the hand of one of the actors who took part all those years ago. If I stretch out my right arm I can grasp the hand of one of the actors who will perform there in the future.

It was a totally magical moment. All the seats were suddenly full of spectators, and on the stage was the classical ancient chorus wearing their masks.

But they were all looking at me, and I was looking at them.

We were looking at one another.

The sun slowly sank down towards the sea's horizon where it set, the audience applauded and started making their way towards the town of Thasos again.

Afterwards, as I sat in the shade of the tall pine trees surrounding the theatre, I experienced a sense of relief that was greater than anything I had felt earlier. I felt inspired, and wanted to sing.

I walked down to the stage again, and had the distinct feeling that the ancient chorus had returned. Every moment of my life was there in the background. Suddenly it started snowing; the wintry morning in Sveg had returned.

The feeling of relief I experienced was associated with the fact that my life seemed to be constituted in a new way. There was a clear meaning in the connections I had discovered – the outstretched hands over time and space.

It seemed to me that in different circumstances one of the members of the chorus thousands of years ago could easily have asked exactly the same questions as I did. And even before ancient Greek drama had become established there had been theatres and actors.

Whoever was the very first actor is something lost in the annals of history; it is a question without an answer. But we know with the tentative certainty that is associated with everything that cannot be proved scientifically that actors emerged from the world of ritual. They were better able to interpret human understanding of the magical dimensions of life – birth and death, natural catastrophes, the sun's constant transit from east to west.

I imagine that the very first actor was somebody like the Swede Allan Edwall. The fact that I don't suggest a woman is because I believe the very first actors were exclusively male. The fact that they belonged to the priesthood supports my belief.

Allan Edwall was able to depict the tragic and the comic. He could alternate between laughter and tears almost without any perceptible change of expression. And there is no doubt that he was always well aware of the presence of an audience. He could metamorphose into a completely different person without losing his audience. He didn't transform the audience. It transformed itself.

Before I left the theatre in Thasos, I was convinced it was Allan Edwall standing down below on the stage as the sun set and the shadows became longer and longer.

I stayed in Thasos that night. The following day I went back to Kavala and continued writing my play.

From that day onwards I have lived with my arms and hands outstretched.

61

A thief and a policeman

LIVING WITH CANCER MEANS LIVING WITH NO GUARANTEES. JUST as the nocturnal wanderings of cats are unknown, cancer cells also travel along dimly lit paths.

We think we know so much, but we are constantly forced to reassess our understanding of the world. If the truth is always provisional, which I think it is, our assessment of how reality has developed down the ages is just as unreliable.

I have devoted quite a lot of my life to studying crime and criminal investigations. My view is that evil always has to do with circumstances, and is never something inherited. I have written about crime because it illustrates more clearly than anything else the contrasts that form the basis of human life.

Everything we do is based on the existence of conflicting forces inside us – between dream and reality, knowledge and illusions, truth and lies, what I want to do and what I actually do. And not least between myself and the society I live in.

It all began early in my life. I grew up on the upper floor of a district court. There were legal sessions every Thursday. I sometimes sneaked into the courtroom despite the fact that I was considered too young to be present, but Svensson the caretaker turned a blind eye. After all, my father was the district judge.

I once sat there as two thieves were being tried after they had undertaken a long journey from Stockholm northwards, stealing things all the way. They had been arrested in Älvros. I still recall being surprised to hear that one of their thefts was of pencils from a kiosk. They admitted that crime, but vehemently denied having stolen two belts from a tailor's.

The simple lesson for a child sitting at the back of the court was that there were consequences if you committed a crime.

Thousands of years ago authors tried to illustrate conflicts within and between individuals; you have to do this in order to depict the validity of a human's personality. One of many ways of doing so is to use crime and its motives.

We think we know what a policeman is and what a policewoman is. We can see them in front of us, in uniform or plain clothes, and they always seem to be heading somewhere specific, or involved in serious and often stormy meetings.

I see something else. An incident some twenty-five years ago changed my opinion of them altogether.

It happened at a street corner in central Lusaka, the capital of Zambia. It had been raining all night, and the road and pavements were soaking wet.

I was waiting for somebody who was late. I looked hard down Chachacha Road without seeing any sign of him, and wondered if I had got our meeting place wrong. Perhaps he had said Cairo Road? Or Katondo Road? I decided on the former, turned off into a side street and headed for Cairo Road.

Having reached there, I started waiting again. It was a Sunday, the shops were closed and there were remarkably few people around. It was very cloudy, a hangover from the previous night's rain.

I suddenly saw a young policeman in uniform, dragging behind him a man who was presumably a thief. Not far from where I was standing was an illegal street market, which was often a haunt of thieves.

The policeman's uniform didn't fit him. His trousers were too long, his tunic too tight. There was nothing comical about what I could see; it was just a matter of a young man having to put up with whatever clothes he had been issued with.

He carried a baton and a pistol. Both items seemed to suit him as badly as his uniform: the baton was too long, the pistol too heavy.

The thief was in his twenties, barefooted, trousers cut short, his scalp covered in patches of eczema. I had learnt that this condition was often associated with poverty and malnutrition.

The policeman was gripping hard onto the collar of the thief's shabby shirt.

There was something touching about the circumstances; both men seemed unsure about what their roles were. I assumed they were on their way to the nearby police station. I had been there once when my car was stolen, and still recall a wall covered in photographs of various criminals. Above it was a headline: 'People we no longer need to worry about'. I asked the duty officer dealing with my case what this meant. He looked at me in surprise.

'Dead,' he said. 'We've got rid of them.'

The policeman in the street abruptly stopped quite close to me. He was still clinging tightly onto the thief's collar, but was staring down at his own shoes, which were brown, dirty and unpolished. Next to where he had stopped was a crippled shoe-cleaner shuffling around on grazed knees and hands protected by plastic gloves. I had seen him before, and knew he could move pretty quickly if needs be.

The policeman said something to the thief, let go of him and put his own right foot onto the shoe-cleaner's wooden block.

Things were beginning to get interesting! The thief stood there motionless while the shoe-cleaner polished away. The policeman wasn't looking at the thief, who I expected to go running off down Chachacha Road.

The policeman suddenly seemed to wake up and said something to the thief that I couldn't hear as a bus went clattering past. To my astonishment the policeman gave the thief a banknote. The thief left – he didn't run but walked off round the corner.

The policeman looked down at his shoe, which was now starting to look quite different. By this time I had forgotten that I was waiting for somebody who was late; the performance being acted out before me was becoming more and more fascinating.

Surprisingly enough, a few minutes later the thief returned. He was carrying a copy of *The Times of Zambia*, which he gave to the policeman who started reading it as he put his other foot up to have the shoe polished. The thief took up his former position, and showed no sign of wanting to run away.

Both shoes were eventually polished. The policeman paid whatever the shoe-cleaner asked for, and when the cleaner showed signs of annoyance at not being given a tip the officer shouted and placed a hand on his baton. The shoe-cleaner was immediately satisfied.

The policeman put the newspaper into his pocket, then grasped hold of the thief's collar again and dragged him away towards the police station. I watched in amazement as they disappeared along the street.

It dawned on me that what I had witnessed had been perfectly natural. In a country that previously had no police officers apart from the English ones conforming to their colonial practices, everything had to be learnt from square one. That applied not only to the policeman, but also to the thief. What I had seen was role-playing, a rehearsal of how to behave in the new circumstances.

It's easy to imagine that police officers have always existed; but of course they haven't. In the early days there were soldiers, non-commissioned officers and jailers. They tracked down offenders who were fined or executed.

Dungeons were only for very special cases. Not until more and more large towns appeared was there a need for a police force, whose role was mainly to control the lower classes and prevent crimes aimed at the upper classes. During the eighteenth century police forces were formed in most European countries, but there is still a lack of what we call police officers in other parts of the globe.

We live in an increasingly divided world in which welfare is improving, but at the same time the gap between those who have access to this welfare and those who have nothing is widening. That is why there will be more and more increasingly specialised police forces.

So being a police officer is a job with a future.

That was perhaps the most important lesson I learnt as I watched the young African policeman in his almost Chaplinesque uniform march off with a thief who was also learning how to play his role.

He wasn't just a thief. He was also taking part in a performance watched by those of us standing on the pavement.

62

Youth

IT WAS A TIME OF LIBERATION.

It was at the end of the 1960s. I was barely twenty years old, I wrote poems and wandered around Stockholm at night sticking them up on house walls and concrete columns. Sometimes they were torn down. I liked that – a reader had reacted, even if it wasn't with appreciation.

In August I would be going on tour with the first play I had written and also directed. It was called *The Playground*, and was a bizarre story about what Swedish society and the world in general looked like from my point of view. Among the characters were the Minister of Finance at the time, Gunnar Sträng; a poverty-stricken Latin American farm labourer called Joao; and the Pink Panther, played by the actor Björn Gedda.

We were going to put on a large number of performances during the autumn. Rehearsals had been complicated by the fact that we were very critical of the Social-Democratic government, and in many cases the organisers were Social-Democratic groups.

After the tour I heard that they had sent out spies to discover how the performances had been received by audiences.

My job during the performances was to take care of practical matters such as lighting and sound, which I did very badly. Sometimes I pressed the wrong buttons on the tape recorder, and the result was either the wrong music or no sound at all. After the shows the cast would glower at me, and I understood them perfectly well.

In addition, in my desperate attempts to find a theatre to finance the whole venture, I had kindly volunteered to be available for a discussion at the end of each performance. It was a promise I would regret, to some extent at least, as these sessions could drag on until after midnight, and sometimes those taking part would almost come to blows. In Karlstad there was such an uproar that we had to put on an extra performance in order to satisfy the extra interest engendered.

I have been excoriated in the mass media for all kinds of reasons – but never as vehemently as I was then because my shoes were worn out. One journalist argued that the hole in the sole of one of my shoes proved I was a left-wing extremist.

On New Year's Eve the previous year I had ended up at a party hosted by people I didn't know at all. It was there that I met the young dancer and choreographer G. She was there with the man she lived with, J, but I didn't know that. We started talking, things clicked, and we exchanged addresses. The following day, a freezing-cold New Year's Day, I found my way to her flat in a house that was condemned to be demolished in Regeringsgatan, more or less where Sweden House is today. When I entered the flat, the man I knew nothing about appeared. He threw a shoe at me, then started twisting G's arm. I left immediately, quite shocked and upset. After all, nothing had happened between G and me. I grew increasingly angry. I went back to the flat and asked the man what he thought was going on. There was no mistaking his jealousy.

Nor my anger.

It ended up in an odd sort of reconciliation. G went to the hospital with her injured arm, J and I went out into the wintry streets.

'There's a remarkable feeling of closeness here in Stockholm, don't you think?' I said.

'What the hell are you on about?' said J, who was an artist and specialised in painting cars. I seem to recall he was very talented.

That was about as close as our relationship got. It was obvious to both him and me that G and I were going to become lovers.

Which is what happened.

It was not my first love. There had been L before that, but this new affair was a great and passionate relationship – it had an extra dimension, something that surprised me and deepened my sensual awareness.

Six months later, a few weeks before I was due to set off on that long tour, G suggested that we should go to Norway and spend a few days walking in the mountains at Rjukan – we had both read books by the Danish-Norwegian author Aksel Sandemose. Telemark was not the area he mainly wrote about, but nevertheless he became our invisible companion.

We took the night train from Stockholm. Somebody stole G's purse at the station, reducing our combined resources dramatically. She wept and said she wanted to stay at home, but despite this setback, we set off.

Somewhere close to the Norwegian border the train stopped for no obvious reason; G was asleep on a bench in the compartment we had to ourselves. I sat looking out into the night, which carried a breath of early autumn, and then looked at G as she slept. For the first time in my adult life I didn't feel alone; in the darkness of that compartment I felt a happiness that was totally new.

We changed trains in Oslo, and from the Västbanestation headed for Rjukan. It was Saturday afternoon by the time we got there. We ate at the only restaurant that was open, then left the little town and started walking. We eventually lay down in our shared sleeping bag outside a barn. It was a lovely evening, but soon it started raining and we broke into the barn. It was our first break-in during our mountain walk. We spoke about Sandemose. G told me about the dances she planned and rehearsed at night in the premises of the Choreographic Institute on Blasieholmen – she had acquired a key without anybody else knowing. I talked about the tour, which would be starting shortly: the first performance would be in Trollhättan, the last one in Malmberget.

Soon after dawn, when it was merely drizzling, we set off up the

steep hills until we came to the mountain itself. I had always associated mountains with snow and cold, but here there was heather
and grey grass growing between lumps of stone. The ground was
soaking wet, and mist glided slowly along the horizon.

We followed a marked path over the mountain, without knowing
exactly where it was leading. We were badly equipped, had only a
minimum of food and absolutely no protective clothing if the weather
were to turn really nasty.

We walked in silence most of the time, accompanied only by a
curlew. It was as if both of us needed to get our breath back. The
love we felt was so all-consuming that it seemed almost frightening.
There simply wasn't room for any words. We were in a world that
in its way could be as vast as space itself.

Towards afternoon the rain grew much worse. It was pelting down,
and the wind was also becoming stronger. There was no protection
at all from the wind; all we could do was to keep going, but because
it wasn't cold we didn't feel afraid.

Eventually the path started sloping downwards. We came to a
building site where a large transformer station was being built. As
it was Sunday, no work was taking place. I managed to force open
the window of a hut so that we could climb inside and dry our
clothes. There were a few blankets lying there, and we wrapped them
around us.

In that icy-cold hut I became aware of what the term eroticism
actually means. In that cold room with our bodies freezing cold we
seemed to have everything against us, but perhaps the reverse was
true, and everything was in our favour.

I remember thinking at the time: *I shall never forget this*. And I
never have.

In the evening a caretaker suddenly appeared. As we had switched
the light on he was prepared for something when he unlocked the
door. By now we had got dressed and were respectable. I gave him
the facts: we were neither thieves nor tramps; we were simply walking
over the mountain and had become soaking wet and frozen through.

He eyed us up and down, and decided to believe us. He went into a neighbouring room – I suspected he was checking to make sure we hadn't stolen anything from the desk in there.

There was a mountain guest house a few miles away; he drove us there and we were provided with food and a room. By the following day we had more or less run out of money; we took a bus back to Oslo and boarded a train to Sweden.

Once again G slept but I remained awake. This might sound like an adjustment of the facts made with hindsight, but it isn't. I really did hope that the experience I had just had was something everybody else should enjoy or have enjoyed – not only our contemporaries but everybody since the beginning of time. Surely our forefathers in their primitive caves or poverty-stricken miners in early nineteenth-century England, to name but two examples that passed through my mind, must have experienced something similar.

At that time it never occurred to me that love is a blessing – perhaps the greatest blessing a human being can be gifted with. It was only later that thought came into my mind.

Nevertheless, one night in August at the end of the 1960s that train compartment was transformed into a cathedral.

Through the window of the train I started to see glimpses of a life that had begun to reveal fantastic secrets to me.

63

The dead body on the bench for the accused

THE REPULSIVE CAN BE ENTICING. FRIGHTENING, THREATENING, but also tempting. Like when you lean over something that smells awful, but is so fascinating that you can't stop yourself sniffing it.

In the Musée des Beaux-Arts in Nantes is a remarkable picture painted by the French artist Jean-Paul Laurens in 1870. It is a competent oil painting, no more than that, created according to the traditions of the time and illustrating a historical event fairly accurately. It is similar in style to that painted at more or less the same time in Sweden by von Rosen, depicting King Erik, Karin Månsdotter and the malevolent Jöran Persson, who wants King Erik to sign a death warrant. Both paintings have an air of Romanticism – the details are real enough, but the picture and its message are essentially false.

In the painting in Nantes, a pope is sitting on his throne in full regalia. Next to him, dressed entirely in black, is a bearded young priest listening to an agitated man who seems to be accusing the pope of some alleged wrong.

It is a picture of the so-called 'Cadaver Synod' of 897, held in the Basilica Salvatoris in Rome on a series of extremely cold winter days. Nowadays the basilica has been renamed as the Lateran Basilica, and the synod is sometimes called 'Synodus Horrenda' – which is understandable if you know what it is all about.

If you observe the Laurens carefully you realise that the pope is actually dead – a cadaver. It is Pope Formosus – the only one in a long series of popes to be given that name – who had been dead for nine months but was extracted from his coffin in order to be indicted by his successor, Stephen VI. The priest dressed in black, whose name has been lost in the annals of history, is assumed to be the former pope's defence lawyer, even if the outcome of the trial was of course a foregone conclusion.

The stench inside the church must have been awful. One can imagine the smell of rotting flesh after nine months of decay.

In those days it was not the practice to embalm dead bodies in balsam. Much of the knowledge acquired by the Roman Catholic Church about the way in which Egyptian Pharaohs preserved corpses had been lost by that time. The Roman tradition was to place them in a sarcophagus above ground. (The word 'sarcophagus' comes from a Greek word meaning 'flesh-eater'.) The sarcophagus was made of limestone, which was thought to accelerate the dead body's transformation into a skeleton scraped clean by worms.

Normally a body would have rotted away completely after nine months, but in its carefully sealed sarcophagus, despite the assumed effect of the limestone, this body would probably have been more or less intact. The dry climate of Rome would have meant that the body would have dried out quickly and the skin become hard, almost like leather, forming a sort of black shell. But the rotting interior organs must have produced an unbearable stench, even for people used to bad smells.

The poor priest must have been suffering the torments of hell as he stood beside the throne, trying to reject the accusations levelled at the stinking body.

Sitting in the background were the bishops and priests making up the jury in this macabre court of justice.

What was it all about? How could the leader of millions of Roman Catholic believers set up a court that was sheer lunacy?

History is full of examples of what one might call 'stories about incomprehensible human beings'. It would be easy to replace the dead body in Rome with something else equally stupid. Despite their claims to be creatures of reason and common sense, people have repeatedly behaved as if there were no rational motives for actions or emotions.

In the case of the dead Pope Formosus and his successor Stephen VI, it is difficult to understand why the living pope dug up his dead and half-rotten predecessor. Dressing up the corpse in full regalia, putting a mitre on his skull and placing him on the papal throne doesn't make it any more comprehensible.

Stephen VI was mentally unstable, we do know that – but not enough to prevent him from being elected pope. Obviously insane candidates were not usually chosen. Corruption and ruthless tactics could result in being elected pope, but people were afraid of insanity, which could lead a pope into paths of action that couldn't be controlled.

Stephen VI was a member of the then Roman aristocracy, and was extremely ambitious and ruthless. Taking his predecessor to court was prompted by a bizarre bureaucratic detail. Stephen VI accused the corpse of having broken an ancient Church law which forbade a bishop to move from one district to another. The early Church considered the bishop of a diocese to be 'married' to its members and that he should stay put. However, if a bishop was elected pope, that was not a move between bishoprics but something different from anything else within the Roman Catholic Church, a detail ignored by Stephen.

Formosus had been a bishop outside Rome. The law suit was set in motion because Stephen VI wanted to defend himself; he had done exactly the same as his predecessor and moved to Rome from an outlying bishopric. He didn't want to risk being dug up after his death, and taken to court, and so endeavoured to have his predecessor's appointment declared illegal so that everything he had done as pope was revoked. That would give Stephen VI a clean sheet, enabling him to place his friends and trusted advisers in positions that would secure his power over the Church and, not least, its financial affairs.

What happened that day in 897 in Rome must have seemed

horrific and absurd. It seems the stench was detectable inside the church for a long time afterwards.

It is not clear whether the outcome of the trial was due to the smell or because everything had been decided in advance, but it took only a few days for the jury to find Formosus guilty of all charges. His papacy was declared invalid.

An even more macabre punishment was that the stinking body had its clothes removed. All that remained on the corpse was the hair shirt, which couldn't be removed because it had become fused with the rotting flesh. In addition the three fingers of his right hand used in blessing congregations were taken away. The corpse was later buried in a graveyard where pilgrims were generally interred.

What happened next is a mystery. There are documents suggesting that after a while Stephen VI had his predecessor's body dug up yet again and thrown into the River Tiber. He soon made himself impossible to tolerate and was imprisoned and later strangled in his cell in July or August 897. He had spent less than a year as leader of the Roman Catholic Church.

These macabre goings-on seem totally incomprehensible: Stephen VI shouting and threatening with his finger raised in the basilica, bishops and priests sitting in the jury, the ridiculous charges and the judgment passed – how could people representing the religious conscience of millions of believers, ambassadors of a God who was both believed in and feared, behave in such a manner? We know that vanity, hatred and other destructive forces can drive people to do incredible things – but we tend to believe that there is a line that shouldn't be crossed.

What were the thoughts of that unnamed priest standing there surrounded by the stench of death? What happened to him later in life? Indeed, how could he carry on living after having been forced by his religious superiors to take part in this macabre farce?

There are people in history I would have liked to meet. He is one of them.

When he was eventually allowed out of the basilica, his priority must have been to free his clothes and body of the stench of death. I think of him as a man who had spent a long time in a fermenting swamp and had finally managed to scramble up onto dry land. I can see him shaving off his beard and the hair on his head in order to be free of the stink.

The image of human beings is and will always be strange. The incomprehensible seems to be an ever-present shadow.

64

A violent north-westerly storm

AT THE NORTHERN TIP OF JUTLAND, WHERE SANDBANKS REACH
out a long way into the sea, is an old church buried underneath
shifting sands. Only the tower sticks out from among the sand dunes,
as if it were the church's gravestone.

I remember the first time I visited the place. As I drove along the
tower suddenly appeared out of nowhere. I stopped and discovered
that the sand surrounding the tower had buried the church itself.

I instinctively realised what the concept of *transitoriness* means.
Before, it had seemed to me closely associated with religion and
something unclear – a way of avoiding calling death by its real name.

But now I saw this solitary tower. Shifting sand everywhere, a few
bushes, and beyond them the sea whose presence was always felt
thanks to its distant sighing sound. Then all of a sudden this tower,
which was fighting stubbornly against the sand and the dunes as
they kept on rising.

There had been a time when the church was full every Sunday
with congregations of poverty-stricken families who lived in the
fishing villages of Skagen. At the beginning of the seventeenth
century the shifting sand dunes became more and more threatening,
like an enemy infantry gathering around the church and preparing
for the final assault.

As a result of a violent north-westerly storm in 1775 the shifting
sands reached the church wall for the first time, and then entered
the church itself. After only another twenty years it had been

defeated. In 1795 the Danish king decided that the church would have to be abandoned. Everything movable would be taken in horse-drawn wagons to Österby Kapell and kept there until a new church was built. The church was deconsecrated and the doors locked for the final time.

The church, which had been standing there since the 1300s, was finally surrendered to the encroaching sand. Today only the tower is visible: the church itself, including the font, which was never taken away as it was carved out of natural stone and too heavy to shift, is buried.

Now the only sound down there in the darkness is the shifting sand, which moves when pockets of air form beneath the dunes. This shifting sand is constantly drifting, conquering fresh tracts of land.

My main reason for going to Skagen was not to see the buried church, but because I intended to send one of my literary characters there – Kurt Wallander, who was in mourning and needed to get away from his normal environment.

I wandered along the endless beaches and imagined how my character would react. It was late autumn: cold, windy, with occa-sional snowflakes drifting through the air, signalling the imminent approach of winter.

I had rented a room in a guest house with no other customers. Skagen was deserted in the autumn; it was a time of great weariness for me, bordering on an unusual feeling of unhappiness. In the evenings I sometimes wondered if I was the one who should be spending time on those endless shores, rather than Kurt Wallander.

On the wall next to my bed were some bookshelves containing a few well-thumbed old volumes. One evening I took one of them down at random. It was printed by the Skagen Boktrykkeri, and was about Skagen – its history, the sea, the fate of people who lived there, and the church buried in the sand. Strangely enough, it had never been opened, and I had to fetch a knife in order to cut open the pages. I lay awake for the whole night and read it from cover to cover.

Shortly before dawn there was a power failure; as this was a frequent occurrence in windy Skagen I had come prepared and lit my emergency paraffin lamp.

What I remember most vividly from the book is how a ship called *Daphne* ran aground on one of the treacherous sandbanks. If it hadn't been for the death-defying heroic actions of a number of Skagen fishermen, the ship would have gone down with all hands on board; instead it was the voluntary rescuers who suffered most.

On 27 December 1862, at about half past six in the morning, the gales that had been blowing all night slowly began to die down. Ragged clouds were racing across the sky. One of the watchmen in the fishing fleet moored in an inlet went ashore as soon as it started to grow light in order to see if the hurricane had caused any damage. Somebody had claimed to see lights on the sea during the night, and it was impossible to know what might have happened in the darkness when the storm was at its height.

The watchman discovered that a large ship had run aground on one of the sandbanks. As the winds had eased, he thought it might be possible to take the crew off the stricken ship. It took just over an hour to launch the rescue boat, and the volunteer fishermen from Skagen started rowing towards the scene – but the currents were so strong that they had to turn back twice. They then tried to send a rope out to the ship, using a primitive rocket launcher – and eventually succeeded. But by then darkness had fallen again, and the would-be rescuers were so exhausted they were unable to do any more.

The following day the wind had eased further, even if the waves were still high and the currents strong. The rescue boat managed to reach the ship, but a sudden gust of wind overturned it. Now it was no longer a case of rescuing the crew on board the ship; it was even more urgent to save all those who had been on the capsized boat.

Another rescue boat crewed by volunteers was launched, and they succeeded in saving two of that crew – Niels Andersen and Jens Jensen Nork – who had managed to stay afloat and not yet frozen to death; but most of their comrades were dead. Their names are listed on a memorial stone raised some years later in Skagen:

Jens Christian Jensen
Niels Christian Simonsen
Iver Andreasen
Anders Christensen Bruun
Christen Thomsen Knep
Jakob Tønnesen
Jens Pedersen Kjelder
Thomas Pedersen

They were all hard-up fishermen, most of them young, and all of them married with children. Some of them can be seen on blurred black-and-white photographs, standing beside their boats. It is difficult to make out their faces without the aid of a magnifying glass.

They were all shy, modest, religious and hard-working human beings.

The crew of the *Daphne* were eventually rescued, but the price had been high. On 31 December, the eight volunteer rescuers were buried; eight women became widows and twenty-five young children became fatherless.

The eight graves were in a row. On top of the coffins lay flowers and in some cases medals awarded to the dead men in recognition of their courage in earlier rescue operations.

The wreck of the *Daphne* was just one in a series of similar incidents. The waters around Skagen are justifiably regarded as a ships' cemetery. Since time immemorial ships have run aground on submerged reefs or been blown too close to land by north-westerly storms.

The fishermen who volunteered to man the rescue boats regarded doing so as a matter of course. Nobody has ever heard of any individual who declined to risk his life in order to save unknown sailors struggling among the breakers. It was routine for fishermen to risk their own lives every day, and when the storms came to risk their lives for others.

One of the most basic features of our civilisation is the readiness to volunteer. Even if rescue operations are nowadays rarely so dramatic and devastating as the one on 27 December 1862, it is still the norm for volunteers to risk their lives to save others in a variety of circumstances.

I often wonder how I would react if a small child suddenly ran out onto a busy road in front of where I was standing, closer to it than anybody else. A child I had never seen before and had absolutely no relationship with.

I don't know the answer because it has never happened. I can only hope that I wouldn't hesitate to run out into the road in a totally unselfish attempt to rescue the child from the speeding traffic.

It should be something one can take for granted, but unfortunately it isn't. People fall down in the street, suddenly overcome by illness. Eventually somebody stops and tries to help, but most people hurry past and pretend they haven't seen the man or woman who fell.

It is a question that has haunted me ever since that night in the guest house in Skagen. Were the rescuers driven by courage? Did any of them even consider it an act of courage? Or was it the realisation that they were entering into the strongest of all relationships? The relationship that is formed when people know they are in mortal danger?

Today that trip to Skagen all those years ago seems almost like a dream. I duly wrote my book, and Kurt Wallander spent a long time wandering around the beaches, feeling mournful, until he met somebody out there in the desolation, the mist and the booming foghorns who drew him back in to his normal life.

I dream about the boat that set out one night in December 1862 to try to rescue the crew of the shipwrecked *Daphne*. In the dream I try to see myself among the oarsmen rowing desperately in their knee-boots and sou'westers.

But I'm not sure if I'm on board or not.

I can't be sure. I'll never be sure.

65

A fictitious meeting in a park in Vienna, 1913

ONE OF THE MOST REMARKABLE ARTISTS OF OUR AGE WAS BORN in 1940.

Pina Bausch was a choreographer who created some of the most notable examples of artistic dancing that I know.

Her black hair was swept back; she was thin and could be fragile. But she concealed an immense primordial power. She was beautiful in a vague sort of way. She was also very stern – but towards herself, never with anybody else.

The most remarkable thing about her was her eyes, her expression. She had a way of looking at you that nobody forgot. When she died in 2009 a lot of people talked about Pina Bausch's eyes.

She looked at people with unwavering concentration, and she was as honest with her fellow human beings as she was with those who chose to dance on her stage in Wuppertal.

I sometimes think I have lived in 'the age of *The Rite of Spring*'.

Last year, 2013, it was exactly one hundred years since Stravinsky, the dancer Nijinsky and the leader of the Ballets Russes Diaghilev mounted the first performance of the ballet *The Rite of Spring* in Paris.

The performance was a scandal. There was such uproar in the audience that Nijinsky, who was standing in the wings waiting to enter the stage, couldn't hear the music. He had to observe the other dancers' movements and count the bars in his head so as not to be completely out of time when he danced onto the stage.

Stravinsky was furious and left the performance before the end, protesting that the audience had made so much noise they had ruined his music.

The Rite of Spring signalled a fundamental change in modern art, showing how it would reflect the twentieth century with its explosive industrialism, technical progress, expanding cities and the vulnerability of individuals in a brutal financial world set to exploit them as never before.

All these new developments are incorporated into Stravinsky's passionate music, with frequent paradoxical changes from something akin to tonal madness to serene calm and even silence. Nijinsky's dancing and the choreography were also something new – the fact that the dancers sometimes turned their backs on the audience aroused people's disgust and anger. It was as if the artists were insulting the audience by abandoning all established conventions.

Sixty-two years later Pina Bausch and her ensemble performed their version of *The Rite of Spring* at the Tanztheater in Wuppertal. I saw it many years after its premiere in 1975. It only needed a few bars of music, a few movements, to make me aware that I was about to see something remarkable.

It certainly was. It was as if Pina Bausch's production was a totally convincing reflection of my own contemporary life and the world I now live in. Loneliness, exploitation, frantic hustle and bustle – it was all there, but with a constant counterbalance in the form of human beings' ability to resist and endure.

Her choreography was a duel. The performance made me feel as if I were part of a resistance movement that refused to be forced to live in a world where people were sacrificed every day at the altar of pointlessness. You are sacrificed because you are too old or too young, too slow or too fat, too black or too ugly. Even if *The Rite of Spring* is a heathen saga, the picture it presents of our time and our society is vividly clear.

Pina Bausch always felt uncomfortable in her relationship with the spoken word, perhaps also the written word. But in dancing and the movements of the body she was able to express herself as she wished.

The audience in Paris in 1913 condemned Stravinsky's music as 'an unpleasant row'. Sarcastically, the composer asked his critics later to point out more precisely where this 'unpleasant row' was. They couldn't, of course. And it wasn't many years before *The Rite of Spring* was performed in a concert version to great acclaim. More and more people had come to realise that Stravinsky's tonal language was an accurate reproduction of all that was new in the world at that time.

Today, we are once again on our way into a new age. In a mere hundred years the world has changed so much it is barely recognisable. It is moving away from industrialisation into what we call, for want of anything better, 'the information age'.

People born in 1913 could not imagine in their wildest dreams many of the discoveries that would be made in their lifetime. Nor could they understand, before it happened, the absurd power struggles that led not least in Europe to the deaths of many millions of people.

About the same time as *The Rite of Spring* had its premiere in Paris, two men were living in Vienna – one of them from Linz, the other from Russia. We can be fairly sure that they never looked one another in the eye and conducted a conversation, but it is highly likely that they passed by one another in one of Vienna's central parks. They lived in different districts, but not far from the park.

The young man from Linz was called Adolf Hitler. The somewhat older man from Russia later took the name Stalin.

Hitler tried to support himself by painting watercolours, which he or one of his friends later sold as postcards. He was often in the park and painted several views of it.

Stalin was in Vienna to study the relationship between Marxism and the national state. He was a member of the Communist Party whose leader was another Russian emigrant, Lenin. Lenin was living in nearby Switzerland.

In 1914 the First World War broke out. Hitler had failed in his ambition to become an artist, and began associating with reactionary and anti-Semitic groups. He didn't hesitate to volunteer for service in the German army, was wounded but survived. After the war he didn't return to Vienna, but settled in Munich.

No doubt neither Stalin nor Hitler had been aware that they had been in the same park in Vienna, perhaps even every day for a long period. Stalin might have noticed the scruffily dressed man painting pictures of trees, fountains and buildings. For his part, Hitler might well have seen the man from Russia walking up and down – stocky, powerfully built and chain-smoking Russian cigarettes.

By the time the Second World War broke out they had entered into a pact, which Hitler broke three years later.

Both these men have gone down in history as being responsible for millions of people's deaths. A long way from walks in the park and painting watercolours . . .

Stravinsky's music and Pina Bausch's remarkable choreography reflect our unsettled times but also the way in which human beings can resist anything that strikes them as destructive.

Hitler and Stalin will probably continue to perch on their respective mountain tops in the collective memory. We can do nothing about that. Tyrants have a remarkable ability to live at least as long in our memories as those we can call good people.

But dare I believe that Pina Bausch and her artistic achievements in the world of dance will still be remembered five hundred years from now? Or will they have sunk in the vast and ultimately all-consuming abyss of oblivion?

I am living in Stravinsky's era, even though he has been dead for a long time. His music lives on. Just as Pina Bausch's dancers will continue to perform their fascinating and sensual artistic movements.

But Pina Bausch herself is also dead.

I wonder if she was worried about the same thing that troubles me. The fact that I shall be dead for so long. Or did she think that death was something that she was unable to recreate in her art, and therefore she didn't bother about what was in store once her heart had stopped beating?

66

The puppet on a string

In 1891 they dug up a street in central Brno, in what is now the Czech Republic. New drains were to be installed so filthy water no longer flowed down the streets.

I recall the name Brno from my childhood, as the city could be found on the medium-wave band of our wireless at home. If I tried to tune in there, all I can remember is a vague buzzing noise – Brno was part of a distant universe.

The street being dug up was called Francouzská. At a depth of four metres the workmen discovered an old grave containing the skeleton of a man. Archaeologists were summoned, and found that the skeleton was surrounded by ivory from mammoths and musk-oxen.

The most remarkable object they found was adjacent to the skull. At first they thought it was a statuette that had broken into three parts during the thousands of years the ivory had been lying there, but on closer examination they were able to establish that it was something unique. Meticulous analysis of bones and soil showed that, like the grave, the object was some 25,000 years old.

What was it exactly? At first the archaeologists couldn't believe their eyes, but the truth was indisputable: the object placed next to the dead man's head was a toy. A doll. A marionette. A puppet on a string.

Although it was broken, it was clear that its head had been movable, like an owl's. The arm – they only found one – had a hole that could be attached to another hole in the body of the doll and moved like a real arm.

So the dead man had a puppet on a string next to his head. They never found the other arm; most probably it had been removed before being buried, or else it had been carried away by earth movements or changes in the level of groundwater. But there was no doubt that the doll was a doll.

When it was dug up, it sent us a message from people living 25,000 years ago. We don't know if the puppet had been used in some form of shadow play or if it was associated with religious rites – but there is also the possibility that it was simply a toy. For a child. Or for an adult who hadn't stopped playing even though he had grown up.

That ancient puppet on a string tells us something about what being human has always entailed. I find it difficult to imagine a more touching and at the same time humorous greeting from people who were living just after an ice age had slowly melted away.

Those of us living today will not be sending puppets on a string into the future. Our legacy is nuclear waste. Our most important task is to try to send a warning to people who might succeed us after future ice ages have passed.

Right now it seems that the only solution is to abandon any hope of creating a meaningful warning, and concentrate instead on preventing future generations from knowing that there is anything there at all. Moss should be allowed to grow on the mountainsides where the troll has been buried. Nobody should remember what was once buried in sealed copper capsules deep down in underground caverns.

People have always tried to create good memories for future generations, and, when necessary, reminders of what was dangerous or evil. But now we live in a civilisation that is not trying to create memories, but to create a form of oblivion instead.

What will be the eventual outcome? An age without memories? Do we still have time to think sensible thoughts? Or is nuclear waste another step along the road leading deeper and deeper down into the abyss?

I don't know. But as a mantra I can now repeat yet again what I have always tried to convince myself of: Nothing is ever too late. Everything is still possible.

We still live in the age of the puppet on a string.

67

Never being robbed of one's happiness

ON 9 MAY 2014 IT IS DRIZZLING SOUTH OF GOTHENBURG WHERE Eva and I live. A change is on the way – I can see that the shallow waters in the Stallviken inlet have started to ebb away, which indicates warmer and sunnier weather. The occasional salmon trout fisherman is standing a long way out from land; they often stand there for hours on end, whether or not the fish are biting, and many of them throw the fish back into the water if and when they do catch one. I envy them their unalloyed joy as they seem to stand there, waiting for everything and nothing.

It is five months since I received my cancer diagnosis, and a couple of days ago I had my fourth and last infusions in this series of chemotherapy treatment. I shall meet Dr Bergman tomorrow, and hear how things have progressed so far.

I got up early this morning – as so often I slept only fitfully. I feel as if I am waiting for a court's verdict, and it's impossible to know whether I am going to be declared innocent or guilty. All I can do at the moment is prepare for the worst but hope for the best.

But as dawn is beginning to break I start thinking about something completely different, just as the blackbird starts singing its reveille from our chimney stack and giving the go-ahead for all the other birds to join in. Instead of preparing for whatever is in store for me tomorrow, I start wondering exactly when I experienced the greatest happiness with which I have been blessed in this life. Is there such a moment? Or is it impossible to choose? The birth of a child, the relief when a severe pain goes away, an assault that didn't result in my death, the feeling that something I have written turned out better than I had expected? I soon decide that it is impossible to choose. Moments can hardly be compared or placed in order. One kind of happiness is different from another.

Nevertheless, I eventually find myself remembering a moment that I think exceeded all other feelings of happiness, even if I don't actually try to make comparisons.

I am transported back to 4 October 1992. Twenty-two years ago. I was aged forty-four and experiencing what were probably the most intense years of my life. I was spending nearly all the time in Maputo, the capital city of Mozambique. I directed at least two plays every year, as well as being mainly responsible for practical aspects of running the theatre.

Most days followed a strict routine. I got up very early in order to work at my desk before the African heat became too overpowering. At about noon I had a meal and then slept for an hour, having first disconnected the telephone and locked the outside door. Then it was time to go to the theatre, where rehearsals generally began at about four o'clock and continued for most of the evening. On the way home I would stop at some restaurant for a bite to eat, usually on my own, which gave me the opportunity to read the only daily newspaper published at that time in Mozambique, *Noticias*. Then I would usually write for a while before falling asleep.

Many of my friends in Europe imagined that I was living a dramatic life; but any drama was inside my head. Never before or after have I lived such a disciplined and in fact rather boring life as in those days.

The previous year I had proposed that we should perform Aristophanes' ancient comedy *Lysistrata*. Needless to say, it would have to be Africanised in order to make it comprehensible to a modern and mainly young African audience, many of whom would be illiterate. The first things to be omitted were every reference to Greek temples and priestesses; instead we would adapt Aristophanes' basic theme about women going on erotic strike in order to force their menfolk to stop going to war.

There had been civil war in Mozambique for over ten years, and many people had been killed. As always in connection with civil wars, there had been extremely brutal attacks on the civilian population – ears and noses cut off, children crushed by being smashed against trees. Everybody in the whole country had friends or relatives who had been affected. There were many reasons why we should mount this play, and I was convinced that up there in his dramatists' heaven, Aristophanes himself would understand how necessary it was to adapt the outline of the play to suit African conditions.

The question was: what could possibly replace the Greek temples and priestesses? One day I was shopping in the central market in Maputo, and when I saw all the women working on the various stalls I realised that this was the answer.

I asked some of the theatre's actresses to spend a few days visiting the market and talking to the women who worked there. It wasn't long before the idea of women withholding sexual favours in order to put an end to the civil war had taken root. Our only problem was that the stallholders didn't really understand the idea of turning all this into a theatre performance; they wanted to do it in real life without delay.

That didn't happen, but we did produce our play. Our Lysistrata, whom we renamed Julietta, was a stallholder selling fish in the market. (The only Lysistrata in our play was a goat of that name. The plan was that the goat should appear on the stage at a critical moment, but we had a lot of trouble keeping it quiet behind the scenes and hence giving away what was intended to be a big surprise. In the end we asked an old goat-keeper for advice, and he solved the problem immediately: 'Put some salt on the outside of the goat's mouth – that'll keep him quiet.' And it did.)

The play was a huge success. For reasons I no longer remember we had decided that the last performance would be on Sunday, 4 October. Throughout the time we were producing our play negotiations were taking place between the legal government of Mozambique and the gangs of bandits – lackeys of the apartheid state in South Africa – creating violent chaos all over the country. The negotiations were taking place in Rome and I don't think anybody seriously thought they would have a successful outcome. Everybody believed the war would continue and there would be no end to the massacre of innocent civilians.

And so 4 October arrived. In the morning a good friend of mine, a journalist, hammered excitedly on my front door. The unexpected had happened! A peace treaty had been signed in Rome. Perhaps the brutal civil war would be over at long last.

When I went to the theatre that afternoon to watch the final performance, the news from Rome had been confirmed. A peace treaty really had been signed. Cars were already driving around in Maputo sounding their horns, as if the national team had won an international match or championship.

As I was walking down the hills to Teatro Avenida I made up my mind what we should do. I sat in the as yet empty theatre with Lucrecia Paco, who was playing the leading role of Lysistrata/Julietta, and suggested what she should say after the final applause had died down. She understood immediately, but asked me to put the right words into her mouth.

'No,' I said. 'The only way you can say this is in your own words. You can't possibly get anything wrong.'

I placed myself in a corner of the front stalls and watched the performance. The goat didn't make a noise behind the scenes and he caused outbreaks of shouting and applause as usual when he suddenly appeared onstage, on the end of a rope. That last performance was very good, and the actors were full of energetic concentration. They were careful not to take things too quickly, and to make sure every detail came across.

The end came at last. The applause was long and loud. At Teatro Avenida the response to final applause is always the same, with the whole cast lining up in front of the stage lights. After being called out onstage for the third time, Lucrecia raised her arms and the applause died down, just as we had anticipated when we discussed it earlier in the afternoon.

I remember her words, exactly as she had chosen them herself:

'As we all know, a peace treaty was signed in Rome today. We can only hope that this terrible war, with all its murders and mutilation, is now over. We must believe that this peace treaty will be honoured. But I promise you that if it becomes necessary we shall repeat our performance of this play again. Like you, we shall never give up.'

It was followed by total silence. There was no more applause. But the audience rose to its feet. In utter silence, they gazed at the actors and actresses who had performed this 2,000-year-old play about a number of women's desperate and courageous struggle against barbaric warfare.

It was the most moving experience I have ever had in a theatre. I have enjoyed many uplifting moments, but never anything remotely like what happened on 4 October 1992. It was touching, but at the same time overflowing with boundless happiness. Conversations between opposing persons really were possible, and a war could be forced to come to an end. I had been present at something that really did make the earth move, when something came to an end and something else started.

I find it hard to recall any incident in my life that was more significant and more filled with joy than that moment in the theatre. Things cannot be compared or placed in order. But that morning in 2014, as I prepared myself for what might be good or bad news the following day, I was overcome by the memory of that all-consuming happiness.

Our theatrical performance had no influence on the treaty that was signed in Rome, but I am convinced that without our work in the theatre, something would have been lost from the process that eventually led to the end of the war. Nobody present at that final performance, either on the stage or in the audience, will ever forget it.

The drizzle continued. I gazed out over the sea and thought that despite everything I had been lucky enough to be present at a moment of boundless joy. Many moments, in fact – but that morning I chose as the highlight our production of *Lysistrata* in October 1992.

Shortly after ten that morning I entered Dr Bergman's office.

Perhaps I was walking out onto the stage. Or maybe I was in the audience and Dr Bergman was sitting on his chair just in front of the footlights.

I knew by now that he always chose his words very carefully.

'We have a breathing space,' he said. 'The chemotherapy has been effective. Some of the tumours have reduced in size, others have disappeared altogether. But that doesn't mean that you are cured, of course. Nevertheless, we have a breathing space, and it could last for quite a long time.'

I am living today in that breathing space. I occasionally think about my disease, about death, and about the fact that there are no guarantees when it comes to cancer.

But most of all I live in anticipation of new uplifting experiences. Of times when nobody robs me of the pleasure of creating things myself, or enjoying what others have created.

Moments which will come, which must come if life is to have any value as far as I'm concerned.

Epilogue

When my father was a district judge in Sveg during the 1950s, he would arrange a court hearing once a month in Svenstavik. Before I started school I used to accompany him there. There was a bedroom for us upstairs in the local court building. I was five or six years old, in 1953 or 1954.

My father once found a man guilty of manslaughter in Svenstavik. He was a lumberjack and had killed a businessman who was widely disliked because he rarely gave credit to poverty-stricken forest workers. Nobody seemed to miss the businessman – but manslaughter was manslaughter, even if the lumberjack was penniless and perhaps in urgent need of help.

My father gave him the mildest sentence the law permitted.

Endless numbers of people surround you as you travel through life. Some you notice briefly, then forget. With others you make eye contact, which leads to a kind of emotional connection. And sometimes you have a conversation with some of these people.

And then you have your family, your friends, your workmates. All those who are close to you. Some move away, or your relationship cools, or they let you down in some way, and friends sometimes become enemies.

But most are simply folk who happen to live at the same time as you do. Millions of people who pay a short visit to the earth, whose stay overlaps your own.

Since being diagnosed with cancer I often dream about walking along streets where lots of people are jostling their way past others. It can be quite difficult to make progress. My dream sometimes places me briefly in a theatre, or a cafe, or in an aeroplane: I am searching for someone. Someone who knows me, someone who is also searching for me.

Then the dream ends and I nearly always wake up with a feeling of great relief. There is nothing frightening about all these people who accompany me or have accompanied me as I journey through life. It is more a feeling of curiosity about who they actually were – I would have liked to get to know so many of them better.

Such as that woman in the Stephansdom cathedral, the tango dancers in Buenos Aires, or the girl in the camp in Mozambique who was reunited with her parents.

And the lumberjack and the businessman he killed in northern Sweden sixty years ago.

All these unknown people exist alongside me. For a short time they have been a part of my life. I share it with all of them.

Our real family is endless, even if we don't know who some of them were when we met them for an extremely brief moment.

relationship